Sisters in Pain

Sisters
in Pain

BATTERED WOMEN
FIGHT BACK

L. Elisabeth Beattie
Mary Angela Shaughnessy, SCN

THE UNIVERSITY PRESS OF KENTUCKY

Publication of this volume was made possible in part by a grant from the National Endowment for the Humanities.

Editorial and Sales Offices: The University Press of Kentucky
663 South Limestone Street, Lexington, Kentucky 40508-4008

04 03 02 01 00   5 4 3 2 1

Library of Congress Cataloging-in-Publication Data
Beattie, Elisabeth, 1953-
    Sisters in pain : battered women fight back / Elisabeth Beattie and Mary
    Angela Shaughnessy.
        p. cm.
    Includes bibliographical references.
    ISBN 0-8131-2151-5 (cloth : alk. paper)
        1. Abused women—Kentucky—Interviews. 2. Wife abuse—Kentucky.
    3. Abusive men—Kentucky—Mortality. 4. Justifiable homicide—
    Kentucky. I. Shaughnessy, Mary Angela, 1949-. II. Title.

HV6626.22.K4 B43 2000
362.82'92'0922769—dc21   99-047706

This book is printed on acid-free recycled paper
meeting the requirements of the American National Standard
for Permanence of Paper for Printed Library Materials.

Manufactured in the United States of America

To the Sisters in Pain
and to our fathers,
Walter M. Beattie, Jr., and Edward M. Shaughnessy, Jr.,
whose devotion to us and to our mothers
and whose acute sense of justice
have cast—as well as created—our lives.

"And you wonder why I didn't rise up and revolt . . . ? I felt lucky to get my shoes on the right feet, that's why. I moved forward only, thinking each morning anew that we were leaving the worst behind.

"To save my sanity, I learned to pad around hardship in soft slippers and try to remark on its good points."

* * *

"It took me a long time to understand the awful price I'd paid, and that even God has to admit the worth of freedom. *How say ye to my soul, Flee as a bird to your mountain?* By then, I was lodged in the heart of darkness, so thoroughly bent to the shape of marriage I could hardly see any other way to stand. Like Methuselah [the family's parrot] I cowered beside my cage, and though my soul hankered after the mountain, I found, like Methuselah, I had no wings.

"This is *why*, little beast. I'd lost my wings. Don't ask me how I gained them back—the story is too unbearable."

* * *

"Plain and simple, that was the source of our exodus: I had to keep moving. I didn't set out to leave my husband. Anyone can see I should have, long before, but I never did know how. For women like me, it seems, it's not ours to take charge of beginnings and endings. Nor the marriage proposal, the summit conquered, the first shot fired, nor the last one either—the treaty at Appomattox, the knife in the heart. Let men write these stories. I can't. I only know the middle ground where we live our lives. We whistle while Rome burns, or we scrub the floor, depending. Don't dare presume there's shame in the lot of the woman who carries on."

Excerpted from The Poisonwood Bible *by Barbara Kingsolver (HarperFlamingo, 1998) and reprinted with the permission of Barbara Kingsolver.*

Contents

Foreword

"Never doubt that a small group of thoughtful, committed citizens can change the world. Indeed, it is the only thing that ever has."

Margaret Mead

This book is invaluable in amplifying the voices of these survivors. Those whose stories so desperately need to be told appreciate the authors' willingness to write this book, not only to commend their survival, but also to help others who have suffered from abuse. My hope is that by reading this book you will see the injustice in the current legal system so graphically described in the women's stories and that your outrage over the lack of protection and enforcement of the law will prompt you to work with policy makers and organizations to hold the judicial system, law enforcement, social service agencies, and others accountable. Loud, irritating noise must be made for change to take place.

Reflecting on my involvement with this almost-spiritual journey, I feel as if I was called to be the conductor of an orchestra. The players performed their pieces brilliantly, and through a collective effort the music could not have been sweeter; for once, "justice pursued, justice granted."

The appointment of women to top leadership positions in the administration of former Kentucky governor Brereton Jones resulted in many of the key musicians being given the right instruments to play. Helen Howard Hughes's appointment as chair of the parole board gave the board an expert on domestic violence. As executive director of the Kentucky Commission on Women in the 1980s, she was responsible for the only research ever done in Kentucky on domestic violence. Allison Connelly's appointment as the state's public defender played a major part. Connelly strongly supported public defender Marguerite Thomas and her team's aggressive efforts in compiling the clemency petitions. My appointment as executive director of the Kentucky Commission on Women gave me access to state officials who could tell me the right music to be played. Chandra McElroy was not appointed by Governor Jones, but her position as rehabilitation specialist at the Kentucky Correctional Institution for Women was paramount in the concert. Sherry Currens, executive director of the Kentucky Domestic Violence Association, helped write the clemency plan (music) and provided critical background information.

Other key musicians were the women journalists who so accurately reported the circumstances under which the women found themselves and who wrote about the system that failed them. Dianne Aprile and Fran Ellers, reporters for the Louisville *Courier-Journal*, and Cheryl Powell, reporter for the *Lexington Herald-Leader*, educated the public about the reality of the women's lives. The supportive and extensive media coverage that the inmates received made Governor Jones's act of clemency easier to perform.

When I first received the women's stories (the dreadful music of their lives), I am ashamed to admit that some parts were too painful for me to read. I kept thinking that if this was too hard for me, how did they survive the horrendous conditions under which their daily lives were composed? I am firmly convinced that every one of these women went to prison for self-defense.

Historically, women have been viewed as nothing more than men's property. Fewer than a hundred years ago, when women married they became legally dead. They could not own property, make a will, have their wages payable to themselves, or vote. However, in recent years, surprisingly, Kentucky has enacted the most progressive domestic violence laws in the nation. The problem is that those laws are not always enforced. The women whose stories appear in this book called for help from law enforcement officers, and many times those officers did not respond. The challenge for us is to change the culture that views domestic violence as an accepted form of behavior and to demand that violence not be tolerated.

Additionally, this book can serve as a catalyst to help imprisoned women across the country. Unfortunately, the tales of these women's lives are not unlike the stories of many other imprisoned women. By exposing how the current legal and social systems fail victims of domestic violence, we can work toward solutions. The public must be informed and inspired to take action (to make music) before we can change the status quo.

From this experience I learned that the power of a small group of people who use their influence to help others can achieve monumental feats. As you read this book and are overcome with emotion, remember that you, too, have the ability to make a difference in someone's life—to create your own music.

Marsha Weinstein

Preface

It wasn't so much their faces as the two or three lines of data that defined their lives. That's what struck me. That's what made me read the Louisville *Courier-Journal* in its entirety on December 12, 1995, despite the intensity of the daylight over my right shoulder showing me that I should have showered and dressed by then, that I should have already started driving the sixty miles to the community college where I taught English and journalism five days each week. That nine women, all ordinary, all now criminals, all imprisoned for killing, for attempting to kill, or for conspiring to kill the men who had tortured them, could be publicly reduced to cases—that their unwittingly theatrical lives would be forever defined as one-acts, as morality plays in which they play victims and villains, but never heroines—hurt me. The facts concerning their crimes and convictions stood out like lettering on marquees, like epitaphs on tombstones. These were the women who Gov. Brereton Jones, an elected official about to leave office, had just made eligible for parole.

That morning I decided to get to know these women and to write about them. That night their collective story was still in my head, and I still felt somehow responsible to them. All I could do, I thought, was to make it possible for their voices to be heard. I asked myself, is my ambition virtuous or arrogant? In the midst of heady, seasonal sentiment, my answer remained unclear.

Another month passed. Since the end of one school semester and the start of another, there had been more information in the newspapers and on television concerning these survivors. I felt certain that I wanted to communicate their individual and collective stories, but my motivation concerned me. Was it my passion for social justice? My need to start another writing project after having put one to bed? Memories of personal experiences that I've tried so hard to forget?

No. I was convinced that those women deserved to be heard. As a journalist, I know that news stories, always dedicated to the simple facts, rarely allude to, much less embrace, the more complex truth. So I sat down and planned a book. First, I decided that the women should speak for themselves. That was essential, as I suspected that opportunities for self-expression had proved rare for them. In addition, no one could narrate the life stories of these survivors better than the women who had lived them. I would conduct oral history interviews, and my text would alternate transcriptions of those tape-recorded discussions with narrative chapters that would incorporate autobiographical accounts written by the women while in prison. But because so much of what those women—the media had begun to refer to them as the Sisters in Pain—had experienced, and because so much of what they would now depend on was state and federal law, I thought that the legal aspects of their cases should also be analyzed. That's when I decided to ask Dr. Mary Angela (Angie) Shaughnessy, a Sister of Charity of Nazareth, who was—and remains—director of the doctoral program in Educational Leadership (which I was completing at Spalding University) as well as that institution's legal counsel, to coauthor my book. She would write the legal chapters; I would write the rest. That was the plan that launched our project.

Since then, a year of conducting interviews that angered us, moved us, shook us, and, above all, instructed us in the insidious, systemic nature of abuse—and a year of arranging our data to emphasize what we see as significant—caused us to reshape our text. We agreed that our emblematic tale with its numerous villains, victims, and survivors required for its full articulation the strength of a single voice. That voice became a blend of our writing styles, of the words of the paroled women who agreed to be interviewed, of our burgeoning sense and sensibility in the arena of abuse, and, most of all, of our experience with the Sisters in Pain and their crusading champions. These champions were the former executive director of the Kentucky Commission on Women, Marsha Weinstein; former governor Brereton Jones; the former chairwoman of the Commonwealth of Kentucky Parole Board, Helen Howard-Hughes; the former counselor for the Kentucky Correctional Institution for Women, Chandra McElroy; and the supervisor of post-conviction services for the Kentucky Department of Public Advocacy, Marguerite Thomas.

On December 12, 1995, I had no idea how psychologically depleting this project would be. But my hope is that the experiences of the Sisters in Pain shared herein, like the squares that make up their quilt, will illustrate a few of our critical social problems that, if ignored, will intensify our collective shame.

L. Elisabeth Beattie

The stories of the nine battered women who became eligible for parole in 1995 fascinated me. As a woman religious, a member of the Sisters of Charity of Nazareth, as a former high-school teacher and principal, as a college professor, and as an attorney, I have seen my share of abuse cases. I have listened to victims who were on their way to healing and to those who were not. For years, I have served as a legal advisor to women abused by members of the clergy, so I was no stranger to the problems of abuse and to other forms of violence. But the plight of these nine women touched something in me. I knew I had to do something to respond to these women, to offer them some shred of understanding and hope, whatever the personal cost. Although I am an attorney, my practice is generally education and employment law, not criminal law, and I wondered how I could offer any practical help. And even if I could think of a way to help, would it be accepted? Would any of these women, most of whom had been raised in fundamentalist Christian religions, agree to meet, let alone trust, a Roman Catholic nun? I'd experienced prejudice and mistrust before, and I was uneasy. Still, that nagging voice of conscience said, "You need to do something."

In 1963, my uncle, Harry Shaughnessy, president of a local clothing union, marched in Selma, Alabama, to the bewilderment of his whole family. When I asked my uncle why he had to do this, why somebody else couldn't do it, he answered, "If I don't do it, who will? Always remember, when you see something wrong in the world, it is your job to do something about it." I trusted that I would somehow learn what it was I needed to do.

I needn't have worried; I found the answer to my question very soon. Linda Beattie had recently graduated from Spalding University's doctoral program in education, which I direct. Linda is undoubtedly one of the best students to complete our program. One day she came to visit me and asked me to coauthor this book with her. Linda believed that my professional knowledge and skills as an attorney would add a needed dimension to the book that she proposed. I agreed to collaborate with her in this project by analyzing the legal issues and procedures for inclusion in the narrative. I am proud to coauthor this book with Linda, and I thank her for having the vision to dream this book into being and for allowing me the privilege of partnering with her.

The original plan was for each of us to write separate chapters; we discussed how this could be done. Should we follow a chapter written by Linda with a legal chapter written by Angie? Should Linda write all of the women's stories and Angie write the latter portion of the book, chapters dealing with the law? Ultimately, the answer emerged: "We somehow have to write it together." And so we did.

The experience of interviewing these women was at once invigorating, in the face of such survival, and humbling, as we wondered on more than one occasion how we could have dealt with the abuse that these women experienced. Would we have survived as they did? We agreed that we did not know.

Finally, a book emerged that we hope tells a story of abuse, violence, survival, and, ultimately, hope. We deeply regret the deaths of the men killed by these women; we do not condone the taking of a life as a response to violence. But we also know, as the Native American proverb states, "You cannot judge a man [or a woman] until you have walked a mile in his [or her] moccasins." Therefore, we have attempted to let these women tell their stories as they perceived and experienced them.

I believe that my Uncle Harry was right. Each of us has a responsibility to do something about injustice and pain. Linda and I offer this work as one attempt to respond to a grave social problem. If each of us will do his or her part, all of us will be able to effect true social change.

Mary Angela Shaughnessy, SCN

Acknowledgments

We wish to thank everyone that we interviewed, as well as the many individuals who advised, encouraged, and helped us to produce this book.

Primarily, we want the Sisters in Pain who permitted us to tell their stories—Tracie English, Teresa Gulley Hilterbrand, Sue Melton, Sherry Pollard, Montilla Seewright, and Karen Stout (Stelzer)—as well as Margie Marcum's advocate, Helen Bowen, to know that we appreciate the courage and the selfless trust with which they've shared their stories.

Two other women, whose patience with our consultations proved endless, former offender rehabilitation specialist Chandra McElroy and former executive director of the Kentucky Commission on Women Marsha Weinstein deserve kudos for their determination to provide hope for abuse survivors and for their willingness to contribute time and energy to our project. In addition, we thank Marsha for writing the foreword to this book.

Former Governor Brereton Jones invited us to interview him at his home; we appreciate his hospitality and the sincerity of his concern for the welfare of the women whose sentences he commuted.

For permitting us to interview them and for providing us with candid comments, we thank Sherry Currens, executive director of the Kentucky Domestic Violence Association; Helen Howard-Hughes, former chairperson of the Commonwealth of Kentucky Parole Board; and Marguerite Thomas, assistant public advocate and postconviction specialist for the Commonwealth of Kentucky Department of Public Advocacy. We also thank Louisville's WAVE-3 television reporter, Connie Leonard, for advising us as we began our research.

Our gratitude extends to Thomas R. Oates, president of Spalding University, who took photos for this book, and once again, to Marsha Weinstein for providing additional photos from her personal collection. Shelly Zegart, a founding director of the Kentucky Quilt Project and of the Alliance of American Quilts, the trustee of the Battered Women's Self-Help Group quilt (now also known as the Prison Quilt) and related archival materials, permitted us to reproduce photos of the quilt and provided us with essays by women's studies scholar Elaine Hedges. We thank her.

A month before completing our manuscript, we decided that a poem articulating various aspects of abuse prefacing each chapter could capture the survivors' anguish in complement and counterpoint to our narrative and to the women's own accounts of their abuse. So we asked award-winning poets from Kentucky to Northern Ireland for permission to reprint their work or to submit original poems for our project. To those writers who responded to our request with enthusiasm, speed, and rare sensibility, we extend out heartfelt thanks. They are Diana Brebner, Kathleen Driskell, Sue Driskell, Jan Freeman, Barbara Kingsolver, Medbh McGuckian, Margaret Randall, Richard Taylor, and Anne Shelby. We also thank Peter Fallon, editor and publisher of the Gallery Press in County Meath, Ireland, and Frederick Smock, editor of the *American Voice* and *The American Voice Anthology of Poetry*, for their enthusiasm in sharing with readers poems that they published first.

John Edgar, executive director of Louisville's Kilgore Samaritan Counseling Center, offered us valuable advice, as did Patrick Kellogg, an Oldham County, Kentucky, pre-trial hearing officer, and other individuals too numerous to list. We thank them all.

The Kentucky Foundation for Women awarded us a grant to help finance this project; we appreciate those funds, which proved pivotal to conducting our work. Angie's sister, Janet S. Kellogg, transcribed our interviews, and Linda's former colleague, Candy Jerdon, and her former student, Debra Salsman, typed our manuscript. To them we extend our gratitude for their diligence, good humor, and fine work.

And finally we thank our friends and families for serving as our long-suffering sounding boards as we articulated the agonies and the enthusiasms peculiar to this project.

Introduction

Pick up almost any newspaper or magazine, flip through radio news reports or television feature specials, and sooner or later you'll encounter the facts. One in four women in the United States is raped during her lifetime, and only one rape in eleven is reported. In 1997, according to the U.S. Bureau of Justice Statistics, 4.5 million violent acts against women occurred, and 95 percent of the perpetrators were men (McCrea and Goldman 1998). The U.S. Justice Department's most recent statistics suggest that 30 percent of the 1,414 women murdered in 1992 were killed by their husbands, ex-husbands, or boyfriends (McCrea and Goldman 1998). Annually, spouses and significant others commit 13,000 acts of violence against women in U.S. workplaces, a figure that translates into five billion dollars each year in medical expenses, catapulting domestic violence into the number-one cause for women seeking treatment in hospital emergency rooms (Kentucky Commission on Women 1997).

And just what is domestic violence? Various individuals, institutions, and organizations articulate different definitions, but suffice it to say that the first widespread definitions of spousal abuse offered in the United States in the 1970s focused on physical violence and its increased frequency. Twenty years later, the National Coalition against Domestic Violence cited domestic violence as "*a pattern of behavior* with the effect of establishing power and control over another person through fear and intimidation. Battering happens when batterers believe they are entitled to control their partners, when violence is permissible, when violence will produce the desired effect or prevent a worse one, and when the benefits outweigh the consequences" (Landes, Squyres, and Quiram 1997).

But no matter its specific manifestations, a significant fact publicized by the National Coalition against Domestic Violence is that "more than 50 percent of all women will experience some form of violence from their spouses during marriage. More than one-third [approximately 18 million women] are battered repeatedly every year" (Landes, Squyres, and Quiram 1997).

Yet it's important to note that abuse of women, although epidemic, isn't new. Western civilization documents the medieval comments of Geoffrey de la Tour de Landry concerning how to punish the "wickedness of a nagging wife." In 1371 he wrote, "Here is an example to every good woman that she suffer and endure patiently, nor strive with her husband nor answer him before strangers, as did once a woman who did answer her husband before strangers with short words: and he smote her with his fist down to earth; and then with his foot he struck her in her visage and broke her nose, and all her life after she had her nose crooked, which so shent [spoiled] and disfigured her visage after, that she might not for shame show her face, it was so foul blemished. And this she had for her language that she was wont to say to her husband, and therefore the wife ought to suffer, and let the husband have the words, and to be master for that is her duty" (Landes, Squyres, and Quiram 1997).

Less than fifty years later, Bernard of Sienna, Italy, suggested that men treat their spouses with the same affection that they show their livestock, a suggestion still regarded, statistics would suggest, as novel by contemporary U.S. culture, which provides three times as many shelters for animals as for abused women (National Coalition against Domestic Violence). In colonial America, a more compassionate culture applied what was later called the "rule of thumb" to situations necessitating the chastisement of wayward wives. Lawmakers still condoned husbands beating their spouses but determined they should do so only with sticks the width of their thumbs (Landes, Squyres, and Quiram 1997).

Historically, Eastern and African cultures have also abused women. Even today, as has been the case for centuries, grooms burn to death brides who are unable to deliver the dowries that their grooms demand. Recent estimates reveal that in India one such woman is killed every twelve hours. Official police records attribute 4,835 females' deaths in 1990 to murder by their disgruntled fiancés, a number that doesn't come close to capturing the thousands of Indian women who succumb annually to "accidental burns" (Landes, Squyres, and Quiram 1997).

Iraqi men often kill female relatives who they even suspect of adultery; Mali and Sudanese men practice female circumcision, an operation performed without anesthesia that results in severe pain, persistent infections, and, frequently, death; and the ancient Chinese proverb, "A wife married is like a pony bought; I'll ride her and whip her as I like," was echoed halfway around the world as recently as 1987 by the comment in a Papua, New Guinea, parliamentary debate that "wife beating is an accepted custom; we are wasting our time debating the issue" (Landes, Squyres, and Quiram 1997).

Patriarchal societies, cultures controlled by men, have traditionally evoked religious doctrine, from translations of the Bible to the teachings of the Koran, to justify battering women. But in the past twenty years, the first social-scientific studies of domestic violence have also identified poverty, marital age (that is, men who marry younger), gender roles, excessive alcohol consumption, stress, having been abused one's self, and having been raised in or currently residing in a subculture of violence as contributors to, if not causes of, the behavior of numerous batterers (Landes, Squyres, and Quiram 1997). And although it is true that women, as well as men, abuse their partners, a 1992 report to the U.S. Senate Judiciary Committee estimated that of the 1.37 million domestic violence offenses recorded in 1991, 83 percent of the victims were women. The Bureau of Justice Statistics (BJS) stated in its 1995 publication *Violence Against Women: Estimates from the Redesigned Survey* (Bachman and Saltzman 1995) that women experience an average of 1 million more violent victimizations annually than do men. And, as reprehensible as is any form of abuse perpetuated by members of either sex against members of their own or of the opposite sex, the overwhelming prevalence of battering of women by men suggests a focus for comprehending and for attempting to alleviate dysfunctional relationships based on emotional, physical, and sexual control.

"A Report on the Status of Women's Health in Kentucky," a 1997 document compiled for the Kentucky Commission on Women, cited 1993 data documenting the fact that every four days in 1993 a Kentucky woman died as a result of domestic violence. And a September 8, 1998, Louisville *Courier-Journal* editorial by Laura McCrea and Honi Marleen Goldman, cochairpersons of Take Back the Night '98, a month-long Louisville-area event focused on public education concerning violent crimes against women, stated that the "leading crime in Louisville [Kentucky's largest city] is domestic violence. The Jefferson County, Kentucky, Attorney's Office prosecuted 5,000 domestic violence cases with the Jefferson County Police Department responding to 11,476 domestic violence calls in 1997." McCrea and Goldman added, "In Jefferson County, 50 percent of the women men murder result from domestic violence acts."

In his 1997 book, *Rural Woman Battering and the Justice System: An Ethnography*, British sociologist Neil Websdale, who studied domestic violence in rural Kentucky, wrote that "[early] research shows that woman battering is as likely to occur in urban as it is in rural areas. . . . Survey research in Kentucky also demonstrates that there are few differences between urban and rural rates of woman battering, except that rural battered women report a statistically greater likelihood of being 'shot at,' 'tortured,' and having their 'hair pulled.'" Additional data, including research by Murray Straus, director of the Family Research Laboratory at the University of New Hampshire, and the Second National Family Violence Survey (1992), reveal spousal abuse to be practiced more in poorer than in wealthier (be they rural or urban) households (Straus and Kaufman Kantor 1994). The latter study revealed that families with incomes at or below the poverty level experience a 500 percent greater rate of domestic violence than do their wealthier counterparts (Straus and Kaufman Kantor 1994). The difficulty of verifying such statistics centers on the fact that abuse victims—ashamed of experiences, injuries, and relationships for which their batterers have convinced them they are responsible and afraid of repercussions from their batterers—often underreport and deny their problems (Powell 1995). Wealthier victims, who are also often more educated, generally possess greater and easier access to private physicians, to alternative living arrangements, to information concerning social service and legal aid, and, of course, to money, all of which allow them more opportunity to conceal or escape their abuse. These findings, however, do not and should not suggest that educational and financial advantages generally available to a group are physically or psychically in reach of all of its members. While the numbers of poor women who experience abuse appear to exceed the numbers of economically advantaged women who are abused, battering can affect all women, regardless of their economic status, age, race, geographical location, religion, or level of education, just as domestic violence shatters each of its victims by stripping her of any role or status until little of her self remains.

It stands to reason, and most researchers agree, that a person's need to dominate intimates with threats and violence tends to decrease in proportion to that person's increased income, education, and interpersonal skills. Men raised in environments to which sociologists refer as subcultures of violence, families and communities that approve physical force as a means of coercion, are more likely to batter than are men taught alternative values. In her *Washington Post* article, "Poor Women Experience High Level of Abuse," reprinted in the May 26, 1997, Louisville *Courier-Journal*, journalist Sandra G. Boodman also emphasized the striking connection between poverty and violence. She cited findings reported in the April 1998 issue of *Orthopsychiatry* that revealed that poor women especially "experience extraordinarily high levels of severe physical and sexual abuse." She wrote that 83 percent of the 436 women with below-poverty-level incomes who were surveyed in this six-year federally funded study, which she deemed "the most extensive investigation into the physical and emotional health" of such women to date, had survived physical or sexual abuse.

Significant, too, is the fact that even though research has linked binge drinking of alcohol, as well as amphetamine use, to violent behavior, cross-cultural studies of the relationship between drinking and violence indicate that social expectations, more than such substances themselves, determine their users' actions (Landes, Squyres, and Quiram 1997).

Focusing on Kentucky, Websdale also said that in "fiscal year 1993 and 1994, Kentucky Domestic Violence Association (KDVA) housed 2,301 and 2,346 battered women, respectively, for varying periods of time. The rural outreach programs from each of the 16 shelters in the state report that many rural battered women cannot or will not use the services or shelters. This suggests there is a potentially large number of rural battered women whose plight is either not known or not officially documented" (1998). These findings again confirm the difficulty of acquiring accurate statistics concerning abusers and survivors of abuse, just as they indicate that the shame and fear that provoke urban victims to suppress signs of their abuse also cause rural women to conceal the truth of their circumstances.

Certainly, domestic violence surrounds us. And, ironically, physical and sexual (in combination with psychological) crimes against women are—even if the economically disadvantaged among us remain at greater risk—equal-opportunity acts. Regardless of their geographical location, race, age, or economic status, each year, at the rate of one woman every nine seconds, women are attacked by their partners (Landes, Squyres, and Quiram 1997), causing "battering by an intimate partner to be the single most frequent cause of injury to women in the United States" (Sipe and Hall 1996). As contemporary society achieves increasing levels of technological sophistication, our information overload includes overwhelming evidence of the pervasiveness of this barbarism that we still struggle harder to ignore than to banish.

Survivors of such violence tend to keep silent. Abusers assure their victims that the violence that they experience is their—the victims'—fault. Eventually, abuse survivors are so beaten emotionally as well as physically that they believe their batterers' excuses. And, when women are abused, people who know them often ignore them. Too terrified to risk involvement, family and friends turn away. Also, ironically, when women are battered, it is the people who don't know them who condemn them the most. An ignorant public perceives battered women to be weak because they "permit" themselves to be tortured. Such pundits call battered women passive and pathetic if they cannot escape their abusers. Battered women could, strangers say, leave, if only they had backbones, if only they would assume responsibility for their fates.

Do battered women frighten us? Certainly, they can anger us. And, apparently, it is easier to pass judgment on abuse survivors than it is to censure abusers, just as it is simpler to turn away from than to confront the complicated faces of abuse. After all, individual cases of battering, if uncovered and contemplated, could mirror other, more familiar conflicts, conflicts closer to home.

It is interesting to note that the predictors of batterers' behavior do not appear to exist for the women whom they abuse. Researchers Gerald Hotaling and David Sugarman, who analyzed four hundred cases of domestic violence, report in their *Journal of Family Violence* article, "A Risk Marker Analysis of Assaulted Wives" (1990), that before their abuse, women cannot be distinguished from their nonabused counterparts. Neither personality traits, age, race, educational level, occupation, number of years in a relationship, nor number of children serve as signals to target women most likely to be abused. And, Hotaling and Sugarman discovered that, unlike men who become batterers, even women who witnessed abuse of one parent by another or who were themselves abused as children do not necessarily gravitate, as adults, to abusive relationships (1990). Not all researchers agree with these authors' findings that a woman's prior victimization retains little or no correlation to any subsequent abusive relationships that she may experience (Landes, Squyres, and Quiram 1997). But a significant aspect of Hotaling and Sugarman's research remains their emphasis that a woman's low or lack of self-esteem may be a consequence, rather than a cause, of her battering.

An increasing phenomenon related to abuse that is not so much recent as recently publicized is that of female survivors of abuse striking back by assaulting or killing their abusers. But as Evelyn J. Hall, a licensed marriage and family therapist who also serves as clinical supervisor of the Counseling Office for Temporary Assistance for Domestic Crisis (TADC) in Las Vegas, Nevada, wrote in her essay, "The Counselor's Perspective," in *I Am Not Your Victim: Anatomy of Domestic Violence*, edited by Beth Sipe and Evelyn J. Hall (1996), "A battered woman usually kills only in self-defense after prolonged severe abuse; she usually has no intent to kill." In the same essay, Hall added, "Typically, a battered woman who remains in a violent relationship for a long period of time is viewed as weak-willed, masochistic, lacking intelligence, or all three. In fact, the opposite is true. She could not survive the years of abuse if she did not have great strength and resourcefulness."

Hall noted that abused women who kill their batterers tend to have "made frequent calls to police agencies for help," but she added that "[trust] in social service providers, healthcare (both physical and mental) professionals, and judicial system representatives is difficult for a woman who has turned to such agents—often repeatedly—to little or no avail." And even though an estimated "22% to 35% of women seen in emergency rooms annually have been injured by battery," Hall wrote that "the medical community has frequently failed to notice, comment on, or intervene in obvious cases of domestic violence" (1996).

From a therapist's viewpoint, Hall said that counseling an abused woman who has killed her batterer "often [focuses] on . . . her legal defense. In most cases," Hall wrote, "the woman is charged with first-degree murder, even though she has no past criminal record." Pointing out the emotional complications of such a client's arrest and of the legal proceedings surrounding her case, Hall wrote, "One issue is how police have treated her. . . . This treatment by the justice system when a woman acts in self-defense extends the wound created by the abuse." She also commented, "The counselor is likely to observe the most severe symptoms of PTSD [post-traumatic stress disorder] as the woman struggles to deal with her shame, degradation, terror, remorse, and anguish about all that has transpired" (1996).

Post-traumatic stress disorder, of which battered woman syndrome (BWS) is a part, is a psychological condition that prohibits people who have experienced extreme fear from distinguishing whether or not a threat remains present. Such individuals, who may otherwise maintain normal psychological profiles, suffer flashbacks of the violence they survived, memories that, because they grow more vivid and painful each time they're revisited, are eventually revised or erased by a form of subconscious, self-protective amnesia. But the "forgetting" that reduces a victim's stress, thereby allowing her to cope, also tends to limit her ability to envision alternatives or to always make what people unable to comprehend her position might deem wise choices (Landes, Squyres, and Quiram 1997). Long-term decision making, stressed Lenore Walker, author of *Terrifying Love: Why Battered Women Kill and How Society Responds* (1989), among other landmark works on the topic, becomes almost impossible for women who, to survive, have been forced to shift their focus from planning their futures to surviving the moment. Walker pointed out that the learned helplessness manifested by most survivors of abuse is the aspect of PTSD that distinguishes sufferers of battered woman syndrome. Because such women suffer abuse no matter what their actual behavior, they learn to regard the outcomes of their own actions, rather than their batterers' behavior, as unreliable. Over time, the increasingly distorted perceptions that permit battered women to develop acute short-term survival skills also cause their perspectives to narrow.

Some scholars, such as Lee Bowker in his article "A Battered Woman's Problems are Social, Not Psychological" in *Current Controversies* (1994), object to the theory that abused women suffer learned helplessness on the ground that domestic violence results from systemic societal, as opposed to individual psychological, dysfunction. Labeling abused women as helpless, argued Bowker and others, serves only to revictimize individuals who, in reality, demonstrate sophisticated survival skills.

But as domestic violence scholars Evan Stark and Anne Flitcraft suggest in their book, *Women at Risk* (1996), battered women's behavior, like the behavior of their batterers, is probably best and most accurately understood as a phenomenon at once social and psychological created together by the partners in abusive relationships and their social networks. To admit that abuse cripples its victims psychologically and physically in covert as well as in overt ways, often for a lifetime, does not and should not negate abuse survivors' awesome emotional and spiritual strength. Because survival, by definition, depends on transcending trauma, eliminating the concept and the terms *victim* and *victimization* from discussion of abuse trivializes, instead of substantiates, battered women and their experiences.

Hall (1996) stressed the importance for women who have killed their abusers of maintaining regular contact with counselors educated in the dynamics of domestic violence, yet she also emphasized that the financial stress of paying for their legal defense adds more strain to such survivors' lives. And even though Hall avoided discussing the fact, women with severe financial constraints often experience few opportunities to obtain accredited counseling that they can afford.

And lack of funds to pay for a private attorney, like lack of money to pay for counseling, can cost a defendant plenty. As Richard H.C. Clay, president of the Kentucky Bar Association, pointed out in his April 11, 1999, *Courier-Journal* editorial, "In Defense of Public Defenders," Kentucky, a state whose public defenders represent more than 100,000 clients each year, "funded its defender system at a little over $5 per Kentucky citizen in 1998. In that same year, [the state] only spent an average of $183 for a public defender to defend a single case. This places Kentucky at or near the bottom of all states in the nation in this area" (Clay 1999). Clay said that a significant factor for such low figures is public defenders' insufficient salaries. He wrote, "Kentucky public defenders can earn only $23,388 right out of law school. This is the lowest starting salary of any of the seven surrounding states. . . . The disparity is even worse in comparison to prosecutors, who are also chronically underfunded. . . . No wonder the turnover is high; on the state level, the annual turnover is 12 percent. In Lexington, the turnover soared in 1998 to 53 percent, while in Louisville it was at 27 percent. These are symptoms of a very serious problem" (Clay 1999). Although conscientious attorneys aim to defend their clients to the best of their abilities, underfunded, overworked legal representatives too often find their abilities, their ideals, and their clients' interests compromised in their efforts to execute intractable caseloads.

Susan L. Miller, an associate professor of sociology at Northern Illinois University, broadened the discussion of how battered women are treated by the legal system by writing in "The Fatal Flaw: Inadequacies in Social Support and Criminal Justice Responses," another essay in Sipe and Hall's book (1996),

Women who use self-defense against violent men generally are treated more harshly by the criminal justice system. . . . Part of this disparity involves a cultural double standard that warns women not to step out of their proscribed gender roles and be violent (like men). The other part concerns the law of self-defense itself. . . . [The] law of self-defense was designed by men, for situations involving typical male action. The law was developed to handle two basic circumstances: a sudden attack by a stranger or a brawl that escalates. . . . The underlying assumptions are that both participants enter willingly, that they are of roughly equal size and strength, and that the event is an isolated incident occurring in a public place between strangers or near strangers where withdrawal or escape is impossible. Most women who kill their abusive partners in self-defense, however, don't fit into these situations.

Miller pointed out that, nationally, before the mid-1980s, law enforcement agents remained reluctant to arrest batterers, as they were trained to believe that domestic violence is a private matter. But advocates for crime victims and for battered women became adamant in their insistence that abusers be punished. She identified the 1984 Minneapolis experiment, a study that concluded that arrest acts as a greater deterrent to repeat violence than does crisis counseling, as the impetus that caused numerous states and Jefferson County, Kentucky, to enact mandatory arrest policies for batterers. But in the almost two decades since that time, arrest has only proved effective in combination with prosecution, and Miller addressed the irony inherent in the fact that police and judges still rarely ask abuse victims themselves, the experts concerning their own cases, what sort of assistance would help (1996).

And as to why so many battered women do not or, ultimately, cannot leave their abusers, Miller said, "The time immediately following the violence is often the hardest . . . for a battered woman to leave, because although [her] bruises may still be fresh, [her abuser's] promises sound even more sweet. It is also the most dangerous time for her to leave. . . . Over 50% of women who leave violent relationships are followed, harassed, or further attacked by their estranged partners. . . . Another study indicates that more than half of the men who killed their wives did so following a separation" (1996).

Miller noted that battered women, whose self-esteem has almost always been warped, if not wiped out, by their batterers, retain the desperate need to believe their abusers' promises not to wound them again, even as they attempt to act more in accordance with their batterers' wishes. For abuse victims believe what their batterers preach: that any assaults they experience result from their own imperfect behavior, a viewpoint reinforced by "[police], prosecutors, and judges [who] have routinely trivialized battering of women by men, thus reinforcing the social message that this violent behavior is acceptable, that somehow the woman 'deserved' it, that she provoked his anger, that she could do something if she really wanted to stop it, or that she was trying to garner some attention for herself." She wrote, too, that "[economic] dependency on the abuser is real. Battered women and their children, once they leave the abuser, often face poverty, short-term shelter stays, inadequate long-term housing options for low-income women, and generally inferior housing and marginal financial help . . . , all of which is exacerbated if the woman has minimal job skills and/or dependent children" (1996).

Most important is Miller's conclusion that the "image of the helpless passive victim, who 'chooses' to remain in an abusive relationship, contributes to stereotypes that belie another truth, namely, that remaining in an abusive relationship can also be viewed as a survival struggle in which a woman is desperately trying to shield her children from harm, maintain daily tasks, and figure out how and when to safely make the break." Miller asked, "What do the acts of resiliency and resistance mean?" And she responded that when society learns to regard women who have been abused as "long-term survivors and crisis-managers" rather than "as passive victims in an unequal power struggle," people will begin to understand battered women's motives and their actual, as opposed to their imagined, choices (1996).

Other issues, such as educating health care professionals to recognize abuse and to provide battered women with service information, such as understanding the effects on children of witnessing battering, such as differentiating between a woman's need to remain with her batterer as her perceived way of protecting her children, and such as the judicial system's determination of her competency regarding custody, are not only significant but also vital. So, too, are such issues regarding battered women's shelters as their adequacy in terms of their availability and in terms of their ability to house not only women but also women with male, as well as female, children.

Across the nation, as well as in Kentucky, programs to aid survivors of domestic violence abound. Plastic surgeons have created Face to Face: Domestic Violence Project, a national program that offers free reconstructive surgery to survivors of domestic abuse whose features have been altered by violence (Rubiner 1996). A new federal law prevents domestic violence offenders from owning firearms. In New York City, special courts have been formed to handle domestic violence cases exclusively, and in Washington, D.C., teams of judges, instead of individual judges for each issue involved, now hear domestic violence cases. Philip Morris Companies, Inc., in conjunction with the National Network to End Domestic Violence Fund, have formed a statewide network, Doors of Hope, to provide for battered women's immediate food, clothing, shelter, and counseling needs, as well as to provide employment training (Dusky

1997). And since 1992 Kentucky's domestic violence laws have been among the nation's most progressive; these laws will realize their integrity when they are recognized and enforced by all of the commonwealth's law enforcers and judges. Public awareness, led by such unprecedented public and private sector alliances as Louisville's Take Back the Night, multiply each year. But until we each understand that domestic violence is not only *a* problem but *our* problem, our mothers, daughters, sisters, and friends will be assaulted. And, one by one, they may, in turn, be forced to fight back.

The Quilting Circle at the Women's Correctional Center in Pee Wee Valley, Kentucky

Sisters in pain, we piece this quilt
From the remnants of our lives,
From patches and scraps and cuttings
Swept up from creased linoleum
And lamentations of dust. From
These wads of gathered lint,
From these frayed leavings, we sew
Tapestries of incest, batterings, and rape
That we and our mothers' children
Fall heir to. Joined, we must believe
They will make us whole.

But no matter what we say
About how ritual and talk
Promise comfort, promise cure,
Survival is the hardest art.
Though each garish square is testimony
To mend the tatters of terror and shame,
These emblems of abuse only sheathe
The teased cotton batting,
The unraveling thread.
As each pierce of the needle
Stitches the fragments whole,
Believe, O believe, this fabric bleeds.

Richard Taylor

Politics, the Prison Quilt, and Parole

It's no secret that as recently as the turn of the twentieth century women were schooled in such domestic arts as cooking and sewing, while, with few exceptions, academic disciplines remained the realm of men. But it's significant to ten Kentucky women who, at the century's close, were paroled from prison that the selfsame form of needlework that permitted pioneer women to express their ingenuity and creativity proved pivotal in communicating the horrific abuse of their descendants. In the spring of 1995 women from throughout the state who had been incarcerated for killing, for conspiring to kill, or for assaulting their husbands or boyfriends, who, the women swore, had for years and even decades physically, sexually, and psychologically battered them—completed a quilt that, in crude but powerful hand-drawn patches, depicts the violent assaults that scarred their daily lives. After sketching on their quilt squares the scenes that still haunted them, those women so recoiled from reliving what they had drawn that every evening they traded their completed squares so that they could sleep. As difficult as it was to harbor images of their own pain, caring for their friends' quilt pieces could be cathartic, they said; protecting others from the emotions that they themselves could not escape permitted them to feel empowered and therefore worthwhile. When the quilt hung on display August 17-27, 1995, in the South Wing Building at the Kentucky State Fair, Gov. Brereton Jones recognized in its grisly-yet-poignant pattern stories that demanded further research. In a matter of months those close investigations led to the New Year's parole from prison of ten women, many of whom had created the quilt. While the inmates' handiwork hung at the fair, WAVE-3, a Louisville television station that produced an in-depth feature series by reporter Connie Leonard on the quilt and its makers for the evening news, referred to the women as "Sisters in Pain," a term by which several of the women began to refer to themselves and to each other. Thus the pastime that had for centuries provided women in the western world a distinct voice was, ironically, the means by which a feisty cohort of contemporary Kentucky women who'd survived persecution by intimates finally made themselves heard. None of these women had quilted before, and it is probable that none of them will undertake such a project again. But through discussing their collective tale of completing the Sisters in Pain quilt, most of the women, in their attempts to educate the public in the dynamics of abuse, have also learned to articulate their own life stories. This is the collective story of those battered women's imprisonment and parole.

On May 16, 1994, Chandra McElroy, a south Louisville native who'd graduated in 1992 from the University of Louisville with a bachelor's degree in counseling and guidance and in 1993 from the University of Cincinnati with a master's degree in criminal justice, started work as an offender rehabilitation specialist at the Kentucky Correctional Institution for Women (KCIW) in Pee Wee Valley, Kentucky. She relished her role as a counselor to individual inmates as well as to groups of prisoners who shared common problems, and the tales that her Emminence, Kentucky, police officer husband told her concerning his domestic violence calls fueled her passion for justice. Stereotypical responses to battered women's plights baffled and angered her: "Everybody always says why doesn't [a battered woman] just leave. Well, how come people aren't asking why is [her batterer] abusing her, why is he allowed to get away with it, why isn't he being taken out of the home and thrown into jail? It's just like in rape [cases]; everybody says, 'She was walking around there' or 'She was wearing that,'" she said. Similarly, McElroy railed against what she regards as the judicial system's chauvinistic attitude toward survivors of abuse: "The main thing is that a lot of their attorneys . . . say [not] to talk about the abuse because that looks like a motive for what happened, when I think [the women's abuse is] the most essential thing to talk about. Or [battered women are] told to take a plea bargain, because if [they] don't take a plea bargain, [they're] going to get the death penalty."

So when two inmates, Sue Melton and Sherry Pollard, each of whom were convicted of murder or of conspiring to kill their abusive spouses, asked McElroy to create a therapy group for battered women, she did. On August 8, 1994, twelve prisoners convicted of crimes related to the serious injury or death of their abusers formed the Battered Offenders' Self-Help Group (B.O.S.H.) at the KCIW. To join the group, an inmate had to meet three requirements: she had to have been involved in an abusive relationship; she had to have been charged with the murder of or with a crime related to the death of her abuser; and as specified in McElroy's July 25 memorandum inviting eligible inmates to join the group, she had to "take responsibility for [her] actions and admit what has happened to [her] and what [she has] done." The memo concluded, "This is the only way the healing process can be fully effective for [participants] and [for] the other members of the group."

B.O.S.H. existed until January 1996 as what McElroy regards a significant therapeutic outlet for women who, until sharing their life experiences with one another, had thought their struggles unique. These women, who considered themselves worthless and who believed that their own behavior, even their own existence, was the cause of their abuse, because that is what their batterers had convinced them was the case, began to sense for the first time their value as human beings. Comparing notes allowed them to see the patterns in their batterers' behavior and in their own responses. The eight to twelve women (after the first few months of meetings, the group consisted of eight permanent members) gathered each Monday afternoon at 2:30 to discuss their experiences; they gained strength from the camaraderie, which they'd all missed as women who were kept isolated by their abusers from family, friends, and organizations—from individuals and institutions—who might have offered help. Their prison sentences ranged from fifteen years to life.

"In general, I think the main thing [B.O.S.H.] helped with was the guilt the women felt for being responsible for somebody's death or serious injury," McElroy said. She added, "Six months after B.O.S.H. disbanded, [the group was still helping] members trust themselves, because they had made some pretty bad decisions in their lives. They were learning how to make better decisions, and [they were learning] how to trust one another."

McElroy described how one of the group's founders, Sherry Pollard, said nothing at all during the first six months during which the group met, then talked nonstop once she learned to trust her Sisters in Pain. And she recalled how B.O.S.H. members grew in their ability to make simple decisions during their first year of meetings. At first, she said, none of the women could even articulate for themselves, much less for one another, their choice of food for dinner, as they remained convinced from their batterers' brainwashing that they were incapable of making the most basic decisions.

"Pulling from my own past, my own home life growing up, I made some pretty bad decisions myself," McElroy commented. "And I saw," she said, "how I could have easily gone down the same path they did. But I chose differently, and I was lucky, so I knew that [these women] could make things better for themselves if they tried."

Two other women thought so, too. Marsha Weinstein, a Louisville activist for women's issues who had once worked as a social worker and who had been appointed by Governor Jones as the executive director of the Kentucky Commission on Women, had determined, in accepting that role, to do what she could to gain clemency for incarcerated women who'd been battered. Weinstein had demonstrated a lifelong passion for curbing domestic violence and its cyclical repercussions that radiate through families as rampant dysfunction; a March 4, 1991, *Time* magazine news brief inspired her to act. The article said that in "December 1990 Ohio's outgoing Governor Richard F. Celeste granted clemency to 26 women convicted of killing or assaulting men who had battered them." Further research informed Weinstein that since 1978 about eighty-nine women nationwide had been granted pardon or parole, and she learned that, according to the U.S. Bureau of Statistics, of all the women in the United States incarcerated for killing a spouse, 70 percent were first-time offenders and the majority of those who had received clemency had not been arrested again.

Weinstein's friend, Helen Howard-Hughes, whom Governor Jones had recently appointed chairperson of the Commonwealth of Kentucky Parole Board, had, in her former role as executive director of the Kentucky Commission on Women, received a federal grant to conduct domestic violence research. This research, despite having been gathered fifteen years before, still constituted, in the mid-1990s, the sole data concerning domestic violence victims in Kentucky. She, too, had vowed to make a difference in abuse survivors' lives.

In early spring 1994, the two appointees, still new to their positions, met for lunch at Flynn's, the Frankfort eatery notorious as the location for striking political deals. The upshot of their discussion, their shared desire to convince the governor to grant clemency to abused inmates, resulted in Howard-Hughes's vow to start reviewing the records of the commonwealth's 116 women prisoners serving sentences for murder, manslaughter, reckless homicide, and assault to determine whether domestic violence had been a factor in their cases. Weinstein returned to her office to contact the governor's general counsel, Mike Alexander, to determine the legal procedures involved in granting such pardons.

According to Weinstein, the mission that she and Howard-Hughes set for themselves suffered from the start because of the popular point of view, especially as espoused by the career politicians, men and women alike, whom she referred to as "the good old boys," who dominated Kentucky politics across party lines. They assumed that women "stupid" enough to remain in abusive relationships deserve their battering and that killing by women cannot be justified, despite any mitigating circumstances, even though men who shoot intruders are absolved for killing in self-defense. Weinstein said that the governor's general counsel informed her that the governor's policy was to grant pardons only to felons who had been out of prison for a decade or more. That policy, in conjunction with the fact that Kentucky's progressive domestic violence laws, passed in 1992, remained largely unenforced two years later due to a pervasive nonchalance concerning the lack of education about or interest in upholding those laws by police, attorneys, and judges, caused the two women to discuss only in private schemes that they believed could be sabotaged.

Meanwhile, the B.O.S.H. Group had met for almost four months when McElroy, on behalf of its members, sent letters to social service and political agency executives throughout the state seeking information about domestic violence. When Weinstein received her letter from McElroy on December 2, 1994, she regarded the request as her opportunity to meet with abuse survivors. By listening to the women's stories, Weinstein believed that she could begin to identify those prisoners whose histories of battering might justify their release. In April 1995 Weinstein met with McElroy and the B.O.S.H. Group, but before she talked with the inmates, she and Sherry Currens, the executive director of the Kentucky Domestic Violence Association, whom Weinstein had brought to the prison with her, discussed several of the prisoners' histories with Betty Kassulke, KCIW's warden. Weinstein, who documented the gist of their three-way conversation for her records, recalled the excitement that she and Currens shared upon learning Kassulke's views. Not only, according to Weinstein, did the warden voice her conviction that several of the B.O.S.H. Group members should be released from prison, but she also agreed with Currens that the 1992 state law known as the Fifty Percent Rule, which entitles victims of domestic violence to a parole board hearing after having served 20 percent of their sentences (instead of after having served the 50 percent of their sentences otherwise required of violent offenders) should be tested. To date, no inmate had been released under that law. During their discussion, Weinstein also learned from Currens that Kentucky law required a legal form to be completed at the time of an inmate's sentencing questioning whether that person had ever been a victim of domestic violence. But that law, Currens noted, like most other domestic violence statutes on the books, continued to be overlooked.

Weinstein cites that meeting with Currens and Kassulke as the occasion when she first understood the extent of battered offenders' legal dilemmas. Attorneys representing women on trial for capital crimes often insist that their clients resist all allusion to any abuse they may have endured, as battering can serve as a motive to kill.

Weinstein gained additional insights from her exchange with Currens and the B.O.S.H. Group. Most of the group's members had lived in rural communities or in urban subcultures "where . . . family, friends, [and] neighbors [believe that no one] should interfere with any man's business," and where the women's batterers had isolated their victims even more by cutting phone lines, by abandoning them without money or transportation, by threatening anyone who might intervene, by nailing shut windows through which the women and their children might have escaped, and even by breaking their victims' toes so they couldn't walk away. A woman's and her children's welfare was, in these women's communities, considered her husband's business, and family members, friends, or neighbors who had later refuted that philosophy had protested too little, too late.

Few of the B.O.S.H. Group members had completed high school, and none of them had attended college. They were all raised in low-income families, and those who wed married into families whose circumstances were similar, if not the same. Like them, their parents and spouses experienced limited formal education. Most of the women, as was the case with their spouses or significant others, had been physically, sexually, and psychologically battered by at least one member of their birth families. Almost all of the women spoke of the presence in their early lives of a fundamentalist form of religion, a theology focused on fear, guilt, and sin. At least half of the group members had been married to men who wore uniforms—policemen and National Guard reservists—and who donned their official garb before they sexually tortured their victims. Those same men killed family pets by snapping off kittens' heads with a jerk of their wrists and by leaving poisoned dogs on sidewalks for their children to find. Such sadistic behavior served as warnings to women who thought that they or their children could escape their abusers unscathed. Yet despite such bloody exhortations and the women's fears, almost every B.O.S.H. Group member had attempted, some again and again, to flee their batterers. The few human, financial, and institutional resources available to the women had proved no match for their abusers, who had calculated their own controlling stratagems for years.

The majority of B.O.S.H. Group members had experienced escalating violence, and most declared having felt resigned to dying sooner or later at their batterers' hands, just as they expressed having felt that such an end would be preferable to further abuse. Ultimately, in most of the women's cases, it wasn't their own torture, but imminent threats by their abusers to murder the women's children—or, it could be argued, in Tracie English's case, her father's killing of her beloved dog—that caused them to confront their molesters.

The B.O.S.H. Group members' experiences presented additional similarities, parallels that they pointed out in their meeting with Weinstein and Currens. Most of their batterers had been friends with, related to, or employed by the only local officials to whom their abuse could have been reported; in several cases, when the women did confide their abuse and request help, their pleas were ignored or their batterers, after being reprimanded, punished their victims by turning on them with renewed vigor. And all of the women, powerless and, in most cases, penniless, remained dependent on legal counsel appointed by their communities, attorneys whose interests may have conflicted, in some cases, with the welfare of the women they represented. Weinstein recalls inmate Karen Stout (now Karen Stelzer) as having asked her, "Why is it that when men go away to war to protect this country they come home heroes, yet when women attempt to protect their children, they are punished and imprisoned?"

Why, indeed, Weinstein recalls wondering. But another group member's comment, "No one cares about us and we have no voice," triggered Weinstein's memory of having read that, in recent eras, women without a political voice had expressed themselves through their handiwork. On the spot, Weinstein proposed to the B.O.S.H. Group that its members do the same, that they design a quilt to depict the battering they'd survived. Weinstein and McElroy said that the women embraced the notion as a means of signaling to other abused women messages of strength and as a vehicle for forcing the public to confront the monstrous truth of spousal abuse. Weinstein then asked the B.O.S.H. constituents if they would permit their common cause as well as their separate cases to be examined before "the court of public opinion." She would contact members of the press, reporters from the print and broadcast media throughout Kentucky, and encourage them to investigate the women's stories. The inmates agreed to Weinstein's plan.

Within a week McElroy purchased material for the women to construct their quilt. It's probably fair to state that when she checked out at her local Wal-Mart the cheap pink and white cloth and the broad-tipped colored markers with which the women she counseled would recreate emblems of their torture, McElroy couldn't have conceived that such a therapeutic exercise, no matter how eagerly embraced by its creators, would within months be exhibited not only across the state and nation but also around the world as a symbol of abuse survivors' stamina. Had she known, McElroy might have bought better materials. And, had the B.O.S.H. Group members known, they might have sketched and sewn with more care. But in the quilt's stark truth rests its power. The crude handiwork that conveys its makers' strength also articulates their truths and signifies their first attempts to trust. A pretty quilt would have constituted a cover-up of the sort that its makers had known all their lives. A more pleasing piece of work would have proven a lie.

One day, while the B.O.S.H. Group members were working on their quilt, Karen received a postcard of the Statue of Liberty. After showing her Sisters the photo of Lady Liberty that her brother had sent, Karen and the women made a pact that, should they ever get out of prison, they would head to New York and meet at the Statue of Liberty, the female symbol of freedom that they agreed to adopt as their own.

As the women's graphic quilt squares multiplied, the reporters whom Weinstein had contacted began to find their way to the Kentucky Correctional Institution for Women. The journalists who came to interview the B.O.S.H.

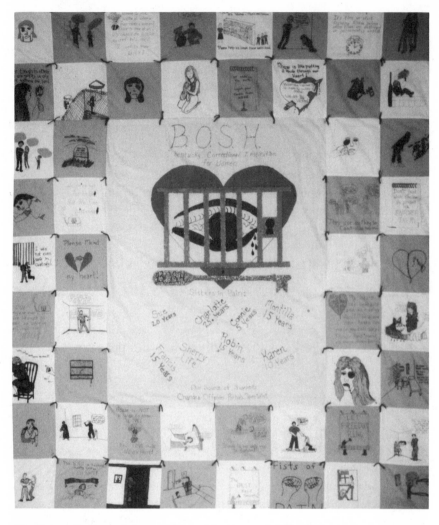

The Prison Quilt, made by members of the Battered Offenders Self-Help (B.O.S.H.) Group at the Kentucky Women's Correctional Institution in Pee Wee Valley, Kentucky. Photo by Geoffrey Carr, courtesy of Shelly Zegart, the Kentucky Quilt Project, and the Alliance of American Quilts.

constituents encountered in the women a united force whose matching blue T-shirts bore a sketch of a human eye staring through prison bars. The state's two largest newspapers, Louisville's *Courier-Journal* and Lexington's *Herald-Leader*, would eventually commit their front pages and many more pages to the B.O.S.H. Group and its members' cases. The positive publicity further encouraged the

Above, Center square of the B.O.S.H. Group Prison Quilt. The square was designed and executed by a Kentucky Women's Correctional Institution inmate who wished to remain anonymous. Photo by Thomas R. Oates. *Left*, Quilt square by Offender Rehabilitation Specialist and B.O.S.H. Group leader Chandra McElroy. Photo by Geoffrey Carr, courtesy of Shelly Zegart, the Kentucky Quilt Project, and the Alliance of American Quilts.

All quilt squares by Sherry Pollard. Photos by Geoffrey Carr, courtesy of Shelly Zegart, the Kentucky Quilt Project, and the Alliance of American Quilts.

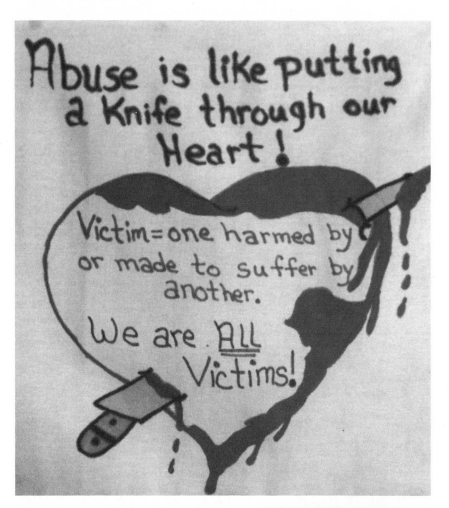

Both quilt squares by Karen Stout (Stelzer). Photos by Geoffrey Carr, courtesy of Shelly Zegart, the Kentucky Quilt Project, and the Alliance of American Quilts.

Both quilt squares by Karen Stout (Stelzer). Photos by Geoffrey Carr, courtesy of Shelly Zegart, the Kentucky Quilt Project, and the Alliance of American Quilts.

Both quilt squares by Sue Melton. Photo by Geoffrey Carr, courtesy of Shelly Zegart, the Kentucky Quilt Project, and the Alliance of American Quilts.

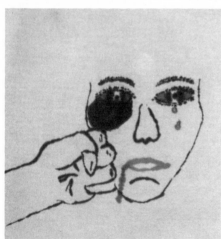

All quilt squares by Sue Melton. Photo by Geoffrey Carr, courtesy of Shelly Zegart, the Kentucky Quilt Project, and the Alliance of American Quilts.

Prison Counselor (Offender Rehabilitation Specialist) Chandra McElroy with the Battered Offenders Self-Help Group at the Kentucky Women's Correctional Institution in Pee Wee Valley, Kentucky. *Front,* Chandra McElroy. *Middle, left to right,* Charlotte Haycraft, Frances Alvey, Sue Melton, Sherry Pollard, and Robin Bailey. *Back,* Connie Conway McMillan, Karen Stout (Stelzer), and Montilla Seewright. Photo by Chandra McElroy.

women to think that their unabridged stories would one day be told, but one of the B.O.S.H. Group's founders, Sherry Pollard, experienced savage repercussions when her former in-laws, outraged that her story should find so public a forum, forbade her eleven-year-old daughter to communicate with her.

But the Sisters in Pain's shared mission strengthened. In addition to executing their quilt squares, B.O.S.H. Group members, as well as other battered inmates whom McElroy counseled one-on-one but who'd chosen not to belong to the group, dictated their life stories to an inmate who typed their autobiographies for them. According to McElroy, the dual purpose of the women's committing their stories to paper was to have the survivors, all of whom continued to express guilt and regret over their batterers' deaths, reflect on their lives as a means of achieving perspective concerning their own roles in their own and their batterers' fates and to have their self-described stories recorded should their cases be reviewed.

By the last week of May 1995, the B.O.S.H. Group members had completed all fifty-two squares of their quilt, and they had also documented their lives. McElroy bought a quilt hanger for her office so that she could display the women's handiwork and, if she liked, focus on a different depiction of pain or survival each week for a year. Karen Stout (Stelzer), whose case Howard-Hughes had reviewed, made parole after a reconsideration hearing based on the abuse that she had suffered at the hands of her spouse. In so doing, she became the first woman in the state to be released from prison under the guidelines of Kentucky's 1992 domestic violence laws. And, in her position with the Kentucky Commission on Women, Weinstein had decided to include her pet project of gaining clemency for battered women criminals in her planning for a state fair exhibit to celebrate the seventy-fifth anniversary of women's suffrage. She decided that the focus of her display depicting women's struggles for freedom would, in addition to suffrage memorabilia, be the B.O.S.H. Group's quilt.

By August, when the state fair got under way in Louisville and McElroy had driven the quilt from her office to the fair for public display, the press had primed the public concerning the dynamics of spousal abuse through news reports, feature stories, and editorials that highlighted the multiple dimensions of the quilt makers' lives and legal cases. Men, women, and children queued to view the quilt, and even longer lines formed after Louisville television stations featured the B.O.S.H. Group's handiwork on the morning, noon, and evening news. State fair officials told McElroy that fairgoers' comments rated the Sisters in Pain Quilt, which would later be dubbed the Prison Quilt, the single most popular piece of stitchery displayed at the fair to date, and on the basis of such unsuspected and overwhelming affirmation, Weinstein staked her mission to attain the quilt makers' release on Governor Jones's sympathy.

She led Jones and his wife, Libby, guests at the seventy-fifth celebration of women's suffrage, to see the B.O.S.H. members' quilt. Weinstein steered the couple to the quilt in hopes of heightening the governor's awareness of the abuses that its makers had survived. She noticed that Jones, upon seeing the quilt, started to cry. The real-life scenario that in a novel or a film script would be cut for seeming artificial and sentimental consisted of Jones turning to Weinstein and saying, "We have got to see about getting these women out of prison before I leave office." Weinstein responded, "Governor, Helen Howard-Hughes and the parole board have begun to review their cases." "Good," said Jones. "This is one thing we *can* take care of." In an interview two years later, Jones commented, "Without the quilt, in honesty, I doubt [the women's parole] would have happened, because [the quilt] made [their plight] very clear. It's possible that Marsha [Weinstein] could have brought the information in the form of letters or petitions, and [their parole] might have happened that way. But the quilt was so easy to focus on. Many things in our society—if they're visual and right there in front of you—you grab them. If they're not visual, and if they're not readily attainable in a busy day, you may or may not be able to focus on them."

By summer's end, Weinstein and Howard-Hughes's campaign had caught fire. On August 22, McElroy and Stout (Stelzer), the latter who'd been paroled in time to see her own handiwork featured at the fair, testified before the state's Legislative Domestic Violence Task Force. They intended their testimony to educate lawmakers about the discrepancies between Kentucky's progressive domestic violence laws and the lax enforcement of those statutes. By October, the Kentucky Department of Public Advocacy had gotten word of the B.O.S.H. Group's efforts, and Marguerite Thomas, an assistant public advocate who also served as a postconviction specialist for the Kentucky Department of Public Advocacy, contacted McElroy stating that she wanted to help eligible abused women incarcerated in the Kentucky Correctional Institution for Women seek clemency. Howard-Hughes asked parole board member Joanie Abramson to review and summarize the files of 120 women who had received convictions for murder, manslaughter, assault, and reckless homicide. The seven-member board met numerous times over the next several months to review the confidential inmate files, along with the information compiled by Abramson and board member Ted Kuster. The board members voted on each case and, ultimately, requested that the governor commute the sentences of nine women, which would make it possible for the board to conduct parole hearings. But before the hearings could be conducted, the families of the men had to be notified and "victim hearings" held in order for the families and other interested parties to express their opposition to the women's parole.

Thomas stated, "Meanwhile, what was happening was [that] I was getting so personally involved with these women. I'm used to dealing . . . with inmates, and they're needy people. These women were well beyond needy, and not only were they needy, [but] they were the best thing to happen in my life at the same time, because they were so wonderful, . . . so pure, so honest, . . . so generous, so compassionate. I don't think I ever hugged so many people in such a short time in all my life. That's all [I] *could* do."

Thomas agreed that she and three colleagues that she appointed would defend the nine inmates targeted by Howard-Hughes, as well as the four prisoners whose cases she and McElroy thought warranted review.

The original group of nine women targeted for early clemency hearings included Tracie English, a Louisvillian who'd been convicted in 1991 of first-degree manslaughter in the death of her father, William C. English. She would be twenty-two at the time of her parole, and she'd been sentenced to prison for twenty years. Charlotte Haycraft, age thirty-four in January 1995, had been convicted in 1994 by a Grayson County court of the murder of her husband, Byron Haycraft. Her prison sentence was twenty-five years. Fifty-four-year-old Mary Ann Long of McCracken County had been sentenced to fifteen years in prison for the death of her spouse, William Long. Her 1992 conviction was "first-degree manslaughter under extreme emotional disturbance." Johnetta McNair, a thirty-six-year-old Lexingtonian, had been sentenced in 1992 by a Fayette County court to twelve years in prison for first-degree manslaughter in the death of her boyfriend, Anthony Thomas Pierce. Margie Marcum, forty-five, was sentenced in 1992 in Martin County to spend fifteen years in prison for first-degree manslaughter in the death of her husband, Marion Marcum. In 1994, a Christian County court had convicted Sherry Pollard of murdering her husband, Danny Pollard. In 1995, the then thirty-three-year-old Pollard was serving her sentence of life in prison. By age thirty-nine, Paula Richey had served four years of her twenty-year prison sentence. In 1991, a Warren County court had convicted her of murdering her husband, Michael Richey. Montilla Seewright had been sentenced in 1993 by a Jefferson County court to spend fifteen years in prison for the first-degree assault of her boyfriend, Roy. By the date of her clemency hearing, she would be thirty-three. And thirty-one-year-old Martina Stillwell of Hardin County had been sentenced in 1989 to ten years in prison for a conviction of first-degree manslaughter in the death of her boyfriend, Darryl "Tiny" Grimes. By 1995, Stillwell had served almost six years of her sentence. Because these women's reports of repeated battering by their victims could be substantiated by such sources as school, state, and hospital records, the parole board had selected these inmates as candidates likely to gain early release from prison. Before the 1992 enactment of the Kentucky Domestic Violence Laws, they would have remained ineligible for parole until they had served half of their sentences, a stipulation of clemency hearings for all violent offenders. But the 1992 revised state law held that offenders who'd been battered by their victims could request a parole board hearing to be exempted from the violent offenders law. The nine women whose cases that Howard-Hughes and the parole board intended to review either had been denied the exemption for abused criminals or had never had hearings; by reexamining these women's cases, the parole board would set a precedent for greater judicial consistency in enforcing enacted laws.

It was late fall by the time the women's defense team fell into place; it was the final months of Governor Jones's term in office, and by all accounts, an air of extreme urgency pushed Thomas, McElroy, and their colleagues to prepare the clemency petitions.

On November 8 and 9, representatives from the Department of Public Advocacy, led by Thomas, filmed at the women's prison thirteen inmates discussing the lives they'd led with their abusers. The resultant videotape, *A Lot of Hurt*, would be shown to the members of the Kentucky Parole Board, as well as to Governor Jones.

On December 11 at 7:40 a.m., Thomas joined McElroy and the thirteen inmates whose cases had been targeted for clemency hearings at the Kentucky Correctional Institution for Women. The warden had been notified by the governor's office that the women whose cases had been reviewed should expect a call that morning from the governor.

Jones's call came fifty minutes later. Thomas remembers: "That morning was one of those life experiences I'll never forget. I got out to the prison the day the governor was supposed to call, and we had no idea what was going to happen. . . . [But I] got to the prison, and it was clear what *was* going to happen. They had already divided . . . the nine [originally designated women from] the four. They had the nine go in the conference room where the conference call was set up. They had the four go to another part [of the prison]. When Jones called, he was wonderful. He was gracious, he was kind, and he just talked. Not one single person said a word. . . . It was just stunning. I really didn't fully understand myself what was going on at the time. The silence was just humongous, and I had this motherly urge to start talking, to say, 'Excuse me, Governor Jones, they're not being rude, they're not being impolite, they're really grateful for what you're doing.' But I knew it wasn't my place to do that. . . . Everybody . . . —every single one of us—thought [the women to whom Jones had just informed he'd granted an opportunity for early parole] would have been exuberant, [and we thought] you would have heard nothing but laughter and yelling and clapping. . . . [But,] there was nothing. It was dead silent. And it was dead silent because four of their [Sisters in Pain] weren't getting out. That's what that silence meant. . . . It was also a defeat, because we had heard rumors that whole week— . . . rumors coming back . . . from the Governor's office— that he was considering pardon. So we had all this mixed up. . . . Was it going to be pardons? Commutations? . . . It was clear from that phone call that only nine [women] were getting commutations, and the next step was [for those women to have their cases heard] by the parole board, which meant nothing was for sure. So it was almost a low. It was almost . . . the lowest point in the whole process, knowing that these women truly hadn't made that big a statement, knowing that they weren't going to get pardons, and [knowing] the whole issue was not really fairly understood because their Sisters were still there." In a statement that contradicts Thomas, Howard-Hughes stressed, "The parole board had access to some inmate and victim files that were not available to anyone else. [Its members'] decisions, after numerous reviews, were based on [each woman's] total file." The four additional inmates whose cases Thomas and McElroy had petitioned the board to review were Frances Alvey, Robin Bailey, Teresa Gully Hilterbrand, and Sue Melton.

After Jones made public the names of those women he'd made eligible to come before the parole board, Howard-Hughes defended the parole board's denial of the other four women's cases by saying that because the women had not been sentenced as violent offenders, they could request early parole without the governor's intervention. But, as Thomas stated, because three of the four women denied parole—Frances Alvey, Robin Bailey, and Sue Melton— had participated in making the Sisters in Pain quilt, anger akin to mourning tempered the joy of the chosen prisoners.

According to Weinstein, Howard-Hughes's original list of women eligible for parole did not include the four additional names cited by Thomas and the Department of Public Advocacy because, in the cases of Robin Bailey, Sue Melton, and Frances Alvey, Howard-Hughes thought that the legal evidence against them outweighed their abusive experiences. Information available to Howard-Hughes and the parole board convinced them that, despite the Department of Public Advocacy's claims to the contrary, those three women's roles in their batterers' deaths could not be explained or justified by their battering alone. And Howard-Hughes's determination to show the public that the crimes of numerous battered women could be deemed acts of self-defense caused her to strike from her list the name of any inmate whose criminal history indicated motives beyond self-defense and whose reconsideration hearings might therefore jeopardize the cases of those women she deemed more deserving of early parole.

Teresa Gulley Hilterbrand's case was another matter. She had been overlooked by Howard-Hughes, as she had arrived in prison after the project started and, while incarcerated, had kept a low profile—refusing to join the B.O.S.H. Group, preferring to write about her pain in private. But in late December, after Thomas had brought Hilterbrand's case to Howard-Hughes's attention and after Hilterbrand had chastised the governor, who had known nothing about her case, on the nightly news, the chairperson of the parole board agreed that Hilterbrand's name should be added to the parole board's list.

Soon after the parole board had voted to grant clemency to the women, the list of whom had expanded from nine to ten, its members received new information concerning Frances Alvey's case, and on the basis of those facts, she, too, a year later, was granted parole. Sue Melton, who otherwise would not have been granted early release from prison, was paroled due to chronic health problems. To date, Robin Bailey is the only B.O.S.H. Group member and Sister in Pain who is still in prison.

But by that mid-December day when the governor called with his news, Thomas had educated all of the women involved concerning the difference between pardon and commutation or parole. Had Governor Jones chosen to pardon the inmates, their records would have been cleared of their convictions and, upon their release from prison, they would have been as free as any other citizens without felony convictions to vote, to fraternize with whomever they chose, and to relocate at will. But instead of pardoning nine of the prisoners, Jones had decided instead to permit them a chance for parole. That is, if, after rehearing each of their cases—this time with the women's abuse histories included in their defenses—the parole board decided to grant the inmates clemency, the women would be released from prison. But, contrary to popular public perception, they would be anything but free. Because a parolee's conviction remains on her permanent record, her continuing status as a felon translates to a lifetime of restrictions. She is not free to live wherever or with whomever she chooses. Her living arrangements must be approved by the parole board before her release, and any travel not only across state but, in many cases, across county lines must be approved for the years of her parole's duration by her local parole officer. In addition, conditions of parole almost always include a parolee's obtaining full-time employment, a difficult task for rural or otherwise-isolated, uneducated women made even more difficult by most employers' reluctance to hire convicted felons. The rule of parole that makes sense for so many types of criminals but that in its cruel irony crippled, for a time, the Sisters in Pain, is the provision that restricts convicted felons from maintaining contact with each other. The B.O.S.H. Group members, who had for the first time in their lives found safety in—of all places—a prison, and who had for the first time in their lives found strength and derived self-esteem from friendships with women whose experiences mirrored their own, would, by gaining their individual freedom, be forever restricted from phoning, writing, or visiting their Sisters in Pain. However, a few months later, Howard-Hughes wrote special memorandums to the women's parole officers exempting them from this rule to the extent that they now may communicate with each other. Parolees must also abide by other rules; they can't, for example, vote or purchase firearms or alcohol. But those limitations were not the restraints that had caused Tracie English, Charlotte Haycraft, Mary Ann Long, Johnetta McNair, Margie Marcum, Sherry Pollard, Paula Richey, Montilla Seewright, and Martina Stillwell to sit in silence on December 11, 1995, after Governor Jones announced his decision.

Thomas commented: "We felt totally gutted at the time. But now I understand [why the governor decided to commute the women's sentences instead of to grant them pardons]. Actually, [his decision] was good for the public, because he could say, 'Here is the process. I'm not just letting these people out. . . . We're going to go through the parole process where everybody has a say-so. The victims' families got to [testify]. We got to prepare [each woman's case] so the parole board [members] could really know who they were paroling. The media was involved. . . . Every single part of this process was open to the public, and it was that that made it . . . beautiful. . . . It was not backroom dealing. . . . [There was] no underhandedness. It was really a good, democratic process that was open to the public."

Later, asked why he'd decided to parole instead of pardon the nine inmates who would, with the addition of Hilterbrand's name, become ten, Jones said, "There were people on the other side [of each woman's case] who were family to the other victims. There were two victims in this situation. Family members of the other victims felt that no, [these women's release from prison] shouldn't happen. . . . I thought both sides deserved to be heard. I was confident that logic and reason were on the side of these women, . . . and [that] they could feel extremely vindicated by having gone through the process. And then [there's] the issue that sometimes develops with a governor's decision that could be termed political. I didn't know any of these [women], and I don't think I ever had contact with them or with any members of their families. But you can't be sure of that when you run for office and go into 120 counties and talk to thousands and thousands and thousands of people. . . . It's conceivable that someplace along the line I might have bumped into one of them, that one of them might have been a supporter of mine in a campaign or something. But there was no reason for them to have a cloud hanging over them. This was, to me, the much cleaner way to do it."

Thomas continued, "The media was waiting for us right after the governor's call. [Prison staff] shuffled us from one room into the media room. And, as I indicated before, I think everybody thought [the Sisters in Pain] were going to come in there yelling and screaming. [But] it was so somber. It was a very sedate, somber crowd. The media knew what was happening, and, when [the reporters] sat down, you could just see them. Their whole faces changed. Their demeanor—it became more than just a quick story [they had] to run back to their stations. They were overcome with the power of these women, [with] the intelligence of these women, [with] the compassion. I don't know; I can't even come up with enough adjectives to describe how powerful the women were that day. . . . The women were their own best advocates."

Nine of the Sisters in Pain handled the news that Governor Jones had intended as a holiday present as the fragile package they knew it to be. Jones would receive public credit for the women's fates, but the parole board would actually determine their futures. Jones hadn't delivered a promise, but he had offered hope. And the women selected to go before the parole board clung to that hope even though the news that their four Sisters in Pain had no immediate chance of parole tempered their excitement.

On December 14, 1995, a *Lexington Herald-Leader* editorial admonished the parole board to "act swiftly on the nine cases commuted by Jones." It further said that the parole board "should examine the other four cases closely to see if they too should be considered for parole.

"Battered women with no previous record of violence are rarely threats to society. Imprisoning them for lengthy sentences serves little purpose.

"The clemency petitions that had been prepared for all 13 of the women contain extensive evidence that they had suffered abuse at the hands of their victims.

"If critical details had been omitted in a particular case, these can be brought out at a parole hearing and the woman can serve out her term. If not, the women should be let free to resume their lives."

The day before, the Frankfort *State Journal* had published an even more strident opinion piece in support of Jones's decision and of the women he wanted paroled. The writer pointed out that "Jones is not the first governor of a state to offer official mercy to abused women convicted of killing their abusers, but his action at the end of his term of office was no less significant. It also focuses public attention on an area of criminal law that is woefully deficient in how the victims of domestic violence are treated by the judicial system.

"A woman who is directly confronted with a knife or gun-wielding man is justified in doing whatever is necessary to protect herself, but a woman repeatedly beaten and injured, confronted with the immediate prospect of further injury and threats of worse, in all likelihood will go to prison for doing whatever is necessary to protect herself.

"That's wrong.

"The victims of domestic violence who act to protect themselves should have the support of society, including the judicial system, instead of the likelihood of a prison cell. Certainly, they should not have to rely upon the end-of-term clemency of outgoing governors."

But even though almost all state and national media coverage of the Sisters in Pain, of their quilt, and of the governor's eventual decision to allow ten of the KCIW abused inmates to seek early parole proved positive, public opinion regarding the women and Jones's decision remained divided. Detractors regarded the battered inmates as individuals incapable of assuming

responsibility for their criminal actions or for choosing to remain in toxic—
even lethal—relationships. Some accused the women and their defenders of
denigrating women by employing the dynamics of abuse as a gender-based
excuse to kill; women, claimed those detractors, should be treated like men
and sentenced in accordance with their crimes. Those same critics called and
wrote their legislators to denigrate Jones for being soft on crime and on female offenders.

Positive and negative, public opinion ran strong. And abuse, a subject
still too often closeted by the secrets that cloak family shame, became a legiti-
mate topic of public education and discussion because of the efforts of Weinstein,
Howard-Hughes, McElroy, Thomas and her colleagues, Jones, and the Sisters
in Pain.

Thomas recalled the day, three weeks after the governor had ended his
phone call by wishing the nine chosen Sisters a merry Christmas, when, one by
one, those women, dressed in their Sunday best, their arms and legs shackled,
met the parole board. "That day was unbelievable. We had no guarantees. We
had the victim hearings, and of course the women weren't allowed to come to the
victims' [families'] hearings. Listening to [the victims' families] was a real downer
again, 'cause [the families' comments] made us feel there was no chance [the
women] were going to get out. . . . [But] I think the [parole] board did an excel-
lent job. They did what they had to do. They put everything on the record. . . .
Usually, parole hearings take three to five minutes, [but the parole board] had [each
of the nine women] in there for half an hour going through everything, . . . making
them talk about the crime [and] talk about the abuse. . . . [For me and my
colleagues representing these women,] legally reviewing these cases and seeing
where the system failed them was hard: Seeing [that] attorneys [gave] such bad
advice to them, seeing [that] their defense [attorneys had] no understanding of
the issue or [made] no attempt at understanding the issue. They [had] tons of
other clients, and they [didn't] have time, whatever the reason. That was depressing—going through [the women's] cases and seeing the lack of understanding and education [throughout] the whole court system. . . . These are
people that hadn't been in the criminal justice system. . . . These were not
murderers, these were not bad people. . . . There's not enough time, days of the
week, attorneys, judges, or jails to hold people 'til trial. . . . It's just a fact of life
that a lot of [cases] result in guilty pleas. . . . Every one of [these women] had a
male attorney. . . . The very fact that [their attorneys were male] stopped [the
women] from getting to know them. When we were making the *A Lot of Hurt*
video, the cameraman was an attorney from our office. . . . [We filmed the
video in] a little room in the prison. . . . Two [of the Sisters in Pain] couldn't talk
because he was a man. [At first,] we didn't figure that out. . . . So, [such women

as the Sisters in Pain] are facing these male attorneys [who don't understand abused women's fears]. Plus, [such women think they *should*] trust anybody that comes. Here's the male authority figure . . . coming to say [they] should plead guilty, so I see [such women's] perceptions [are that they're] forced to plead guilty. But I also understand that from the legal [perspective, such attorneys are] saying [pleading guilty is] in your best interest. . . . I saw all of the terrible holes in the system I work in."

On January 4, 1996, each of the ten Sisters in Pain who shared their life stories with the parole board in Roederer Correctional Complex, a nearby prison for men, made parole. In her January 5, 1995, *Lexington Herald-Leader* article, Cheryl Powell, a reporter who had written a series of news and feature stories on the women and their bid for clemency, wrote, "Many of [the] public defenders cried as their clients appeared before the parole board yesterday. Although the media were allowed inside the hearings, attorneys and family members were not; they had to watch on closed circuit TV from a nearby room at Roederer Correctional Complex. . . . After each woman answered questions, the room was cleared so board members could vote in private. The women were called back in to hear the decision."

Parole board members voted unanimously to release Tracie English, Mary Ann Long, Margie Marcum, Johnetta McNair, Montilla Seewright, and Martina Stillwell. Charlotte Haycraft, Sherry Pollard, Paula Richey, and Teresa Gulley Hilterbrand were also paroled, but in their cases the board's votes were split. Board members tied in their votes concerning Sherry Pollard's release, but Howard-Hughes cast her tie-breaking vote in Sherry's favor. And finally, one by one, from mid-January through mid-March 1996, the Sisters in Pain who were granted clemency were released into the care of relatives who transported them home.

The B.O.S.H. Group officially disbanded on February 20, 1996, but the paroled Sisters' swan song occurred the next week, on February 27, when Thomas, McElroy, Weinstein, and Linda Smith, the attorney whom Thomas had acquired to defend Tracie English and Sue Melton, accompanied Tracie English, Johnetta McNair, Sue Melton, Montilla Seewright, and Karen Stout (Stelzer) to New York. The women's parole officers granted them special permission to appear on the nationally televised *Donahue Show* and to remain together long enough during their two-day journey to celebrate their freedom at the Statue of Liberty.

Between December 1995 and February of the new year, the Sisters in Pain's fame had spread beyond Kentucky. After *Time* magazine and the *Washington Post* published articles about the women and the B.O.S.H. Group's quilt, national television talk show hosts called Weinstein to book the women for their programs. But before leaving prison, the Sisters in Pain had told McElroy that they wanted to avoid sensational publicity; the only interviews to which they would agree would be those that they thought might help the public to better understand the dynamics of abuse. So, as the women's appointed representatives, McElroy and Weinstein screened all media requests and declined all talk show appearances except for that of the *Donahue Show*. The paroled women believed that Phil Donahue would be a journalist who would treat them with respect and who would address the subject of domestic violence with integrity. Later, two of the women, Tracie English and Karen Stout (Stelzer), decided that they could help educate the public about abuse by appearing on other programs, such as the *Montel Williams*, the *Maury Povich*, and the *Sally Jesse Raphael* shows. Weinstein joined Karen on the latter television personality's program. But most of the Sisters in Pain would continue to shun publicity.

Thomas refers to her trip to New York with the Sisters in Pain as the most moving experience of her life. But as she explained, the event did not begin well. "WAVE-3 wanted to follow us up there [with their] cameras, and we were so worried about that because [we feared] it would come out on TV like this glitzy trip to New York. . . . The [women] get out of prison and now they're going to New York, all expenses paid. We thought that would feed right into a negative perception [on the part of] the public. So, I guess I was preoccupied with what this was going to look like.

"In reality, we hadn't seen each other for a week or two. Once these women made parole, they weren't allowed to see each other. What's so important about that fact is that they had been this cohesive group in prison. Like in an AA [Alcoholics Anonymous] meeting, . . . they helped each other all the time. Even if they weren't actually in counseling together, out in the [prison] yard, at dinner—wherever—they were there for each other. . . . They got out of prison, and they had nothing. They did not have the support group at all. They went back to their same old lives where they had no support. They went to parole officers who didn't care whether they went to counseling or not, . . . [who] were not supportive of trying to understand their issues. [Parole] was completely pulling the rug out from under them, and I didn't understand all that was going to happen to them until I was on the airplane between two of them and I'm ready to [say], 'Isn't this great? Here we go!' [But] an hour into this thing, I'm crying, 'I want to go home!' I can't believe how depressing it is. [The women] haven't seen each other for this length of time, and they are unloading, and it's not, 'Life is great.' It's, 'Life is horrible.' You know the Karen Stout [who claims to have been assaulted after her release from prison] story, . . . and Montilla had daughter . . . and son problems and . . . housing problems. Then the [woman] behind me [said], 'I can't get in this group, [and] I can't do that.' Johnetta McNair,

Members of the B.O.S.H. Group and friends in February 1996 after appearing on the *Donahue Show. Seated, left to right,* Sue Melton and Tracie English. *Standing,* Lucy Jones (Governor Jones's daughter), Linda Smith, Marguerite Thomas, Karen Stout (Stelzer), Gov. Brereton Jones, Johnetta McNair, Phil Donahue, Marsha Weinstein, Chandra McElroy, and Montilla Seewright. Photo courtesy of Marsha Weinstein.

her time was running out to get a job. By the time we were landing in New York, I was just very, very depressed. There again, you'd think it was going to be great. We'd get to New York and walk around. Well, it wasn't like that. [The women] wanted to go to the hotel and lock themselves in a room and commiserate with each other. They could care less where they were. They could have been on Mars, they could have been at Kentucky Dam Village—it really didn't matter. They just wanted each other. Then we had the other problem: they couldn't go out anywhere because they were on parole. So it wasn't like we could even go sightseeing. We had to be in by dark.

"But, by the next morning, things turned around. . . . This is an unbelievable story. The *Donahue Show* had arranged for us all to have private suites, beautiful suites. . . . These women had been living in prison for four, five, six years. . . . [But, in Manhattan,] nobody stayed in her room. They all stayed in

Members of the B.O.S.H. Group on the ferry to visit the Statue of Liberty in February 1996. *Front, left to right,* Tracie English and Chandra McElroy. *Middle,* Karen Stout (Stelzer), Sue Melton, Montilla Seewright, and Johnetta McNair. *Back,* Marsha Weinstein and Linda Smith. Photo courtesy of Marsha Weinstein.

one room. They all camped out, blankets on the floor. . . . They bonded that night—they got it back together—and by the next morning it was a whole renewed attitude.

"That morning of the taping, [staff from] the *Donahue Show* took us over to the Statue of Liberty. Riding over on the ferry, Montilla was just a nut. She's the funniest person I've ever met. She was joking and laughing . . . with the bus driver, she's joking with the ferry pilot . . . and she's the group leader. She's gotten everybody rolling. Then, all of a sudden, the ferry gets up close to the Lady. . . . She's just been cleaned up, and it was sunny. It was silent. It was similar to a religious experience, it was that moving. Everybody started crying and talking, giving thanks for making it happen. Everybody's . . . sharing in the moment. . . . [And] this just goes to show who these women are and what makes them tick. At that time, the first thing they thought was, 'We have to get something for Governor Jones,' . . . 'We've got to thank the man that made this happen. What can we do?' We started kicking around ideas, and we came up with flowers. And I said, 'Why don't we get him [a flower] for everybody he got out?' Then, when we were on the island, we got him a [replica of the] Statue of Liberty. I don't think I've ever cried so hard."

Above, Members of the B.O.S.H. Group at the base of the Statue of Liberty in February 1996. *Left to right,* Chandra McElroy, Tracie English, Montilla Seewright, Sue Melton, Karen Stout (Stelzer), and Johnetta McNair. *Below,* The Statue of Liberty, February 1996. Both photos courtesy of Marsha Weinstein.

That afternoon, during the taping of the *Donahue Show*, the assembled Sisters in Pain met Gov. Brereton Jones for the first time when, on camera, he walked onto the stage. A couple of the women hugged him, a few shook his hand. They gave him his flowers and his statue and after the taping, they had their pictures taken with their governor, the one man who most of them trusted.

Several months later, when discussing his experience appearing on the *Donahue Show* with women he'd helped parole, Jones's eyes welled up again. "I get all emotional talking about it because it's just so important," he said. "[These women encourage all of us to] never give up hope. . . . One person or a small group of people can make a major difference; that's the way all the major accomplishments [in] America have taken place. . . . These women refused to just be quiet and serve their time, so I think they deserve the credit."

A few months following their parole, we asked the Sisters in Pain to tell us their life stories. Several of them could not—or would not—be contacted, and a few were reluctant to go on record with information that they feared could somehow return them to prison. But six of the Sisters in Pain and one Sister's advocate—the woman who, for a decade, has lent her voice to that Sister's cause—agreed to share with us their oral recollections as well as the life histories that they dictated or wrote while incarcerated. Despite the hurt triggered by recalling their abuse, these survivors said they now see their roles as helping other battered women realize that they are not alone and as helping the public to understand the dynamics of abuse. Therefore, the chapters that follow consist in large part of these Sisters' spoken and written words. We have chosen for these survivors to speak for themselves; narrators removed from their first-person experiences could never recreate the raw power of their stories, and these survivors, silenced too long, deserve to be heard. The grammar, punctuation, and spelling of the women's language is not always the standard American English of the classroom. But their words, preserved as spoken and as written, convey messages that, if altered, would fail to be as strong or as clear.

Waiting for Daylight

I was like you, a child full of light, dreaming
of starlight and swirling dresses, slow dances,
picnics in the sun, and someday a house
on a wide green lot, children I'd raise
on lullabies and lemon drops,
a man with gentle hands.

His eyes pulled at mine, his hands,
shoulders, grin sweet as a boy's.
Moving to the music,
I never heard the words.
you are mine now you belong to me
Dizzy with longing, weak
with sweet fevers, I took
his jealousy for passion.
Passion, I took for love.

Knowing now where the road leads,
I'd turn back. But then, awash with love,
loyalty, blind hope, always on the brink
of hell and a bright tomorrow—
do you forsaking all others
take this man till death do you part

The first time he hit me just once
but hard, to show me, he said,
who was in charge. Then he slapped me.
I was slow with supper. I talked back.
He flung me to the wall. I promised
I'd do better. He promised
never anymore *sorry sorry sorrow*

Bad weather will come back.
There's a storm brewing
behind his eyes. Rage

gathers like thunderheads.
His face darkens in its shadow.
I run for cover but he finds me,
thunder in his fists,
lightening in his palms.
Hair tooth belly bone blood skin
sparrows sparrows caught in the wind

I grow numb, paralyzed, a climber
trapped in snow. Now he'll kill me
if I leave. He'll kill me if I stay. I pray
he'll hit me down enough I'll slip away,
slide slow and easy down some deep
silent river, and not come back this time.

Bad storm tonight. Tonight
he keeps me up all night. He pushes
the gun into my mouth. The children
stumbling sleepy confused the boy
cries out he knocks him the gun
the girl he turns I

hair tooth belly
bone blood
sorry sorry sorrow
sparrow shot silence scream
sirens far away

Now in this room I wait.
I have seen my children
torn from me, crying for me,
I have seen my own death
in my lover's eyes.
I have seen him that I love
dead by my hand. I have seen
all this and live.

I stand in the yard with the others.
I feel the sun on my arms.
I listen for music. I wait for daylight

and dream of a house, a wide green lot,
my children with me,
some sweet day,
singing,
safe.

Anne Shelby

Lyrics written to accompany a musical composition by Steve Rouse based on the experiences of the Sisters in Pain and reprinted with the permission of Anne Shelby.

Sherry Pollard

Staunton, Illinois, a prairie village not far from the battered city of East St. Louis, where Sherry Pollard was born, stretches as flat and wide and absolute as most midwestern towns. In fact, its tidy streets laid out in grids must serve as models for scouts earning badges for compass mastery or for memorizing the basic concepts of Euclidean math, for parallel and perpendicular are precisely how Staunton's avenues and sidewalks stretch north, south, east, and west before they intersect. Even the citizens of Staunton, the men, women, boys, and girls whose pursuits cause them to dash down the wide, cracked sidewalks or to dawdle in front of Main Street's five-and-dime picture windows, staring at plastic fans or Lucite flowers—at pairs of just about anything celluloid selling two for fifty cents—seem preordained by some inner compass to walk within limits, to cross only at lights, and to live and die by the creeds of the churches, Catholic and Protestant, stationed at Staunton's most prominent corners.

That's how Staunton struck us, anyway, as we cruised its streets around noon, Central time, July 27, 1996. We'd driven from Louisville to interview Sherry Pollard, who, since her release from the Kentucky Correctional Institution for Women in Pee Wee Valley, Kentucky, had been living with her youngest sister, Joyce Robinson, and with Joyce's husband and children in a tiny clapboard house on a straight and narrow Staunton side street. But, before we arrived at the Robinsons' home, we stopped in town for lunch. The corner pizza place, the kind of eatery that probably predated pizza itself, proved a good choice. Comforting waitresses, the sort that could be forty, fifty, or sixty, not to mention any age in between, wearing comfortable shoes served comfort food thick with cheese and cookie-sweet crust by the bottomless deep-dish pan. And again we contemplated the principles of math as we stoked ourselves for the interview. Our mission, as well as our appetites, caused us to chew on the word "circumference." Anxiety over whom we would meet, over what she might say, and over what we, in turn, *should* say, translated into too much pizza. This would, after all, be our first interview, and we wanted it to go well. We'd just finished reading Sherry's own story, the life history she'd written in prison, and this is the story we'd read:

Opposite: Sherry Pollard and her current husband, Alan.

"I was born on January 22, 1962, thirteenth in line in a family of fourteen children. I have little to no recollection of my childhood.

"My mother worked nights and slept during the day. My father never worked due to the fact that he was medically disabled. I was closest to my sister, Mary, who is two years older than me, and [to] my younger sister, Joyce.

"As a child I was a loner; I stayed to myself most of the time. I spent two years in kindergarten, but I don't know why. In middle school I was an average student and I dropped out of high school in my sophomore year.

"At home I had a lot of responsibilities since the older kids all worked. I cooked, cleaned and looked after my little sister. I remember those years as being very sad for me. It seemed that I felt sad almost all of the time.

"When I was thirteen, my older brother returned home from Hawaii where he was stationed while being in the service. I'd never had a relationship with him at all. [He] was in his twenties at the time, and he was living at home. It was at this time that he began an incestuous relationship with me that continued for several years.

"When I quit high school, I was pregnant with my brother's child. I'd met Danny Pollard by that time, who was a student in the same grade as me.

"Danny and I were married on March 7, 1979, when I was four months pregnant. Danny and I had discussed this situation of my being pregnant with my brother's child prior to getting married. He offered to marry me and tell everyone that it was his child. We both agreed that we would never tell anyone any differently about the baby.

"Things went pretty well for us until the baby died at the age of nine weeks old of SIDS [Sudden Infant Death Syndrome]. It was then that Danny started attacking me in my sleep—not physically, but mentally. I didn't realize until then what my problem was. I'd been having trouble sleeping, and I'd wake up very upset and frustrated, crying. While I was sleeping he'd say things to me like, "[Your brother] is coming to rape you," and "Maybe you just want to fuck him, but if you do, I'll hurt you and him both." Shortly after Holly's death I woke up and discovered him saying these things to me. I waited until we'd gone out for a ride to confront him about this. Danny started accusing me of taking up for [my brother], and he was giving me hell. We had a wreck. Because of the things Danny continually held over my head about the incest with my brother, I felt that I wasn't even worthy to live. His mental abuse broke me down to the point that I began to feel that I didn't deserve my next breath.

"Things seemed a little better for Danny and I. In June, 1981, we had a son, Danny, Jr. Then one day Danny came home and found the man we rented from in our apartment and he went off on me. He accused me of having an affair with the landlord, and I did all I could to explain to him that he was there fixing the bathroom pipes. Danny picked me up and threw me across the room at the couch, but I missed the couch and hit my head on the coffee table. My face was cut right above my right eye. I jumped up and ran to the bedroom. Danny came after me and pushed me down on the bed, telling me he'd never let me out of the house again. I struggled with him for over an hour and finally somehow managed to get away from him."

Sherry, like the majority of women who suffer abuse, did not think to call the police or other sources of help. As she said often, her husband was a police officer and her father-in-law had been the chief of police. Sherry's actions reflected her belief that blood is, indeed, thicker than water. Her inability to get help during the early stages of her battering contributed to the tragedy that ultimately claimed her husband's life.

Sherry's story continued: "I left the house and went to work. While I was at work I got an emergency phone call saying that Danny had taken a bunch of pills trying to kill himself. First, I called the police and they told me to meet them at the house to let them in. As it turned out, he took a bottle of Tylenol. The police told me that it would make him sick but that he would be fine.

"Danny and I moved to Florida a few months later. My father had died after the Tylenol episode, and Danny and I seemed to get closer. But while in Florida, Danny started seeing a girl he had met in a bar that he and my brother-in-law had stopped in one night on their way home from work. When I asked him about her, he denied it and came back at me with accusations that I was having an affair with someone at work. I kept insisting that I wasn't, and then he started throwing up the situation with my brother. He said, 'If you'd fuck your brother, you'd fuck anybody.' Danny kept insisting that he didn't trust me.

"Danny and I went into a period of arguing that lasted for months. He told me that things were this way because of me and my brother. We decided to move back to Kentucky, and at that time I was pregnant with our daughter, Amie Jo. Amie was born in May, 1983.

"When we got back to Kentucky I started to work at McDonald's, and Danny went to work at Mid-Continent Spring Factory. We were getting along a whole lot better, and I started to feel like we were at long last becoming a REAL family.

"Around the first of 1984 I became pregnant again. Like all of the rest of them, this pregnancy was also high risk. I had an awful lot of problems carrying this baby and, in my sixth month, the doctor had to take the baby because he wasn't living. When I lost this baby it was devastating for me emotionally. It brought back all of the feelings I had when I lost Holly. Even though Holly was fathered by my brother, she was still MY LITTLE GIRL!!! She was part of me. It makes no difference to me regarding her loss that she was fathered by my brother. The pain was, and still is, very real.

"I was so scared to talk to Danny about how I felt. I knew that he would throw [my brother] up to me again. I just waited until I knew that he was asleep, and then I'd cry quietly to myself. I felt that I had no one I could talk to about my pain; I felt like an outcast in my own home.

"By the end of 1985 I decided to have my tubes tied because I could not stand the pain of losing another child. Danny was totally opposed to my having this surgery and refused to talk to me for weeks. When I attempted discussing the issue of sterilization with him, he'd say, 'You'll have a baby for your brother, but not for me. What kind of women does that make you?' I never answered him aloud, but I answered it to myself. I felt that I wasn't a woman at all, but a cheap slut who would let her brother get her pregnant. With Danny constantly reinforcing these feelings to me with his . . . words, I just knew that he and I were both right about me. My feelings of worthlessness grew and grew. I came to feel that I wasn't good enough to be his wife or anyone else's, for that matter. I was so ashamed and lonely. I began to question myself as to whether or not I deserved to have two such beautiful children. Since I had already lost two children, I became determined not to lose these two as well.

"As time went by, I became closer and closer to Danny, Jr., and Amie Jo. I never dreamed that we could be so close! Little by little I built my entire world around my two children and my husband. I lived my life to make the three of them happy with no regard for myself. It was seeing them all happy that gave me my happiness and pleasure in life. I convinced myself that I had to prove to them that I was worthy of them. Eventually, I got to the point that I'd do or try anything to make them happy.

"Once again things seemed to be improving in our lives. I felt like I'd finally found what was missing from my life all of those years. It was my family. They were the only thing that had meaning for me. When I stood back and looked at them I knew that I had FINALLY done something right!!!

"I started having a lot of medical problems and the bills began to take us over. I started to learn the hard way that I couldn't manage money well at all. Eventually, we had to file bankruptcy, and this sparked a lot of problems between Danny and I.

"My migraines seemed to come more frequently as the arguing and fussing Danny and I did increased. In the past I smoked a joint to ease the pain, so as the migraines increased, so did my usage of marijuana.

"By 1989 it seemed that things between Danny and I were a little better. But then I learned that I had to have a hysterectomy. I knew that this was going to set Danny off, so I delayed telling him. By this time Danny was a Police

Officer for Oak Grove, Kentucky. I was then working at Mid-Continent Spring Factory. When I was finally able to tell Danny about the needed surgery, things got very tense between us. He spoke often of wanting another child, and I put off the surgery for a year, even though he and I both knew that the idea of another baby was impossible. I had the surgery in December, 1990. After this he and I talked a lot about adopting a child, but we never did check into the idea too much. He told me on several occasions that, had I taken better care of myself, I'd probably still be able to have one myself.

"His comments cut me deeply inside. Once again I started to feel like I was responsible for everything that was wrong in the life we shared. I was feeling totally inadequate. So I started all over again trying to prove myself worthy of him. It didn't matter this time. He even started telling me that I was letting myself get fat and that, as a cop's wife, I should look good beside him. I started skipping meals, but nothing helped. The harder I tried, the more he complained.

"By the time my mother died in 1991 I noticed that Danny was starting to seem distant. I first thought that it was because he was so close to her. It became normal for him to get a phone call and then leave for hours at a time. I consoled myself with the knowledge that he was a cop and had to work a lot of hours.

"In August, 1992, a man showed up at work and showed me some pictures of Danny and his 'wife' at the lake that were taken earlier that same day. Danny had even taken our children with him! My daughter confirmed it later that some woman was with them at the lake. After I put the children to bed, I asked Danny about it all and he admitted to it.

"The next day I moved out and took the children with me. I'd cried all night long out of the hurt and humiliation of what he'd done. After a couple of days he convinced me that it was over with and that he wanted me and the children back home. Everything was fine for about two weeks, and then I found out that he was seeing her again. He convinced me that they were just friends and that he was worried about her because she was in an abusive marriage. He told me that her husband had raped her when she went back home after their affair. I showed no sympathy for her. I even went so far as to make a comment about the fact that I didn't care what he did to her. This made Danny terribly mad at me. He ripped my gown off and put his gun to my head asking me, 'How would you like to be raped?' He then proceeded to rape me. It was the most humiliating thing he'd put me through up to that point. I spent the next two hours in the shower, crying. I felt dirty, ashamed, hurt, and terrified. The next morning I couldn't even face the children. That night I took a bunch of pills, attempting to kill myself, but all they did was make me sick for two days.

"Danny started to bring his girlfriend to the house. They'd be there together when I got home from work. One day I came home and found them asleep together on the couch in front of our daughter. It was then that he told me it was his house and he'd do just whatever the hell he wanted to. I smoked a couple of joints to help me cope with her being there. Later that night he told me that it was time I saw how a REAL woman acted in bed. He handcuffed me to a chair in our bedroom and I had to watch them having sex. This was even more degrading than the rape. For me, this was the final straw. I had no self-esteem left. I couldn't even think straight. I stayed in a daze most of the time, and I couldn't even seem to grasp the smallest of ideas. I couldn't even deal with my children. I felt dead on the inside. I felt that I was in his way, but I couldn't leave him because he said he would take the children away from me. Since he knew what he did about me and my affair with my brother, I just knew that he really could do just that. And he would not think twice about taking my two children away from me.

"Shortly thereafter I went to work one day and called my brother. I told him to call work and tell them anything that would get me off work, because I knew that I could not stay there. He said that he would, but only after I promised that I would meet him and talk to him about what was wrong, since I was crying and almost hysterical. I intended to do just that but, when I left work, I [didn't] remember a thing until three days later when I discovered that I was in Western State Hospital. It turned out that I'd tried to shoot myself after wrecking my truck. I told Danny that when I was released I was going to take the kids and move to Illinois [to live] with my sister. Before I could get released, he went and filed for divorce and custody of the children.

"I went to Illinois for about a week. While I was there, I talked with Danny and the kids every day on the phone. Once again he convinced me that everything with 'her' was over. He convinced me that he and the kids missed me terribly, and that they all wanted me back home.

"I went back home because I could not stand the loss of my children from my life. Danny and I slept in different bedrooms for a few days, but it didn't take long before things returned to where they left off. It wasn't any time at all until he was bringing her to the house again, and if I dared to say something about it, he'd wave his papers in my face. He said to me, 'You can leave if you want to, but the kids are NOT going with you anywhere, and you'd better remember that, when you leave this time, I'm going to tell them everything—all about how their mother is a slut who slept with her brother and even had his kid. They will hate you and you'll never see them again.' Danny knew that they were the only thing I lived for, and that the kids were the only hold he had left on me. Every day things got a little worse.

"Eventually, things got so bad that I had to go start picking [Danny's girlfriend] up. If I went anywhere, he made me take her with me. I could not go anywhere without either him or her with me. Then he moved her into the house. I was made to have sex with them. Everyone knew about their affair. His co-workers even made jokes about it on their private channel on the police radio. I felt that they were all playing a sick game with my life and my feelings. It was as though everyone was standing around trying to see how much more I could take before I'd snap.

"I tried to talk to [Danny's] boss at one point and was told that it was only a phase [Danny] was going through. He said, 'Hang in there, and it'll all work out.' When Danny found out I did this, he blew up. He accused me of trying to get him to lose his job. He said, 'You better keep your mouth shut, or everyone will really know what you are.' He made me go rent dirty movies, and I had to even take along my shadow, which is what his girlfriend had become to me.

"On several different occasions, she and I both tried to leave him. I'd get the same response every time. He'd threaten me with losing my children and exposing my ugly past. He also had something on her, and I'm not sure what it was. It was enough to keep her around.

"Around Christmas of 1992 we found out that she was going to have Danny's baby. This was just another thing he had to shove in my face at his will. He kept reminding me that she was going to have the other child that I would not have for him. By this point, I was hopeless. Nothing seemed to matter to me. He'd taken everything from me—my dignity, self-worth and self-respect. I had nothing left. I was empty, lost, confused, hopeless, and helpless. I was nothing more than an empty shell living in his sick world. I no longer felt human, and I was not even capable of being a mother to the two children that I loved more than life itself. By this point, I was living off of coffee, cigarettes, and marijuana. I had no appetite, and the smell of food made me sick. I lost a lot of weight very fast! My insides were so nervous that I shook all the time. I had trouble sleeping, and, when I was able to go to sleep, it was only for one or two hours at a time.

"In January, 1993, I called his sister. I told her that I couldn't take it anymore and that he was going to have to make some kind of choice. I was getting undressed that night, getting ready for bed, and he told me that his sister had called him and told him what I'd said. We had a huge argument over the incident. He put his gun inside my vagina and told me, 'If you ever say another word to anybody else, I'll give you the fucking of your life.' I saw something in his eyes that I'd never seen before. He was not the sort of man to 'play' with a gun. I had no doubt that his threat was in reality a promise. I was so afraid of him!!! I had absolutely no doubt in my mind that he would use that gun on me.

He told me that he would have his cake and eat it, too, and that there was nothing anyone could do about it. He always reinforced his 'ideas' with the fact that I should consider myself lucky to have him.

"I was upset all night. For as afraid as I'd been in the past, I never knew so much fear until then. The next morning my brother, Jerry, called. He could tell how upset I was. I finally told him what had happened and that I was scared of Danny, but that I couldn't leave him. I told Jerry that I knew that this whole situation was going to come down to someone's death, and that I expected it to be mine. Jerry assured me that everything was going to be fine. He promised that he was going to talk to Danny and that everything would be taken care of. On January 4, 1993, Danny was killed as a result of that talk.

"After talking on the phone with my brother, I realized that my kids were late for school. I took the kids on to school, and, while driving, it hit me that Jerry said he was going to talk to Danny about our situation. After what happened to me for telling his sister, I got really scared for the two of them (my brother and husband) to talk. I didn't know what would happen to me when I got home if Jerry talked to Danny about our personal life. I stopped at a pay phone to call Jerry and stop him from going to my house. All I got was an answering machine. I was supposed to go to work for my manager's training program, but I was too scared. All I could think about was what happened last night and that Jerry was going to talk to Danny. I was upset and crying, and I went back home. I thought maybe I could stop Jerry before he said anything to Danny.

"When I arrived home, Danny was still in bed. Jerry had not been there yet. Danny hollered from the bedroom and told me to bring him some coffee. I threw some water on my face and then took him his coffee. I sat the coffee on the table and sat on the edge of the bed with my back to him. I was crying and trying to hide it from him. Nothing was said for several minutes and finally he said to me, 'Honey, I'm sorry about last night.' Then the phone rang, and it was one of our creditors telling us we missed a payment on Friday, and this was Monday. Would we be in today? I told them yes, and then I hung up the phone. [Danny] started yelling at me, saying that I'd never change and that he might not be sorry after all. When he sat up I got scared, so I very quickly ran out to my truck and left for work. I just knew that everything was getting ready to blow up again, just like it [had] last night.

"I cried all the way to work. I didn't care anymore if Jerry did talk to him and let him know I'd told someone else. I just knew that all of the abuse had to end. I couldn't take another minute of it. Again, I was going on coffee, cigarettes, and marijuana. Nothing I did seemed to be right. I could not even think straight enough to try to reason with [Danny]. I had not committed a crime; I merely forgot to pay a bill, which should not [have] surprised anybody, given everything I was living through at the time. But the reality is, I am sure that there would not have been any reasoning with Danny by this point, anyway.

"When I got to work, I tried hard to concentrate [but the] events of last night just kept racing through my head. Jerry stopped over and asked if I was alright. I said, 'NO!' I told him that I was scared and tired and that I just wished it was over. Jerry told me they'd been to the house (he and his friend) but [had gotten] no answer. He said the cruiser was in the drive and [Danny's] dog was on the back porch. Jerry figured that maybe Danny was in the shower or something, so he was going to go back over there. I told him to be very careful, because Danny was really mad when I left the house. I told him I felt like I was going crazy and that all of this shit just had to stop. Jerry asked me where Danny kept his gun in case he went for it. I told him he kept it next to the radio.

"Jerry and his friend left not long after they got [to our house]. Sometime close to 11:45, I got a phone call from my brother's friend. He said, 'You need to go home.' Then he hung up on me. My insides went to pieces. I called Danny's girlfriend to see if she was ready to go, since I was supposed to pick her up on my way home. But she was still in the bed. So I left to go home. A thousand things were running through my mind. I didn't know if Jerry and Danny were into it, or if Danny was going to be mad as hell and waiting for me.

"When I got home and went into the house, it was very quiet. I called for Danny. There was no response. I laid my books down on the couch and noticed that the dog ran down the hallway. I saw Danny laying there. I ran next door to where another officer lived to get help.

"I was taken to the hospital and treated for shock. For the next several days I could only think about my children and wonder why Danny had to die. I couldn't deal with it. He died when we were so upset with one another and I had so many unanswered questions that I'd never have any answers to.

"Between the Monday that he died and the day of his funeral, which was on Friday, I was interviewed several times by the police. Many others were interviewed as well. All day Saturday I spent reviewing the events of the last couple of weeks and trying to figure out who killed [Danny]. When it hit me that Jerry and his friend must have had something to do with it, I got scared and confused. I didn't know what to do. I could not be sure that they had done it. Somehow, all of the pieces fit together in my mind. Jerry didn't want to go to the funeral, and, when I saw him, he wouldn't look me in the eye. I was supposed to meet the detective the next day, Sunday, along with Danny's boss. I made up my mind that I was going to tell them about Jerry's supposing to go talk with Danny. I wanted to tell them why Jerry was going over there. I wasn't going to tell them that I suspected anything else, because I just wasn't sure.

"I was nervous and confused, so I took some of the medicine that they had given me at the hospital. Then I took two Sinequans so I'd be able to calm down and think clearly. Nothing seemed to help, so I smoked a couple of joints.

"When I went for the interview, I tried to explain what I knew about Jerry's going over to my house to talk with Danny. At first, I was fairly comfortable. I knew all three of these men, as they were all friends of ours. They asked me to make a statement, because they would need it to go out of state to Nashville to talk with Jerry. By this time, all of the drugs were kicking in. They gave me some questions to answer on paper. The detective tried to help me, but I was getting more and more confused. The drugs were kicking me hard."

It appears that the only way that Sherry knew to cope with tension was to turn to marijuana and drugs. Sherry is a small person, so the effects of her drugs were probably magnified. She does not recall any efforts on the part of the police to deal with the effects of the drugs that she took or to wait until she had "come down" before continuing to question her. Usually, statements given under such circumstances can be thrown out of court and/or recanted. But Sherry recalled that when she stumbled over her remarks during her question-and-answer session, she was told to write her answers and then to read them into a tape recorder.

"They asked me to read my answers off to them on tape, when they read the questions to me. When I got done, the detective went and got me a cup of coffee. When he returned, he asked me if anyone had explained my charges to me. I had no idea what he meant until he told me that I was under arrest for capital murder. I dropped my coffee. I could not believe what he'd just said. I couldn't remember what I said in my statement that would cause them to want to arrest me for murder.

"He then told me that I could either let my sister-in-law, Barbara, keep my children, or [my children] could go to the state. He called [Barbara] to come and get them. I can barely remember seeing the children before they took me to jail. I didn't eat or sleep that night.

"The next day two public defenders came to see me. One of them said that he was representing my brother who'd been arrested the night before. The other one said he might be representing me. I tried to answer all of their questions. They said that their office probably couldn't be representing both of us, and that they may have to get an outside attorney for me. A few days later, they told me that they had some woman attorney in mind and that they'd call her. They called her and then told me that she said she didn't have time for a capital case.

"On January 28, 1993, I was sent to Kentucky Correctional Psychiatric Center for an evaluation. I was scared and confused from the Sinequan I was taking. I didn't tell them anything about the abuse. I was too ashamed of it all.

"I was returned to the jail on March 3 and was told that the attorney had agreed to take the case. Up until this time I had a pretty good relationship with Amie, but Danny, Jr., was pulling away from me. It was killing me on the inside, but I tried to give him some space.

"The attorney finally came to see me and seemed anxious to help me. She said that she understood about the abuse and that we'd wait to see what the evaluation showed. In the meantime, she was going to have someone from the spouse abuse shelter to talk to me. No one ever showed up. After the evaluation came back, the lawyer said she wanted another evaluation to see if I'd fall under the Domestic Violence Law. But this was never done, either. The attorney kept reassuring me that everything would be alright. She promised me she was going to talk to someone to get an expert opinion about my state of mind at the time of my giving my statement to the police. Again, this was never done. Then it came down to my not ever being able to get her on the phone. She'd tell me she was coming to see me, and most of the time she never showed up. By this time, my relationship with Amie was rocky, and I'd received a letter from Danny, Jr., telling me that he didn't claim me for his mother anymore. That was my last contact with him to this day.

"My children were all I lived for, and now it seemed as though I was to lose them both. Everything I'd gone through to keep from losing them was for nothing. Danny was still going to win, and I was going to lose my children.

"My sister-in-law was insisting that I was upsetting Amie with my phone calls and, if I didn't stop, she'd get my parental rights terminated. So now all of my phone calls to her were being taped to prevent the termination of my rights. I felt like I was still having to fight to be with my children.

"My attorney was still promising me that a murder charge would not stick when I discovered that I had a second charge of robbery. My husband's police radio and gun had been taken from the house. Now I was facing the death penalty. I'd started off taking 100 mg. of Sinequan, and by this time I was taking 300 mg. All I wanted to do was sleep. When I was awake, I felt like I was in a daze. But all along my lawyer kept telling me I wouldn't get any time." Sherry said that she was led to believe that she would not be doing hard time, so when told that she and her brother could face the electric chair, she agreed to plead guilty.

"A few short days before the trial was due to start on February 14, 1994, our attorneys came to see us. They told us we'd been offered a plea bargain—me, a life sentence, Jerry, life without the possibility of parole for 25 years. It was a package deal. Either we both took it or neither of us got it. We had until morning to make our decision. All of a sudden, my lawyer is saying that if we go to trial, my brother will get the death penalty, and there'd be a good chance

I would, too. Her change in attitude scared me to death. All along, she'd said I'd come out of this alright. She assured me that I wouldn't be too old when I got to meet the parole board in 12 years. She promised me that if I were a good prisoner, and since I had no record, I'd go to a halfway house in a couple of years.

"On the day I went to enter my plea, my attorney took me into a room and explained to me that the robbery charge was being dropped, and that I was pleading guilty to conspiracy to murder. I told her that I just could not go into the courtroom and plead guilty in front of my children to having their father killed when I did not do that. She reminded me that it was a package deal and Jerry had already entered his plea. She told me that I had no choice.

"A couple of weeks later, I was taken to [the Kentucky Correctional Institution for Women in] Pewee Valley. I received a record card, which stated I was charged with "Murder HB [House Bill] 76," so I wrote to [my attorney] and asked her why. She told me that she thought she'd made it clear to me that I pled guilty to murder, not conspiracy."

Sherry added, "Up until this point I've only interjected here and there about my children. The last section of my story is devoted to them, for they are the beginning and the end. They are all that matters.

"I'm not sure I can find the words to explain how I feel about them. I love them so much that I would die for them without giving it a second thought. Since I lost my first daughter, I had a tough time bonding with Amie Jo and Danny, Jr. I was so scared that God would take them away from me, too. But as they grew older and I became more comfortable with them, my love for them grew deeper and deeper every single day. I was and still am so terribly proud of them. My children and I spent all of our time together. When I wasn't working, I was with them. I always believed parents should raise their own children and not let other people do it for them."

As she continued her story, Sherry expressed her pain at not being allowed to see her children. Yet she knew that if she tried to contact them, she could lose her parole and be returned to prison to serve out the time remaining on her original sentence.

"When they were little, I'd play with them, color with them, even get into their little swimming pool with them. When they got bigger, we'd go for walks and ride bikes together. We'd take turns racing. Sometimes, I'd walk beside them while they rode their bikes.

"When Danny became a police officer, he spent so little time with them. I'd spend even more time with them to make up for his absence. There is not a doubt in my mind that Danny loved them. He just didn't have the time to spend with them. Danny worked odd hours and put in a lot of overtime, but I know he loved them with all his heart, just as I did.

"Danny was a very strict parent. He almost never allowed them to go spend the night with their friends or let their friends stay at our house. Danny was extremely hard on them about their school work. Since Danny and I were never really good students, he was determined that his children would do better for themselves than we did. I saw my son get some pretty hard whippings over his grades. I always felt that the kids were doing the very best that they could, so, whenever possible, I'd sign their papers with the bad grades before Danny got the chance to see them. He'd give them whippings with a belt that no child should ever get.

"At the ages of 7 and 9 the kids were expected by their father to keep their rooms clean. When Danny got into one of these cleaning moods, he would demand that the entire house be cleaned from top to bottom. He'd give the children about 30 minutes to clean their rooms, and then he'd go to inspect. He'd call them to the living room and, if their rooms didn't suit him, he'd completely destroy them and have them go back in and start over. Danny, Jr., and Amie Jo would stand there with tears running down their faces, asking me, 'Why does he do this?' My insides fell apart every time we went through this. All I could do was hug them and promise them that everything would be alright. I'd help them as much as I could. Danny would threaten me if I tried to stop him. If the kids didn't get it right, they'd get ten of the hardest licks you have ever seen. Then they got another ten minutes to get it right. If it still didn't please him, he'd whip them again. He'd dare them to cry and send them back to their rooms to clean some more. I'd wait till he went outside, and then I'd run in there and help them. I felt so sorry for them. Most of the time they'd be sitting there with everything they owned dumped out all around them. They'd be crying and asking, 'Why is Daddy being so mean to us?' I'd always felt like I'd let them down when this happened. I'd kiss them quickly and then help them until Danny caught me. Then I'd have hell to pay for weeks over it."

Clearly, the way that Danny disciplined his children could be construed as child abuse, especially his practice of doling out multiple whippings in a single day. Still, even today wives are reluctant to report their spouses' child abuse. As she indicated a number of times, Sherry believed she could not get any help from law enforcement agencies, because Danny was a police officer. She also expressed her fear of repercussions from Danny if she tried to summon help.

Sherry wrote, "When Danny's girlfriend became part of our lives, that included her son, as well. Danny showed him more attention than he did his own two children. He'd play with [his girlfriend's son], but when Amie and Danny, Jr., tried to join [in] and wrestle on the floor with him, like they saw him doing with [his girlfriend's child], he'd get so much rougher with our kids.

They'd usually end up walking away crying. Danny would call them big sissy's [*sic*] and make fun of them. He'd treat [his girlfriend's] son like a piece of fragile crystal and ours like they were less than nothing. He always paid more attention to her son than to our own children.

"One night at dinner [his girlfriend's son] spit Coke from a straw at Danny, and [Danny] laughed. He thought it was so cute. Then, when Danny, Jr., did the same thing, [Danny, Sr.] got mad. He threw his whole glass of Coke at Danny, Jr., and then told him to clean it up. He got up from the table to go wipe the Coke off of him, and I followed him. I asked him why he did that, since Little Danny was only playing with him and trying to get some attention from him, too. Danny got mad at me and shoved me up against the wall. He said, 'I don't give a damn, but he's going to clean it up.' I went back to the kitchen and told my son to finish eating. He didn't make the mess, and he didn't have to clean it up. Little Danny said, 'No, I'll clean it up, because Daddy said to.' I gave him a big hug, and Little Danny said, 'I was only playing with him, Mom.' I told him that I knew that and I'd clean up the mess. Danny and I got into a huge argument because he heard me say I'd clean it up. By the time I got back to the kitchen, Danny's girlfriend had it cleaned. This transpired about a week before Danny's death.

"The very next day Little Danny came to me and said, 'Mom, why don't you and me and Amie just leave Dad and let him have [his girlfriend and her son]?' When I looked at him he had tears in his eyes, and all I could do was give him a big hug. I told him that I loved him and Amie. I told him that I could leave, but if I did, he and Amie would have to stay there with their dad. It drained all of the life from me to have to tell him that, because I knew that he couldn't understand why they could not go with me. They never knew that their father filed for custody of them when he filed for divorce. Danny, Jr., said they didn't want to stay there without me. I promised him that I'd never leave them. Danny just got to where he did all he could to turn the children against me. He was slowly turning the last things that meant anything at all to me away from me. I just wanted to die, because I knew that the children were not going to trust me or believe in me, since I could not take them out of this house of pure hell.

"At one point Little Danny told his dad that he was going to turn him in for child abuse if he whipped him again. Danny got really mad and told him if he wanted something to tell the police about, he would sure give him something worth telling them! Danny told Danny, Jr., and Amie Jo that there was a special paper that parents could go to the Police Department and get that gave them special permission to whip their kids. Danny even had his [police officer] friend . . . tell them the same thing so that they'd believe it. I feel that, when

[Danny's officer friend] told them this, he thought that it was a big joke. Little did he know the depth of the conversation."

Sherry's story concludes: "Since being in prison, I have completed the Parenting program and Reaction Emotive Therapy Group. I am currently in the Books Behind Bars Program, as well as [in] the Jaycees. I have worked in the kitchen, and [I] am now employed with Correctional Industries Printing Plant in the bindery department.

"I have spent approximately one year in each of two group therapies. One is a general counseling group, and the other is the B.O.S.H. Group, which is the Battered Offenders' Self-Help Group.

"My brother, Jerry, remains at Eddyville doing a sentence of life without parole for 25 years, and the third co-defendant . . . was given 5 years probation and lives in Nashville.

"[The brother with whom I had an incestuous relationship] and I have no contact, although I did write him after I got here, and I am enclosing his reply in this [parole] packet. I asked him why he did what he did to me all those years ago.

"If I can get released, I intend to go to Illinois to live with my sister. I'll stay in counseling as well as pursue family therapy. I still have contact with my daughter, and I believe she will come to live with me. My son remains alienated from me. I will definitely finish college, . . . I want to be a Medical Administrative Assistant.

"Recently, my daughter asked me what it meant to have a contract on your head. She said that [a relative of her father] and a bunch of her friends said that now I have a contract on my head. I am scared of the environment that my children are in.

"I am seeking clemency for the purpose of reuniting my family. I feel strongly that no justice is being served here. I am doing everything I can to improve the type of person I am, and I will never stop doing that. I pray that the Board will consider my plea for clemency and understand that I will abide in whatever directions are set forth."

Sherry was granted her freedom, but it appears that she has lost her son and, perhaps, her daughter. However, she remains hopeful that, as her children grow older, they will want and will seek contact with her.

Knowing what we knew about a woman who'd survived such abuse by so many people made us wonder how Sherry would perceive us. Linda had spoken to her several times over the phone to arrange the interview, and during those calls Sherry had always sounded polite but quiet—almost shy. That was the persona we met in Staunton, too, a petite, reserved woman with permed brown hair and enormous, deep-set eyes, a woman with measured speech and a Mona Lisa smile.

Montgomery Street, where the Robinsons live, is less than a ten-minute drive from the restaurant where we ate, so following our lunch we found the street, the house, and Sherry. When we arrived, Sherry's brother-in-law was asleep on the living room couch, and his children, who were watching cartoons while dressing compliant kittens in doll clothes, circled their sleeping father while screaming war whoops at decibels that should have, as the saying goes, awakened the dead.

Sherry led us to the kitchen, a straight shot through the living room, where we plugged in our recorder. As Sherry responded to our questions in her low, steady voice, the living room war cries escalated. At times, we were invaded. If a doll dress got stuck on a kitten's head or if a child demanded an adult audience for an impressively shrill experiment, the preschool troops would surround us, stilling Sherry's speech. And fifteen minutes or so into our discussion, Joyce arrived home from work. Uninvited, she joined us at the kitchen table, eager to enter the conversation. The compulsive perfectionist in Linda railed against such interview conditions, but Angie, raised in a large family herself, invited the spontaneity that Linda, in the end, came to accept, if not appreciate. For Linda witnessed Sherry's patience when Sherry's nieces lunged at Sherry's lap. And when Sherry would demure or falter in her desire to sanitize or reinvent her past, Joyce would interject a firm directive. "Say it the way it really was," she'd tell her sister. And, if Sherry couldn't, Joyce would.

Late in the interview, toward the end of an emotional conversation, Linda asked, "When you were being abused, did you turn down any offers of help?"

Sherry replied, "Oh, yeah. The one sitting here at the table, Joyce. My sister in Nashville. The friend that I worked with. I guess I didn't want to believe that my relationship with my husband had gotten to that point."

Linda: "Did they encourage you to leave?"

Sherry: "Oh, yeah. I had left after the incident where I tried to commit suicide."

Joyce: "I had her up here once. Couldn't keep her."

Sherry: "He convinced me to come back."

Joyce: "You need to rephrase that. He didn't *convince* you. I think he *coerced* you. Say it the way it really is."

According to Sherry, she still didn't know, when we interviewed her, what role her brother Jerry had played in her husband's murder.

From his prison cell, Sherry's brother, Jerry Mathenia, wrote a letter supporting his sister's release. In this letter addressed to Helen Howard-Hughes, he described the events as he recalled them: "On January 4, 1993, Sherry called me, crying hysterically and trying her very best to define the Abuse that her husband had committed on her on that night before. She told me that he [Danny] had handcuffed her to the bed and raped her and Sodomized her with his Police Service Weapon [a 9mm handgun]. He had penetrated her Vagina with this Lethal Weapon only to satisfy his perverted sexual fantasies. . . . I had no other alternative but to make the trip from Nashville, TN to go talk to Danny about what had happened and to try and talk some sense into him. I felt an obligation as a brother to stop this Abuse. When I confronted Danny about this, he just made the smart remark that, 'She's my wife and I'll do want [*sic*] I want!' . . . At that time, Danny had reached on top of the refrigerator and pulled a knife on me and had tried to stab me in the chest. I moved as quickly as I could to avoid being stabbed only to be stabbed in my upper left arm. At that point in time, I then fought with him to take the knife away from him until he went down on the floor and could not fight me anymore. At that time he told me he was sorry and I left him there on the floor still alive. I regret now that I never attempted to call 911 for him. . . . I strongly feel that if he were not a Police officer in Oak Grove, he would have been jailed and prosecuted to the fullest the law would allow. . . .

"By allowing her parole so she can get out and go to one of my family's homes, she will be able to receive a call from me so that I can tell her how very sorry I am for taking Danny's life. God knows that I never intended for it to go that far. Please tell her for me that I am truly sorry for what I have done. I can only hope she will someday be able to forgive me."

No one has said whether Jerry's letter made any difference in the parole board's decision to act favorably in behalf of Sherry's request for parole. What is known is that her former in-laws spoke strongly against it at her hearing. Sherry was paroled but her life did not continue as she'd planned.

The question of the missing gun and the radio continues to plague Jerry. He stated in conversation with Angie that he never saw the items and that he didn't take them. The fact that they were never recovered, he said, is suspicious. Yet the robbery accusation is what catapulted his murder charge into a capital-murder charge. Capital-murder charges are generally brought only in cases that are particularly gruesome, or contain such aggravating circumstances as the commission of another felony (in this case, theft) at the time of the murder.

During our interview with Sherry, Linda asked, "So the three of you— you and Joyce and Jerry—never really discussed what happened?"

Sherry: "No."

Linda: "Do you think you ever will?"

Sherry: "I don't feel that I have the right to ask. I don't think it's my place to judge. I think, if he wants to bring it up, I'll listen. I'm not a pushy type of person unless someone brings it up. You bring it up, you've opened the door—Honey, I'm in there."

Sherry's last remark shows the caustic cynicism that can pepper her speech, revealing that brains, wit, and anger can hold their own with her reserved alter ego.

When Linda asked, "Are there things that, as a convicted felon, you can't do that you would like to do?" Sherry replied, "I really *had* considered running for President." Then, in a tone less flippant, she added, "No alcohol. No drugs. Nothing that's not prescription. Can't vote. Didn't do that, anyway."

Linda: "You can't serve on a jury, either."

Sherry: "No, I can't. I don't think they'd want me up there."

Convicted felons lose many of their civil rights, one of which is the right to vote or serve on a jury. Even after a sentence is completely served or one's parole is completed, the convicted felon cannot exercise some civil rights. Of course, a convicted felon always carries the designation of being a criminal. The only way to have one's civil rights restored is to obtain a pardon from the state governor, or, in rare instances, from the president of the United States.

Our joking, edgy exchange stopped when Sherry began talking about the B.O.S.H. Group that she and an inmate friend, Sue Melton, founded with the help of prison counselor Chandra McElroy.

Linda: "After you started the group, what did you find beneficial about it?"

Sherry: "I guess being around other women that had been there. A lot of times you could start talking and just look at one of the others, and they knew what you meant without saying anything. There was a lot of things that you could share in there that you couldn't out on the yard in prison. You can't talk to people out there unless you want [your words] everywhere twisted and turned."

Linda: "What was your involvement in making the Sisters in Pain quilt?"

Sherry: "That's a tough question to answer, because I guess I was excited about doing it, but I knew there would be a lot of feelings stirred up when we did do it. Karen Stout [Stelzer]—her and I made the pattern up as far as what it was going to look like. But everybody in the group ended up doing their own squares. We worked on it three or four months. I guess we first actually started talking about it in one of the B.O.S.H. groups, and then we decided we needed extra time to work on it, so we ended up working on it twice a week—once for our group and once for the quilt."

Linda: "In your mind, what was the purpose of the quilt?"

Sherry: "Therapy."

Linda: "Did you think about an audience for that quilt outside of prison? What did you hope it would do?"

Sherry: "Open people's eyes. Maybe somebody in that situation, after seeing that quilt, would get enough courage to leave."

We asked Sherry, who, at the time we interviewed her, worked the grave-yard shift at a truck stop on the outskirts of town, how difficult it had been for her to find a job. It's a real catch-22, she said, having to hold down a job as a condition of parole while having to confess, on job applications, to being a convicted felon, a category of applicant most employers choose to eliminate. She told us how, during her first few weeks in Staunton, she'd applied to work at every store and factory in town. But on every application she'd told the truth when asked if she'd ever been convicted of a crime. The result: no one wanted to hire her. But Sherry's final application, at the truck stop where she'd then been employed for some weeks, hadn't even raised the question. So the truck stop manager hired her on the spot. But according to Sherry, she started wor-rying that her parole officer might drop by to check on her some night when she was working, a terrible way, she thought, for her employer to learn the truth. So after a week or so on the job, she told her manager that she did, indeed, have a criminal record. "For theft?" asked the manager. "No, for murder," Sherry replied. "Oh. Well, then," said the relieved manager, who kept Sherry on.

When asked what the most difficult aspect of rebuilding her life had been since her release from prison, Sherry said, "I guess when I was in prison I knew I couldn't get to my kids. But now that I'm out, that's the hardest part. Out here I can get to them, but, legally, I can't, unless I want to go back to prison."

Joyce spoke up. "We have recently gotten phone calls. My husband is here all day long, and he has gotten most of these phone calls where they ask for Sherry, and he says she's not here, and they hang up real fast. It's a female voice, and—you know how people talk out of their noses—real nasally? It's that type of voice. I can't say that's.[the person in Danny's family I think it is], but that's the way [that person] talks."

Sherry: "[A member of Danny's family] has recently called my parole of-ficer. She needs to know what kind of supervision I'm on. She doesn't think the supervision I'm on is strict enough."

Linda: "Why do you think she would be calling here?"

Sherry: "To make me miserable. To make me call [her back] to violate my parole."

Linda: "She can call you, but you can't call her?"

Sherry: "No. I can't have any contact with the victim's family. But if she calls here, there's nothing I can do."

Linda: "Have you settled into a life with your sister?"

Sherry: "I think so. It wasn't as hard to adjust as I thought it was going to be. Of course, leaving Kentucky and being up here—where not too many people knew me, anyway—kind of helped. Every now and then some people will come into the truck stop from Kentucky or Tennessee, and they'll look at me. I've even had a couple of them ask me if I'm from Kentucky. One man told his wife: 'I told you it was her.' But they never said a word to me."

Linda: "May I ask you why you haven't changed your last name?"

Sherry: "I was asked that by a counselor in prison. Right before I left he said I should change my name. I thought about it, but there's two reasons why I don't. One is that if I change my last name, I feel like my kids will feel like I'm abandoning them. Maybe I'm wrong, but that's the way I feel. And two, it wouldn't do me any good to change my name, as far as trying to get away from my in-laws. I will be easier for my kids to find under this name."

We turned, then, to Joyce.

Angie: "You've made an enormous commitment here. I know Sherry's your sister, but can you talk about how you felt through this whole thing—trying to get her out of an abusive situation, seeing her charged with a crime that she says she didn't commit, and bringing her up here?"

Joyce: "Well, you already know I tried to get her out of the house [she shared with Danny Pollard]. I had her up here once. I tried to convince her she needed to stay up here. My other sister and brother said, 'Well, if she really wants to go, we can't keep her.' But I said, 'I'm telling you now—if she goes back down there something bad is going to happen, and I don't know to whom. Nothing good is going to come out of that house; I'm telling you that right now.'"

Angie: "Why did you feel so strongly?"

Joyce: "Because it had reached the point of no return."

Angie: "Did you know that from observing your sister, or from things she had told you, or from knowing your brother-in-law—her husband?"

Joyce: "From knowing him, how he was. I never liked him. I made no secrets about it to anyone, including him—*especially* him. Knowing her and knowing that she would do anything to keep her children—they were the only reason [Sherry] went back to Kentucky. I tried to tell her. I tried to convince her. I did tell her that I knew he had already filed custody papers and was going to take the children away if she didn't come back. That was the turning point after which I couldn't convince her. I said: 'You've got to get away from him. Your children have minds of their own. They're old enough now, and they know exactly what went on in that house. It may have been behind closed doors, but you can't hide from children. They pay too close attention. They know, and they're going to come 'round eventually. Is it really worth risking lives?' I knew it was going to come down to that, only I thought it was going to be her. And I think, if my brother hadn't stepped in, it *would* have been her. I have no doubt. I have no doubt in my mind it would have come to that."

Linda: "What do you remember of your childhood? Sherry says she recalls little before age thirteen."

Joyce: "I have the same problem remembering too much before I was five. I know I have blocked it out but, for what reason, I don't know. I know some day I will remember—sooner or later, good or bad. But because I'm the youngest, I don't remember a lot of what happened to the older children. By that time, my parents were very old to be new parents. I never remember my father working—ever. He was always disabled as long as I can remember. My mother worked odd jobs here and there, usually washing or cooking or something like that, but she never really held down a job. We moved around every year to a new place. It was not what I would call a stable environment. It was not what I would call a supportive environment."

Linda: "Were you subjected to physical abuse from your parents?"

Joyce: "I can't say that I actually remember any physical abuse, but I have a fear—and it's way back in the back of my mind—that something happened. I really do. I really believe it. It happened to all of us. It started with Danny at the top and worked its way down. I can see it in all my brothers and sisters, whether they want to admit it or not."

Angie: "You said you knew your brother-in-law. What kinds of things did you observe in your sister that made you suspect abuse?"

Joyce: "She withdrew from her family. We were close growing up, and we hardly talked on the phone anymore—not even on birthdays or at Christmas. If I did call down there, she was never happy. You can hear things in people's voices and just know they're not themselves."

Angie: "Were you afraid, Sherry, that any more contact with your sister would cause you to tell her the truth?"

Sherry: "I couldn't fool her. On the phone: Quick—say what you want and get off, because [Joyce] was perceptive. I thought it was a secret. I thought I was doing good."

When we left Sherry, Joyce, and Joyce's husband and the household's youngsters and pets—the latter still fueled with electric energy—the now lavender-edged sun sat low on the horizon. In that slanted light Staunton looked even more like a board game than it had at high noon, its geometric zoning a real-life rendition of Monopoly's tidy, low-rent suburbs. Do not collect $200. Do not pass go. Go directly to jail. Sherry's new setting struck us as apt. In many ways, her life had been determined by a role of the dice. And here she was on Montgomery Street, a.k.a. Baltic Avenue, having lost everything but still hoping to rebuild.

We both liked Sherry, and we wished her the best. We believed her. We believed that she'd experienced every abuse that she'd described, and we believed that she hadn't murdered Danny Pollard or even conspired to kill him. As dysfunctional as Sherry's birth family had been, she had in her sister, Joyce, as well as in her brother-in-law, strong family support that many battered women lack. In Sherry's case, one family ally meant salvation—or at least a chance to start over again.

When we had asked Sherry whether Danny Pollard's coworkers had been aware of her abuse, she had said, "I know they were because I could sit and listen to the scanner at night when he was working. The police had their one channel they got all their calls on, and then they had their private channel. I could sit and listen to them on that, and they'd joke about which woman Danny was going to go home and have sex with that night. Everybody thought it was a real big joke. They all knew what was going on. They *all* knew."

Perhaps Sherry's marriage to Danny Pollard had paralleled her teenage abuse. Perhaps her entire family had known for years that one of her brothers had raped her—repeatedly—for years. But since both of those men in Sherry's life were protected by families and coworkers who kept shameful secrets, Sherry suppressed her secrets, too, denying the truth until she could no longer feel or even recall the first thirteen years of her life.

Considering how Sherry was raised, and considering how she was raped and impregnated by an elder brother, her desperate escape into what would become an abusive marriage isn't surprising. Nor is it shocking that she would cocoon for years in denial, her essential mechanism for maintaining sanity, if not for prolonging her very survival. But it is difficult to comprehend that several outside parties—indeed, that officers of the law—would treat at least one woman's agony, as well as her children's misery, as a sick, sexist joke. It's equally appalling to think that attorneys and judges could assume such cavalier stances with the broken lives in their charge. Dysfunction within families can take generations to coax to the fore and to cope with, much less to cure. But corruption run rampant in institutions and within professions, when brought to the public's attention, should be cut to its quick. Hacked away. Rent. Torn asunder. Fried.

"I never wanted to tell anybody about what was happening to me," Sherry had said, "because I felt like there had to be something I'd done to deserve what [Danny] had done to me."

Sherry Pollard had dressed as her husband had told her, had behaved as her husband had told her, and had sacrificed her dignity and her humility, if not her humanity, to save her children's souls. But at the time of our interview, custody of Sherry's children had, after all, been rescinded. In most ways that mattered, release from her bondage had cost Sherry her world. "At first, I stayed with him because I was afraid," she'd said, "afraid that with even just one child, at the time, I couldn't make it on my own."

What a world, we commented, wherein female children are still raised to think that they and their dependents can't survive without a man. What a world, we said, where, in too many places, that belief is not myth, but still-sad truth. And what in the world, we, in our approach to our own city, wondered—as Louisville's corporate high-rises loomed before us, lighting up the night—is the answer to a problem as prevalent and pervasive as apathy itself?

Laborare Est Orare

I haven't forgotten all those fearful years
when work was prayer. There was nothing to

hope for in all that torture, but there I was
hoping for something to save me. He came so

close to killing me. And I kept telling myself how
much he loved me. What did I know about

love? Even then, I could strip old pine floors,
bake bread, plant those gardens which sustained

me. Bury another child. Go through all the
motions of making things work. Is prayer ever

only for believers? I came so close to finding
my own murder as an answer. Now, here is

this world I have worked so hard for. This
earth is no heaven, but it has its places where

I can find peace. Love, when I think of you,
there is never enough work to love you within,
    there is never enough prayer.

This is such radiant life, and I am thankful:
    Laborare est orare. Work is prayer.

Diana Brebner

Excerpted from The American Voice Anthology *(Univ. Press of Kentucky, 1998) and re-printed with the permission of the* American Voice.

Karen Stout

We arrived in Sonora, Kentucky, at about 8:00 p.m. on August 2, 1996, long after what sidewalks there were had been swept clean and rolled up for the night. The town—a crossroads, really, just a couple of exits past Elizabethtown heading south from Louisville on I-65—appeared deserted. No kids, no cars, no stray animals, even, to populate the dusty streets. Karen's clear, terse directions took us straight to an old apartment by a railroad track, a narrow house cut up and converted into dirt-cheap rentals the size of trustee prison cells.

Jimmy, Karen's youngest son, still a teenage boy, was curled on the couch when we entered. His eyes never left the aging RCA console across the otherwise empty room except to acknowledge with a squint us middle-aged, smiling women. To him, we must have seemed as patently foreign but not half as fantastic as that of the Hollywood starlets whose sexy, comic antics filled his surreal screen.

Karen greeted us with an apology for Jimmy's presence and proceeded to seat us at her table, the sole stick of furniture to suggest that their almost vacant living room also served as their dining room, even as it acted as a chipped and barren marker to delineate the edge of their closet-sized kitchen. A bedroom portal yawned off the main room, and during our interview the runt-sized remnants of a litter of tortoise-shell kittens that emerged when we arrived would continue to leap from the bedroom's depths, testing their claws on the massive arms of the couch, their makeshift scratching posts. The apartment's only light other than that from the television screen's steady glare shined thin and white from a single bulb dangling naked and dusty above the table where Karen seated us in straight-backed, splintered chairs.

"Sorry about Jimmy. I tried to work out something so he'd be somewhere else, but I couldn't," Karen said. Neither, she said, could she talk freely to us about her abuse when her son, who'd never heard just how much she'd endured, would overhear our conversation.

We glanced at each other, alert to the danger of a long-planned interview destined to be destroyed by a censored conversation. But Angie, acting on a hunch, pulled cash from her purse. "How about a hamburger?" she asked Jimmy, whose focus switched in a flash from his sitcom's two grinning models to Angie's extended bill. "You bet," he said, escaping into the evening's darkness that, absent streetlights or moonlight, was at last absolute.

Somewhere in Sonora, Kentucky, on that hot summer night, a fast-food franchise must have rented Jimmy a cool booth and some company for the cost of a meal. At any rate, he stayed away from home until sometime after we left, allowing Karen to recount her life to the sound of cats scratching, trains thundering, and our shifting chairs' rhythmic creaking in the dim, eerie light.

"Will you discuss in detail all the abuses your husband committed against you?" we asked.

"That's kind of a hard one. That's twenty years' worth. It mainly started out on the weekends. He would wake me up if I was asleep, or a lot of times I would play possum to try to avoid conflict when he got home. He would just physically beat me up and drag me by my hair. Several times he would put a rope around my neck and drag me through the house."

For several hours Karen spoke into our recorder. Her eyes stayed on ours as she talked, switching audiences as tact required, too polite to acknowledge or too honest to care that tact itself constitutes an incongruous counterpoint to the insult of abuse. And Karen's voice never wavered; she recited her tale in a steady, throaty voice that, almost devoid of modulation, mimicked the sound of a soul submerged. Asked to backtrack, Karen did. She described her life, before her parole, like this:

The fourth of seven children born to conservative Baptist parents outside Akron, Ohio, Karen claimed a close but financially restricted family. Her father taught school, her mother worked odd jobs "to make ends meet," and on Sundays, family days, Karen, her parents, and her siblings played ball or attended church picnics. But as Karen related an ideal, storybook childhood, her further comments constructed a more complicated, isolated youth of few friends, strict supervision, and parental insistence on her adherence to rigid, rigorous moral and dress codes, as defined by the family's church.

As she spoke, Karen pulled out her copy of her fifteen-page life history that she'd written while in prison. We'd read it before, but while Karen left us for a moment to round up her cats, we reviewed it again. On the first page, Karen had written, "When I was in the fifth grade, my oldest brother began molesting me. He had sex with my sister, and for a long time Kathy was scared that she was pregnant by him. She and I would talk about what was happening to us, but we never told our parents because our father had a bad heart and [my brother] always said, if we told, Dad would have a heart attack and die. He also molested my brothers. [The brother who molested me] was into very perverted sex. He made me urinate on him. Most of the time he took me to the attic where it was very dark to make me masturbate him. This is when I learned to fear the dark and to detach myself during sex and pain."

Therapists claim that such dissociation, an instinctual survival technique, can become permanent as people pad their psyches from further pain. Reading her story and listening to her tale made us think that this was the case with Karen, whose speech resembled that of a veteran flight attendant reciting safety regulations by rote. Did she believe her life had been, or did she think that our inquiries were, the stuff of a futile mission? Her facade remained that of a weary woman older than her years but younger, somehow, too; a slight, long-haired, blue-jeaned, and T-shirted woman in her early forties with wide, brown circles under her eyes and a story that, despite its dramatic climax, seemed unable to conclude.

Continuing her story, Karen said that after high school she enrolled in a nine-month business-college program that she completed in six months in order to escape the city. Her parents limited her opportunities to meet new friends, especially men, so she returned to her high-school sweetheart, Jim Stout, whose frequent, violent claims on her she confused, she said, with love. She'd met him the summer before her senior year and didn't much care, she added, for his deviant friends. Yet she couldn't help thinking that his cramming her in a school locker and leaving her there until he thought she'd learned her lesson for talking to another boy somehow sealed his declaration that she belonged to him. On another occasion, though, he pushed her out of a tree for the same offense, for once again speaking to a boy. Soon, she said, he didn't allow her to talk to girls, either. Nor could she abide her parents' wishes, or her grandmother's, whom he cursed, without being slapped or slashed. "And then," Karen wrote in her prison account, "he started talking about marriage."

She wrote that on St. Patrick's Day of her senior year Jim convinced her that they should have sex. While parked in his car at a drive-in, he promised her that their intimacies would lead to a wedding. But intercourse couldn't take place that night, recalled Karen, because her private parts proved too small. Nevertheless, on November 23, 1973, Karen and Jim were married. Their sexual problem remained, and Jim attempted to resolve their dilemma by coating Karen with cooking oil, a practice that soon resulted in her experiencing acute, recurring infections.

Early in their marriage, Jim aimed at a military career that, according to his wife, had to be postponed until his police record, which Karen claims he had destroyed, could be "cleared." His charges included "attempted murder, discharging a firearm within city limits, unlawful transaction with a minor, and rape." She added, "He'd lost his license due to driving under the influence," but, she concluded, "Subsequently, he did gain entrance into the army."

Karen commented that before his army appointment, while waiting to enlist, Jim began to act violently. She wrote that her sister had taken Karen and Jim into her home, thereby creating a household that Jim determined to control. According to Karen, Jim's drinking binges escalated. First, he killed his sister-in-law's dog. Then, when after a party she poured out his half-empty glass of beer, Jim attacked her. Karen wrote that she came to her sister's rescue, that a brawl ensued, and that she and her sister escaped in the end by car. The two sisters fought over Karen's determination to stay with the man whom she had married. She'd been raised with the belief that marriage means a lifetime of for better or worse. God would punish transgressors, and her parents would back Him up. The fact that her bargain continued to worsen, with no better days or nights in sight, still didn't grant her permission, Karen believed, to divorce.

So Karen returned to Jim and they moved, this time to reside with his family that, before their arrival, consisted of Jim's grandmother, mother, uncle, brother, and brother's girlfriend, all packed wall-to-wall in a three-bedroom house. In her autobiographical sketch Karen said, "We shared a bedroom with his brother and girlfriend, and the odd part about the situation is that none of the bedrooms had doors. Jim and I went off into the woods to have sex. We lived like this for about three or four months until he entered the service."

In her written account, as well as in telling her tale, Karen paused at this point in her story to explain her former husband as best she could. She felt sorry for him then, and she feels sorry for his memory still, she said, because she mourns the psychic pain that made him so mean.

Karen pointed out that Jim and his twin brother were illegitimate and didn't meet their father until they were five, when he took his sons on a picnic and chose that occasion to christen Jim with a souvenir smack. Jim also told Karen that his twin had always been their mother's favorite. Referring to her husband in the present tense, Karen said, "Jim, my husband, looks exactly like his mother, and she just despised him. She would buy a brand new bike for [his brother] and give Jim the bike [his brother] broke." And Karen commented that she herself had observed her husband perform all the physical labor in his family because his parents and siblings all claimed to be disabled by a crippling bone disease. "Violence appeared to run in the family," Karen concluded. "[Jim's brother] was a very violent man . . . and his wife had to just disappear with their kids to get away. Jim and [his twin's] father was an alcoholic, combined with the fact that he wasn't part of their lives.

"As for my mother-in-law, to me it seemed she hated my husband. I honestly don't feel they ever loved one another. Later on in our marriage I'd have to talk Jim into even going to visit his mother. She never cared for me and we learned to just tolerate one another. . . . Several times during our marriage she tried to get Jim to leave me, promising she'd help raise the children he and I had together. Jim always said, 'You never raised me. How can you raise my kids?' She would send money or gifts to Jim and the boys for holidays, but never [to] me or my daughter. Eventually, Jim yelled at her about this, and she started sending to [our] daughter, too."

Karen summarized her assessment of her spouse's family's interactions by saying, "Jim was able to get close to my parents. I wonder if it wasn't out of his resentment and jealousy over how close I was to them. Jim had a pretty close relationship with his grandmother, but she took up for me and he resented this, too. When she passed away he reminded me that I had no one to protect me now. Eventually, my father passed away and Jim seemed to grow more bitter toward me. He felt like he'd lost his own father."

A few days short of their first anniversary, Karen gave birth to a boy. Jim had entered the army by then, and the couple had moved into a trailer of their own. But instead of welcoming his son, Jim claimed that the boy, whom they named Bill, wasn't his. Jim commanded Karen to keep the child in his nursery as long as he, Jim, remained in the house. Karen commented that for a year Jim refused to hold, much less to see, his son.

Her trauma over her husband's rejection of their child hurt as much as the physical damage that Bill's birth had caused her, Karen said, adding that the size of her vagina had once again become an issue, this time creating such difficulties that she delivered the placenta a month after her baby's birth. She said that her doctor, declaring her body had endured enough trauma, advised Karen to abstain from intercourse until she healed. But Karen wrote that, just after her hospitalization, her brother-in-law beat and raped her. "Jim caught him and kicked him out with a knife," she remembered. "Jim blamed me for the rape and beat me."

Karen said that Jim demanded that she resume regular intercourse with him, a command that resulted in a second pregnancy. She wrote, "Jim was so upset over my being pregnant again that he tried his best to beat the baby out of me. He swore [that this baby, too,] wasn't his. I went to stay with my sister and had the baby in Ohio. I stayed there until Jim appeared and forced me and the kids to go home with him. Nadine arrived prematurely by five weeks and was born with lots of problems."

Despite her belief in the sanctity of marriage at almost any price, Karen reported that it was then that she began plotting her escape. She fled twice with her children, but both times Jim found them, brought them back, and beat Karen for her transgressions. To ensure that she wouldn't succeed should she again try to leave, Jim padlocked the trailer doors from the outside and took the telephone with him whenever he left.

But after a while Jim neglected to lock in his family. Whether his behavior changed due to carelessness or due to contempt over her past failures to free herself and her family, Karen couldn't tell. But one day she seized another chance to run by snatching up her babies and bolting through the unlocked door. And once again Jim located them, she wrote, returned them to their prison, and broke the three smallest toes on each of her feet—insurance against her further attempts to flee.

The next time that Karen got pregnant, Jim went wild and, in his fury, beat her until she miscarried. "Jim got scared and put me in the bathtub and brought the waterhose from outside to flush the baby's remains out of me. At my next gynecological check-up, the doctor never mentioned there being a problem."

She added that soon thereafter Jim fought with their landlord and the local sheriff. The upshot of their battle was the family's purchase of another trailer, a home they moved to Radcliff. It was then that Karen realized that, despite taking birth control pills, she'd become pregnant again, a fact that, after five months, she could no longer hide from her husband.

The account Karen wrote while incarcerated reads, "[After] the baby had begun moving and Jim could not beat it out of me, he performed an abortion on me. He tied me to the bed and used a wire coat hanger on me. When he got the baby out he mutilated it right in front of me." We asked if the baby had been alive when her husband aborted it, and Karen replied, "I was bleeding a whole lot and I wasn't really alert. I could see what it was, and he made a point of telling me the baby was alive. I don't know for sure. The baby didn't cry or make any noises. You could tell the sex of the baby. It was a pretty good-size baby. It was bad enough that he took the baby out of me. He then began to dismember the baby. He didn't kill it quickly. He took the arms off, then the legs off, before he took the head off." Karen wrote, "I nearly bled to death and Jim became panicked. He tried the hose-in-the-bathtub trick again, and this time it didn't work. Then he packed me on the inside with ice. Still, this didn't work. I was so terribly upset, and Jim gave me some of my medicine (I took Phenobarbital and Dilantin for seizure disorder) and, because I was so devastated, I took the rest of the medicine that I had in the house. The bleeding just would not stop and I had to go to the hospital. I was admitted to Ireland Army Hospital on Fort Knox to be treated for the abortion. I was then released to Hardin County Hospital's Psychiatric Unit because of the pills I'd taken. Ireland could not keep me . . . because I was classified as non-ambulatory. It was at Hardin County [Memorial Hospital] that the abortion was documented as a 'gross criminal abortion.'"

But the military police dismissed Jim Stout's actions. Karen explained that because her husband swore that the abortion had been performed by a couple, by military colleagues whom he disliked and therefore attempted to frame, the police neither suspected nor accused him. And because, Karen stated, the military police told her that a person could not be convicted without authorities having found fingerprints in Karen's body, the couple that Jim cited were not even questioned.

It should be noted that, while it is true that evidence linking a perpetrator or perpetrators to a crime is required for a conviction, it is not legally necessary to have fingerprints, particularly inside a person's body. The testimony of witnesses also constitutes evidence. If Karen's statement is accurate, it would appear that no investigation occurred. It is doubtful that Karen, knowing the truth, would have stood by and watched them be arrested and/or tried. Once the abortion became history, the drama continued.

At home, Jim's violence toward his children escalated. On one occasion when their daughter Nadine irritated him, Karen claims that Jim hit Nadine, causing her to fall and hurt her head. Karen drove Nadine to Ireland Army Hospital, where she was examined and released. A month later Nadine's skull swelled and split from the injury, requiring two years of intermittent hospitalizations.

Karen reported having found herself pregnant again, the result of a vicious cycle that she said she couldn't break. Jim hated children, she wrote, yet he demanded sex. And once again, when he saw that his wife, who still took birth control pills, was pregnant, he beat her as he had so many times before in hopes of aborting the baby. Karen wrote, "But midway through the pregnancy, he stopped beating me. It was almost like it suddenly dawned on him that I was pregnant. I gave birth to a boy that we named Christopher. Christopher was a beautiful child and had such a beautiful laugh. Jim was crazy about him. In fact, he wouldn't let me touch the baby when he was at home.

"When Christopher was four months old he'd stayed awake very late one night. I finally put him down to sleep at about three a.m. and then went to bed myself. Jim and I had an argument about me insisting that the baby go to bed, and I was so tired I went on to bed and left Jim up, very angry.

"Christopher was on a very rigid feeding schedule of every four hours, but, when I got up at six a.m., he appeared to be sleeping so soundly that I decided not to wake him. . . . I got the kids ready for the day, and, by the baby's ten a.m. feeding, he still had not awakened, so I went in to get him up. When I picked him up he was stiff. I collapsed onto the floor in shock and then crawled over to the phone and called Jim at work. I said to him, 'The baby's real bad sick and I need an ambulance.' Sometime later Jim showed up at the house with the police and the coroner. They wrapped my baby up like a sack of garbage and [the coroner] slung him over his shoulder and took him away. I was so shocked and hurt at the time that it never occurred to me to wonder how Jim knew to send the coroner to the house. The official cause of death was listed as Sudden Infant Death Syndrome [SIDS], and the coroner listed the time of death as one p.m., which could not have possibly been the case.

"After Christopher's death, Jim was angry at the world. But, especially, he was angry at me. He kept saying, over and over, 'If you hadn't gone to bed, Christopher wouldn't have had to die!' I thought that he meant that I could have prevented the crib death, but now it seems that his anger would have been unleashed on me rather than our innocent baby. . . . He blamed me entirely for Christopher's death."

In a two-sentence aside Karen's written account continues: "Jim had moved his girlfriend . . . into the house. She stayed for about six months, and I was glad, in one respect, for he wasn't quite so sexually demanding on me."

According to Karen, it was soon after Christopher's death that Jim wanted to expand the couple's sex life by engaging in "swapping," exchanging partners with other couples and engaging in group intercourse. Karen wrote that because she refused to participate in such activities, her husband had her raped by a couple whose acts caused her to be hospitalized for three and a half weeks with a rectal hemorrhage. She claims, though, that when she tried to file charges, the police discouraged her on two counts: The rape, they advised, had occurred in "the wrong place" on her person for any accusation to result in an indictment; and because the couple who Karen cited as having committed the crime had been transferred by the army to Germany, "the police didn't feel that it was worth the expense to the government to bring them back."

The rest of Karen's story reads: "One time I remember while my daughter was at Lexington University Hospital and [our oldest son] Bill was staying at my parents' house, Jim came to pick me up to come home and change. He decided to pull off the road on the Bluegrass Parkway, and he told me to get out of the car. I did as he said, but I had no idea what he had in mind. He got a rope out of the trunk of the car and said he wanted to show me something. We locked up the car, and he took me into a wooded area off the road. He really didn't seem upset, so I wasn't alarmed. I had not been home, so there was no way that I could have done anything to make him punish me. After walking for quite a while he started talking about how we were going to make love in the woods like we used to while living with his family. He said that he wanted to rekindle our marriage. I tried to tell him I didn't want to when he threw me down onto the ground and I hit my head on a log. I was dazed for a couple of minutes. He began to tie me up with the rope to some trees and [he] took my clothes off. I was laying on sticks and rocks and he kept laughing. I screamed at first, but he was right. We were too far off of the road for anyone to hear me.

The look in his eyes scared me, and I honestly thought he was going to kill me. He picked up a branch and began whipping me all over with it. The more I cried and begged him to stop, the harder he whipped me. He found a bigger branch and started to insert it into me and move it in and out. It hurt so much because of the size and the bark on the wood. Then he put it in my rectum and did the same. At this point I prayed that he'd just kill me, the pain was so unbearable. It seemed like this went on for a very long time, and then he started to rub his penis all over my face and body. Then he very violently had sex with me. He pushed me so hard with each stroke that I thought I would die. After he got done, he put on his pants and left, and I was still tied to the trees. He said he would leave me there to rot and the bugs would eat all of my flesh and no one would find me. I begged him to let me go, and [I] cried, but he just walked away. I laid there for a really long time and the bugs did crawl on me and I could hear noises, but I didn't know what was coming. It was almost dark and I had cried until I could not cry anymore. He finally came back and sat down beside me. He said that I was not to tell a soul what had happened or he would really leave me there the next time. I promised not to tell if he would let me go, and he untied me. I put on my clothes and saw that I was bleeding, but I didn't tell Jim. I was terrified that, if I told him, he'd tie me back up and leave me there. All the way home he kept reminding me not to tell a soul or I would die a slow, horrible death and no one would find me. I couldn't wait to get to the shower and wash. I felt so dirty, and it seemed as though I could still feel the bugs crawling on me. I was literally covered with bites and scratches.

"For many days it was impossible for me to use the bathroom because it was so painful. I finally had to take some of the stool softener I had from being pregnant so that I could use the bathroom. I feel so terribly ashamed of this, and I know that [now, by revealing this incident,] I am breaking a promise. I pray that God will understand and forgive me.

"On several occasions Jim portrayed a rape scene while having sex. He'd put on his black ski mask that he kept in the drawer and then tie and gag me after I went to sleep. He didn't want me to make noise and wake the kids. I knew that I couldn't scream, anyway, for if one of the kids woke and saw this, he'd kill them and me, too. So I kept my screams inside to try to protect the children. He'd cut my pajamas off with a knife and then rub the knife all over me, poking me with the point. He was always careful not to cut me with it; he just threatened to. He would put alcohol all over me to cleanse me, even putting it inside of me with a syringe that he got from the hospital. I felt as though I would lose my mind it burned so badly! I would focus real hard at the picture on the wall and accept the pain of what was coming next. He'd use cucumbers, squash, or sometimes his shotgun to insert inside me and then move them in and out. He even used dried corncobs that felt like sandpaper inside of me. While he did this, he would masturbate himself over and over again with that mess going all over my face and body. I couldn't help but gag, and [I] even choked once because I started to throw up, and with a gag on I couldn't get it out. This was a routine for him a couple of times a month that seemed to get longer each time he did it to me.

"One time Jim wondered what would happen if he stuck a small mouse up inside of me. I guess he wondered if he could get it back out. He took a pipe from the garage and while I was tied up he inserted the pipe. Then he shoved this small mouse down through the pipe with a string attached to its tail. Once the mouse was at the end of the pipe he removed the pipe, leaving the mouse inside of me biting and scratching to get free. I wanted so badly to scream, but nothing would come out. I was so shocked and angry at what was happening, but I just couldn't let the kids see this horrible sight. He finally pulled the mouse out, cut off its head, and laid it on my face. I don't remember much after that." But, during our conversation, Karen added, "I got an extremely bad infection because he left the dead thing inside for quite some time. I was tied up to the bed, and then he took it out and put it on my face and then he raped me. There was times when he would tie me to the bed and he would rig up this thing with a battery and some battery charger cables, and he would put the cables on my private areas and turn on the juice to see how much I could take before I passed out. . . . He would beat me with a paddle he made. . . . It got to the point that he could not sexually perform normally. It always had to be a rape scene or something really devastating."

Karen wrote, "I became pregnant with our last child, Jimmy. During this pregnancy that Jim vehemently protested, he performed a ritual cursing of the child. He tied me down and lit candles, then cut a big X into my stomach with a hot knife, thereby cutting and burning me at the same time. During this pregnancy I was diagnosed with uterine and cervical cancer with advanced endometriosis. Jim forbade the corrective surgery, saying that it would make me less than a whole woman. I had an awful lot of problems during this pregnancy, so much so that the doctor thought the baby would be born a monster. He would not even let me watch my son be born. I named him after his father, and Jimmy was born on September 5, 1980.

"Jim left the service in 1981. I was working two jobs, and this is when I suppose that Jim started to abuse Nadine. Jim and Jimmy were very close. Nadine and I were having problems medically since we are both epileptics and our medication was not being regulated. I eventually had to have emergency surgery for the cancer—eighteen months after the diagnosis.

"Jim had two run-ins as a result of his sexual abusiveness that did not involve me. He was in a bar on two different occasions and violently grabbed strippers each time. One was left with a bruise on her buttocks and the other a bruise on her breast. Both times Jim was roughed up pretty badly by the bouncer and told not to come back.

"We had been living in a subdivision for a while and Jim hated it. We had to be so careful of his every abusive move. He'd had to resort to gagging me with socks and tape in order to keep the neighbors from hearing anything.

"Jim went to work for the Civil Service as an instructor, but because of student abuse charges brought [against] him, he was asked to resign to keep his record clean and have the ability to obtain other Civil [Service] work. He quit, and a few months later [he] became a mechanic for Civil Services, which is what he remained doing until his death. The student abuse charges were [made by] male students for verbal and physical abuse.

"We moved to Rineyville in 1985 to a house that was virtually isolated. . . . It is accurate to say that this is when the nightmare turned into a living hell for me and my children.

"Jim's abuse became more violent. He also developed a very paranoid personality to the degree that he installed motion detectors and wired the windows shut. He gave 'medicine' to each family member every night. We lined up like a bunch of robots to take it. We had no choice. I found him frequently coming out of one of the children's rooms in the middle of the night. He'd say that he was checking on them.

"He began mutilating animals in front of me and the children to intimidate us. He was raising Samoyeds and was bringing them to our bed and having sex with them in front of me. The dog would try her best to wiggle her way under me to get away from the pain he inflicted on her, but I could never help her; I was tied up myself. He tried to get one of the dogs to have sex with me, but it didn't work, thank God. He hung a cat in the yard with its little feet barely touching the ground until it died. He made Nadine hold animals while he shot them and let the blood splatter all over her."

We asked Karen if she thought her spouse had tortured and killed animals to teach her and their children a lesson. "It was directed to whoever found them," she said. "Sometimes it was just to show how he was going to kill my children. . . . Some kittens, he just popped their heads off. . . . Nadine [would choose] which kitten she wanted to keep, and then the next day the kitten would be headless. . . . My daughter wanted a white, long-haired Persian cat, and I looked for years and years and found her one. That [cat] made it only six months. Jim left it dead on the sidewalk so she would find it . . . when she went out to school."

Karen wrote, "Jim kept trying to kill me while he continually bought more and more life insurance on me. He tried over and over to poison me with wintergreen candy until I found the bottle in the cabinet marked with the skull and cross-bones. Then he started rigging up the car so that the brakes would go out. Since he was a mechanic, this was not a problem for him.

"My husband got brought up on federal extortion charges resulting in his being placed on federal probation for two years and having to pay restitution. The charges were reduced to official misconduct. He was not permitted to have guns or weapons, nor was he allowed to leave the area without permission. Our house was loaded with his weapons and he never got permission to go anywhere. My son Bill threatened to tell on Jim for the guns and Jim took the guns to [a local shop] to protect himself.

"Approximately one year prior to Jim's death, he found a new way to torture me. After [I had] surgery on my breast, he would punish me without leaving noticeable marks by squeezing the breast. It would send so much pain through my body that I would almost pass out. When I didn't work [outside our home], I didn't care if he blackened my eyes or left bruises because I could make sure no one saw until I was healed. He would break or crack ribs by kicking me with his army boots on, and after seeing the doctors wrap [my breasts] a few times, he just started wrapping them himself. Once he wrapped them too tightly, and since I couldn't breathe too well, I wound up with pneumonia, and, in the hospital, my lung collapsed. He got really mad at me one time and locked me in a metal cabinet . . . and then opened up a jar of spiders. I am terrified of spiders, and they got on my legs and I passed out from fear. I knocked the cabinet over trying to get out, but he left me in it all night. He shot at me a couple of times, leaving holes in the wall not far from where I was. He even shot at me with his crossbow and a broadhead tip (it has a bunch of razor blades on the tip) . . . and barely missed my leg.

"Things came to a head one Wednesday night in December when, on the way home from church, one of Nadine's friends [whom Nadine] had confided in told me that Jim had been having sex with our daughter. I went into an emotional tailspin. I had believed that I was the only one being hurt and that I was [a barrier] between [Jim] and my children. But this was not so.

"When I got home, I went straight for the gun in the bedroom. I confronted Jim in the living room with what he was doing to our daughter. I pulled the trigger and the gun did not go off. It wasn't loaded for the first time ever in the history of having it in the house.

"When Jim got me calmed down, he assured me that [his sexual molestation of Nadine] had only happened two or three times, and he swore that it would never happen again. I believed him, but [I] moved him out of our bedroom and [I] moved Nadine in. It wasn't long until Jimmy was begging to move in as well, and I allowed him to come in and sleep on the floor near [Nadine and me]. Bill's room was in the basement, and I discovered that he was keeping a board up against his door. Our lives had become a genuine living hell.

"Then Jim must have gotten to Nadine. She started begging me [to allow her] to sleep in her own room, [promising] me that 'Daddy wasn't trying anything' with her. After a while I relented, and she went back to her own room.

"[In March,] Jim had surgery on his shoulder. While coming out of [anesthesia in the recovery room,] he motioned for me to come close to him. When I did, he grabbed me by the neck and told me to get him out of there now. He said that I [hadn't] told him it would hurt that bad, and it was all my fault that he was in such horrible pain. The nurse had to help me remove his hand from around my throat so that I could breathe. She told me that it was just the pain medication, and she asked me to leave.

"We went to visit my mother that summer, and Bill and I were wearing long-sleeved shirts. My mother figured out that we were bruised . . . and [she] questioned us. She began acting strangely toward Jim. When we got home, Jim tied me up and cut me up from the middle of my chest down my side, trying to figure out how much I'd told my mother. He cut me so deeply that he could not stop the bleeding. He finally sewed me up himself and then gave me an injection of the dog's penicillin. I had no idea at the time how dangerous this was. For a very long time I could not move my arm or the scar would . . . open.

"One thing was apparent. Jim's cover was blown. His abusive deeds were no longer a well-kept secret. But by this time I could no longer stand the hell I'd lived in for twenty years. He had punched, kicked, and beat the hell out of me. He'd slammed me against walls, pushed me down stairs, and [pushed me off] the garage roof. He'd tried to poison me, drown me, burn me, and cut me up. He made me have sex during my period, made me perform oral sex on him, and inserted me with everything from vegetables to guns. He'd hooked me up to batteries with live wires to shock my genitals. He'd beat me with paddles while he masturbated on me. He tied me up and put bugs on me. He'd killed my unborn baby. He had sex with our only daughter. He physically abused our oldest son. I just could not take any more. I decided that I would drive him over the edge and force him to kill me. I wanted to die, and this was the only way out. Somehow, I had to get out and save my children as well. I knew Jim's point of no return, and I knew that I could push him over that point.

"I devised a plan to save the kids. I gassed up the car and parked it in the driveway for Bill to make a safe getaway. I put some things in it that I knew they'd need. I told Bill that as soon as he heard the shot, [he should] grab the other kids and run for the car. I told him not to come back for ANY reason whatsoever until after he knew for certain that the police had his father in custody.

"Bill was so distraught that he confided the entire situation to his girl-friend. Later, his girlfriend would be charged with complicity to murder for her knowledge. But she was granted immunity to testify in court. One of Bill's friends got involved. He hid in the barn and he had been given a bag by Bill. When Jim came out of the house, [Bill's friend] got scared and ran up on Jim and stabbed him once. Jim came into the house and I was just waking up. I'd taken some Benadryl earlier for an allergic reaction, and it [had] knocked me out cold. I saw that Jim was bleeding, and I rushed up to help him. We made several calls to 911 before any help was sent. . . . Jim drew his last breath in our dining room and was pronounced dead at the hospital. It was August 17, 1992.

"The kids and I clung together as though . . . stuck [with] glue. In a few short moments, our life ended. The twenty years of control left me incapable of making even the smallest decision. I relied on my mother and my brother, Keith. I had no idea how to go on. On August 29, we were arrested."

Karen said, "When they took me in this room they fingerprinted me, and that was the first time I knew I was arrested." After she was fingerprinted, she was taken to jail and, she added, "When I got to jail I had to put on the uniform and give them all my clothes and stuff. They didn't strip-search me. They knew I had already OD'ed [overdosed] . . . [at] the Police Department. I had ate everything that was in my purse."

Asked if she was given any medical attention, Karen replied, "They just told the inmate that was in my room, 'If she stops breathing, knock on the door.' [My cell mate] told me that two days later, when I woke up." Asked to describe the condition of her cell, she said, "[The county jail]: We had four beds on both sides and we had about twelve people in there. They were sleep-ing on the floor, throwing up all over the place. It was not a special treat at all. The guards were okay after you got to know them, but most of them were afraid of me, so they wouldn't even come around the bars. They just sat there and looked through the bars, and then [they would] leave. . . . You stayed in your cell with the cockroaches. . . . There was more roaches than inmates."

Karen told us that when she walked out of the holding cell, a man who said he was an attorney announced that he would represent her. She described dealing with several lawyers, and she claimed that she had been defrauded of certain monies due her. However, it should be noted that a person convicted as a party to a murder cannot profit in any way, including gaining an inheritance, from that murder.

Karen also said that she felt browbeaten by the prosecutor and aban-doned by her own attorney. The prosecutor focused on the calls that Karen had made to 911. "He said that the deceit and the lies started with the 911 tapes," she said. Eventually, Karen was found guilty of complicity to commit murder, and was sentenced to ten years in prison. She reported that the jury was told that she was already eligible for parole.

"Jimmy went to stay with my mother and my sister. Later, the judge gave custody of Jimmy to my brother-in-law. This was a man who had never been able to get custody of his own children. [Nine months after Jim died, my brother-in-law] died of a heart attack. My mother and sister now have temporary custody of Jimmy.

"My life began to unravel during the trial. I learned that Bill had been sodomized by his father. The shock sent me reeling. I found out that my daughter had been pregnant by her father once at the age of thirteen and once again at fifteen. Her father [had beaten] her, as he had . . . me, to cause her to miscarry. Jim had been molesting her [when she was] about four or five years old, and [he] had started having sex with her [when she was] twelve. He also sodomized her and forced her to perform oral sex. Nadine has become a self-mutilator and [she] suffers from anorexia. She is now pregnant and is looking forward to her baby, although she refuses to marry the baby's father. I also learned that my husband abused Nadine's boyfriend. Jim stabbed him with a fork, dropped a large pumpkin on his crotch, burnt him with cigarettes, and pulled his hair and ears.

"I found out that all of the teachers at school were terrified of Jim. They wanted someone with them whenever he came around. I knew that the people with the military feared him, but I was shocked to learn that school officials feared him and never once notified me of their suspicions." Teachers in Kentucky are required by law to report suspected child abuse to Child Protective Services.

Karen continued: "[Bill's friend] was charged with capital murder. Bill, his girlfriend, and I were charged with complicity to capital murder. Bill's girlfriend had two additional charges of obstruction of justice since she left the area and could not be found to testify at [the friend's] trial. As I stated earlier, [Bill's] girlfriend was given full immunity to testify. My daughter was also charged with complicity to murder, but her case remained in juvenile court because of her age and because [she was] found incompetent by a psychiatrist . . . She spent twelve months [in a Morehead, Ky., facility], but while awaiting the trial, [she] was housed in Owensboro where she attempted suicide. [From there she] was sent to Riverdale Hospital for seven months, [before being] released [to] my mother and sister's care until the proceedings in September 1993.

"I was convicted of second-degree manslaughter. [Bill's friend] ended up being convicted of reckless homicide, as a result of a trial by jury. He was given credit time served—eighteen months. Bill [was convicted on a charge of] complicity to commit reckless homicide, and [he was] given credit time served—twenty months. I was brought before the grand jury on a charge of complicity to first-degree rape of my daughter. [But, after testifying] that I had no [involvement in or prior knowledge of her rape], I was not indicted.

"I arrived at KCIW on September 20, 1994. Shortly thereafter I met the Parole Board and received a serve-out on [my] ten-year sentence. The Parole Board seemed more concerned about the rape charge than the death of my husband, and I was never indicted on the rape. The Board was not even aware of [my] abuse, which was really so overwhelming in both [my] and [the friend's trials], as well as [in] both of the juvenile proceedings. The abuse was not even disputed in any of the court actions."

Karen described being sexually harassed and assaulted while in the Kentucky Correctional Institution for Women. At one point, Karen stated that another woman raped her: "At Christmas time, they gave out big candy canes. Very big ones. A lot of women used them for other things besides eating them." We cannot verify the truth of Karen's accusation, but none of the other Sisters in Pain, when asked, recalled any such occurrences and denied any sexual harassment or contact. In fact, most reported feeling safe for the first time while in prison.

"Since being incarcerated, I have been working for Correctional Industries, which is an OJT [On the Job] training program. I am taking ceramics classes, and I attend Residents Encounter Christ, a program that is sponsored by Chapel Services. I attempted to go to AA [Alcoholics Anonymous] . . . to learn more about Jim's problems in an attempt to understand. But it didn't help. I regularly attend church and have completed the Emmaus Bible study course. I am regularly attending the B.O.S.H. [Battered Offenders' Self-Help] Group, and I am in one-on-one therapy besides. I am taking the Mail Box Bible Study. I took and passed Introduction to Auto Technology. I spend personal time helping other residents study for their GEDs [General Education Diplomas, and I am] writing letters for them for such things as shock probation and visitation with their children. Several of those personal investments of time have resulted in positive outcomes." Karen spoke of the Sisters in Pain quilt, which she helped make: "[Even] though verbally we weren't opening up, it was our way of telling someone there was a problem in our lives. And it was our way of telling other women, 'Don't keep [your abuse] shut up.'"

Karen recalled that in spring, 1995, she tried to keep quiet the fact that she was going up for parole. "In prison when you come up for parole, people mess with you. They try to get you write-ups and everything else, so that, when you get to the Parole Board, people [will] mess with you." On June 12, 1995, Karen made parole, and she was released on July 7. She expressed profound gratitude for Chandra McElroy's B.O.S.H. Group, and for Marsha Weinstein's vision, both of which, she said, boosted her self-esteem.

Concerning her relationship with her children, Karen wrote, "Today, my relationship with Bill is strained. This is a result of the influence of his attorney and therapists. Bill and I had always been terribly close before this happened. We did everything together, and we truly enjoyed one another's company. My prayer is that someday we'll be able to recapture some of what's been lost through this ordeal. We . . . remained very close until they transferred him from the juvenile facility. I promised that I'd protect him, no matter what. Then they moved him to the adult jail and he continually grew more distant. His attorney had filed an order for no contact, so I was unable to write him or see him at all. He began to seem so bitter and angry. He asks my mother about me all the time, but he doesn't come to see me.

"Nadine and I have our ups and downs. She is bitter and angry with me for confronting her father about his sexual abuse of her. She feels that I violated her trust. The abuse got [a lot] worse for her after I confronted her father. Nadine is my gift from God because she nearly died. During her struggles with the brain swelling, when she was blind as a result of the swelling, I held her tightly to me to protect her from her fears. I breathed life into her when she could not breathe on her own. Three different times she was pronounced DOA [dead on arrival]. One-third of her brain was badly damaged, and I prayed . . . for a miracle to let her live and have a healthy, normal adult life. Now, with her pregnancy and anorexia, I am very proud of her two-pound weight gain. The doctor convinced her that the baby was gaining weight, not her. She is a joy to me. All of my children are.

"Jimmy has vowed not to ever return to Kentucky. I will see to it that he never has to. He doesn't feel safe here. He and I are pretty close now. He was a daddy's boy, but my little baby. I spoiled him rotten when I could and spent lots of time with him.

"I am so terribly sorry for the death of my husband. I am also very sorry for the way that it happened in that [it] damaged so many lives. I never once intended for my husband to die. I planned for it to be me. I triangulated my son [Bill], who rose to protect me from the demon we lived with. I was so beaten down mentally, emotionally, and spiritually at the time of Jim's death that my only thought was to save the children and let me die. It was my release from this control and the end of my torture that I was seeking. I have never found that release, for even in death he controls my thoughts and dreams or, shall I say, nightmares. Unfortunately, the whole thing backfired and the wrong person ended up dead.

"Nadine intends for me to live with her and has already procured a two-bedroom apartment. This will be fine with me. I look forward to spending time with all my grandchildren as they come along. Eventually, I will move to Ohio and raise Jimmy. I am in hopes and prayers that all of my children will attend family therapy with me. We all have unresolved issues that cannot be laid to rest until we have some quality time to devote to this cause.

"My life is going to be spent helping women who are being abused. I am learning so much! I know now that women are supposed to have orgasms and that women are not meant to be sexually abused. I know now that I have the right to a life that is free from abuse. I will carry the scars on my body for the rest of my life, but I am devoting every minute of every day to healing the scars that no one can see. I am speaking of the scars on my heart."

Karen's story hadn't ended as she'd hoped it would. Of course, it hadn't ended at all. Yet six months after her parole Karen knew she couldn't go home again to Ohio. And, except for Jimmy, who did, despite his vow, return to Kentucky, she remained separated from her children. There was no family therapy. There was no counseling of any kind. Counseling, after all, costs.

What money Karen made she earned working for the Elizabethtown attorney who had represented her in court. She ran the law firm's bankruptcy department, she said, for a salary lower than that of the office receptionist.

Karen still had plans to help battered women. She spoke about an idea she had to network hospitals via a computer link. "Abusers," she claimed, suddenly growing more animated, "get away with abuse because they're not going to take you to the same hospital. They're going to take you to different doctors, different hospitals, so nobody knows you're having repeated freak accidents. I want it to be so that when [medical personnel] punch up a lady's name they can see a social security number and they can say, 'Hey, she's had several other [injuries]. Look at this case before sending that woman home and right back into that guy's arms.'"

Excited, Karen continued in a stronger voice, "I want children to be taught what abuse is. Abuse is not just a black eye. Our quilt depicts that. We tried very hard to depict sexual abuse, physical abuse, and emotional abuse. And emotional abuse is very hard to depict on a quilt, but we tried, because each one of us was subject to all that. These poor little kids [all around us] are in emotional abuse so much that they don't even know what it is. Why can't we teach them what it is? I know I should stop [talking about this]. At the Domestic Violence Task Force I got so encouraged when . . . a lot of [the state senators] asked the right questions. But then they walked right out of there and did nothing. I got so discouraged because I thought maybe for once somebody really cared. The quilt made somebody really care. Maybe the quilt needs to come back and get . . . notoriety again. Stick it up somewhere in the Capitol building if that's what it takes. I don't know what it takes."

Karen referred to having visited the Statue of Liberty with several of her

Sisters in Pain since her release from prison and to having realized for the first time during her visit that the book that Lady Liberty is holding isn't the Bible, but a volume of secular laws. Karen said, "Here I am, standing inside of [the Statue of Liberty], on the very top, and I can't even hardly catch my breath, and I'm looking, and I see she's carrying a book of laws that don't even protect women. It was just such a kick. I'm, like, 'Come on, now! We've got to do something to support her again.' She was very supportive of the laws, or she wouldn't be carrying a book of laws. Why don't our laws protect women as well as men? If a man shoots an intruder, he's a hero. But when a man lives in a house and he threatens your young and you retaliate against him, you are pond scum and put in prison for life. It's a double standard. It should be justice for all—not justice for men and screw the women, which is basically what it is right now. It's justice for men and, if you've got enough money, maybe a little bit of justice for women. But, for the most part, women get the longer sentences and the most stringent guidelines and everything else."

We asked Karen whether she'd come to terms with her nineteen-year marriage, her husband's death, and her four-year imprisonment. Turning the thin, gold wedding band that still encircled the scarred third finger of her left, nail-bitten hand, Karen said, "The Bible says you're supposed to be submissive to your husband, and I didn't understand until after he [Jim] died and I went into counseling [in prison] . . . that being submissive doesn't mean doing things you know God wouldn't want you to do. It's doing things you think God would want you to do, and God's not going to punish you for what someone else does to you.

"My pastor, after I got locked up, he said I had everybody's blood on my shoulders from the church, because a lot of people left the church . . . People were leaving the church, and he blamed me for it." But the prison chaplain, Karen said, had convinced her of her innocence.

Karen added that she could now distinguish love from abuse, but she said that she would continue to wear her wedding band until she felt like a survivor, until she could believe that, even in death, Jim Stout no longer controlled her.

She spoke of her hopes of seeing Jimmy graduate from high school. She didn't have plans beyond the next few years, she said, because she was sure she wouldn't live. She described her illnesses—all major—and the assaults she'd endured since her parole. She'd been raped since her release, she claimed, just as she'd been molested in prison. And others had attacked her, she assured us, attempting battery and rape. Later, Chandra McElroy, Karen's prison counselor, told us that the prison physician who had examined Karen had pronounced Karen's torso the most battered body he'd ever seen. So we concluded that although we'd never know the extent of Karen's difficulties after her parole, her self-identity as a victim still defined her.

During our late-night drive back to Louisville, we spoke of Karen's sister, who had at first tried to convince Karen to leave Jim Stout, but who had then abided by her promise to Karen that she wouldn't interfere. We talked of Karen's mother, too reticent to intrude beyond asking about her daughter and grandchildren's bruises and broken bones. We referred to the physicians and to the police who had witnessed Karen and her daughter's horrific wounds and had dismissed them as accidents or as anomalies too troublesome to pursue. We talked of Jim Stout's employers who, according to Karen, had deemed him too abusive for his military job, but who had deemed their interest in him finished when they ended his army career. We spoke of the teachers and administrators at Bill and Nadine and Jimmy's schools, all of whom, Karen said, feared Jim Stout. We spoke of the police that Karen had called early in her marriage—of the officers of the law who had refused, she said, to help her, because her problems were "only" domestic disputes. We discussed Karen's trials, which did not permit her to introduce as evidence any mention of the abuses she'd endured. And we discussed Karen herself who, convinced throughout their relationship that Jim Stout must have been right, believed she deserved her living hell, a fate even her religion had endorsed. We knew that while none of these people or institutions could be held responsible for Jim Stout's behavior or for the fact that he was now dead, any or all of them could have helped Karen and her children and even Jim Stout himself if they had considered even one of the Stout family's problems to also be theirs. And finally we spoke of the men and the women we knew who had commented, when they learned of our interest in Karen and the other women whom Governor Jones had paroled, that they simply didn't understand why a battered wife couldn't or wouldn't leave her spouse. We discussed how we could offer, as response, the stories of Karen's thwarted attempts to flee—punished, as they were, by greater imprisonment, by broken toes, and by Jim Stout's threats to kill Karen's family. "Go ahead, leave me," he'd say. "When I kill your mother or your brothers and sisters, I know you'll come back for the funeral." And we could point out that Jim Stout, like most batterers, isolated his victim without any contacts, credit, or cash. But could we, we wondered, convince men and women so fortunate as to have never been so harmed of the fact that the most insidious aspect of abuse is its ability to alter its victim's perspective? Karen had spoken of learning to focus, while being tortured, on a picture hanging beside her bed. She had reported how her survival had depended on her ability to transcend her pain by nailing her very existence, as it hung in the balance, to that portrait secured to a wall. In the end, all we could conclude is that Karen had not been able to see beyond the boundaries that confined her, and that not once in almost twenty years had anyone ever offered to help her tear those barriers down.

Not Listening, Hearing

I begin hearing him
when he is six miles away,
as he punches out, thermos clanking
inside his steel lunchbox.
On his way to the truck,
he turns when his buddy yells to him.

I hear a strike against the raspy matchbook,
a sizzle like a Roman Candle just
about to take off.
He and his buddy
joke and spit.
A boot grinds a stub into the gravel.
One butt
still afire,
is flipped through the air,
whizzling, it falls through the naked
limbs of bush and settles underneath.
there it smolders,
raises a thin sexy wisp of smoke.

I hear it burning, him burning
and driving now, he pulls into
the tavern where he will order whiskeys
and sit for two hours, and think, think,
but already, he's driving home
and I'm crouched behind
my bed.
It is not yet dark. I am
holding a hammer, though when
I look over at the clock
his time card is still
in his hand.

Kathleen Driskell

Teresa Gulley Hilterbrand

On August 3, we headed out again, this time for Morehead, where we were to meet Teresa Gulley at the Holiday Inn. Teresa, who'd remarried since being charged with her crime, now goes by the surname Hilterbrand, and we'd rented a room with a conference table and chairs so that when Teresa's second husband, Jimmy, arrived with his wife, we three could retain some privacy as Teresa recounted her life. But too much time elapsed as we waited in the motel lobby. The coffee shop closed; the hands of the clock above the registration desk kept crawling past, then way past, our appointed rendezvous hour; and the cars in the parking lot continued to move on, failing to even hesitate in front of the lobby's double glass doors. Finally, the office phone rang, and the desk clerk motioned us over.

Jimmy had phoned to tell us that Teresa, then in the midst of a panic attack, couldn't come after all, but he added that we were welcome to find the Hilterbrand house, if we were willing to interview her there.

The land around Morehead is rural and rolling and not well marked for the convenience of strangers. In other words, we took a wrong turn or two before finding the right road, the road that boasted the warning "Congested Area" on a bold, black-lettered sign planted in the ground a country mile before a couple of single-story buildings rose to bracket the horizon. Past that sign and around a few curves, beside each of which stretched tobacco fields interrupted by an occasional abandoned car or ramshackle house, we finally found the Hilterbrand home, a modest, split-level brick rising from a lush, rambling yard.

As soon as we opened our car doors children appeared, children clamoring to show us the squirming kittens and puppies that the youngest among them clutched to their chests. Like the scene in *The Sound of Music* in which Baron Von Trapp's boys and girls assemble to perform, the Gulley and Hilterbrand offspring lined up at attention, awed, we assumed, by the sight of strangers.

Jimmy, the blood father of four of the brood and stepfather to the rest, emerged from the house, then led us all inside to the living room where he took his low-slung seat before the television and where the children resumed their stair-step formation in front of the wide bay window. Awkward minutes passed as we waited for Teresa. Jimmy watched his satellite-dish special while the children sneaked us nervous smiles.

Finally, a tear-stained Teresa emerged, clutching the belt of her robe in one hand and a box of Kleenex in the other. She sat on the sofa and apologized for her anxiety. But with each word she spoke, she shook more tears into her lap and onto the green shag carpet. She lit a cigarette and smoked to try to calm herself, and in hopes of reassuring her, we told her once again that our mission was to hear and understand her story and to thereby help others to understand her situation, too. She nodded but continued to cry, Jimmy continued to watch TV, and the children continued to stand in a row, still entranced by our tape recorder and bland city speech.

A half-hour passed before we dared ask Teresa if she could indeed endure an interview and before we indicated that the interview that we proposed required that we talk with her alone. She agreed to try, and after Jimmy and the children left to spend the afternoon outside, our conversation began.

Teresa Elaine Gulley Hilterbrand was born in West Liberty, Kentucky, in Morgan County, on Valentine's Day in 1959. But she spent her first twelve years in Crittenden, Kentucky, in Grant County, and on her twelfth birthday she moved with her family to Lewis County. She told us that, as the second oldest of fourteen children, she grew up filled with shame and fear. She even titled the autobiographical essay that she wrote while in prison "Fear," and that memoir details what Teresa still can't discuss without crying.

Before our visit Teresa had sent us the story that she had written while incarcerated, and the phrase that stayed with us after we read it and that haunted us still as its shaking author sat beside us attempting to collect herself is "Mommy [has] big hands." Those words launch a sentence that lists, according to Teresa, how those hands, when in contact with their daughter, landed bruises, raised welts, and drew blood. Teresa refused to articulate to us her childhood abuse in anything but snatches, aborted references to physical and psychological battering that ended in frantic pleas to keep secret the sick and ugly truth about a still-living, still-feared parent.

But it's significant that Teresa states that battering began before her first marriage, so significant that omitting its mention would perpetuate the sort of crippling lies that permit such abuse to continue. So the childhood that Teresa could not discuss we reconstruct here from the written account that she sent us.

Of her mother Teresa wrote, "I feared this woman, literally. There were times I wish I'd die, there were times I wish I'd have the nerve to kill myself, there were times I knew she'd kill me with one more blow, and there were numerous times I hated that woman and just knew I couldn't possibly be her daughter. I never said any of this out loud. But she did speak out loud when she constantly told me she hated me, and when she said she wished I hadn't been born."

In her essay, Teresa recounts incident after incident in which she claims her mother's irrational anger struck its victim as humiliation and pain. At age three or four, Teresa wrote, her mother, holding Teresa while frying bacon, became infuriated when sizzling grease splattered on one of her daughter's legs and Teresa began to cry. Because of her tears, she wrote, her mother beat her. On another occasion Teresa had soiled her slip by playing on a rusted slide. Upon seeing the stain, her mother "beat me from shoulder to legs. Blood was pouring from my rear and my thighs, mostly. I was kept out of school for three to five days, and, when I returned, I was sent in a culotte slip under my dress with Vaseline on my legs so the slip would stick." Another time, after Teresa complained that she was cold, she stated that her mother forced her to stand behind their stove until she fainted from the heat and awoke to the burn of butter being applied to her seared forehead, nose, and cheeks. Teresa's essay reports that such physical punishment as sitting in tubs of freezing water, sleeping in empty baths, licking her own urine off the floor, and sucking her soiled underwear after being scared severely enough to defecate scarred Teresa's childhood and now constitute her memories as surely as her mother's words molded Teresa's self-image. "I lived by names she called me—not the one she gave me at birth. I was fat, ugly, a bitch, a whore, a slut, and a tramp," she wrote.

Teresa said, too, that she would be beaten for "a bad grade in school" or for not doing homework that she was not allowed to bring home, anyway. "I was kept home from school a lot," she wrote. "I know I was kept out of school as a punishment for liking school. But I didn't like school—I loved it. It got me away from her."

She wrote, "I won the spelling bee at our school in seventh grade and received $10.00. Mommy bought me a dress and shoes and she told me I looked like a fat, ugly cow, and she sent me off to compete in another bee. I won third or fourth place because I couldn't understand what the announcer was saying. I cried my heart out and I wished that one moment to have Mommy to hug me. But when I got home, instead, she told me she knew I couldn't do it and she didn't know why she let Daddy waste gas to take me to town or why she spent that money on me for a dress and shoes I'll never wear again. 'Now,' she said, 'take [your] stupid, ugly ass to bed.'"

At age twenty-one, Teresa married Rick Gulley. But sixteen years, four children, and a second husband later, Teresa still quaked when we mentioned her mother, the woman she recalls as having such powerful hands.

Throughout our conversation, Teresa continued to smoke and sob, but her panic subsided. She said she met Rick Gulley one night—she recalled it was Thanksgiving—in 1979 when he appeared at her trailer door. "I kindly told him to get lost," she said. "I said he was one heck of a smart ass and I just wanted him out of my house." So Rick disappeared, but he returned the following March and asked her for a date. She refused, but he asked if she'd reconsider if he stopped drinking, and she said yes, she would.

So Rick abstained from alcohol, and he and Teresa began to date. But two months into their relationship, Rick resumed drinking. "I wanted to break it off with him," Teresa said. "But he kind of jumped my case, and said, 'I gave up drinking for you, I gave up my friends for you.' I went back to my place and he went straight for the booze and got . . . sloppy drunk and he come up to my trailer. I felt sorry for Rick. He never thought he could do anything. I thought I could save him."

The thought that she could change him is what caused Teresa to agree to marry Rick, just three months after they met. She'd been working two jobs as a fast-food waitress and as a department store clerk, and he'd been helping intermittently on his brother-in-law's farm. But by the time they were wed, in August 1980, Teresa held the only job between them. She waitressed, and the couple survived on her tips.

While she worked, Rick would spy on her through the restaurant window while sitting in his car. Teresa said he'd fly into jealous rages if she spoke too long to her customers. "It didn't matter if it was a man or a woman," she said. "I thought he loved me. I know he loved me, and in the beginning I did believe that maybe he did this out of love." Like so many battered women, Teresa saw the physical abuse Rick heaped upon her as just punishment for some misdeed. If a man truly loved her, surely he would punish her only for her own good. But Teresa said that, after several years, she came to realize that Rick's behavior exemplified emotions far from love. We asked her how she had reached that conclusion. "Throughout the years I had some counseling," she said. "I'll tell you the best. We had an instructor at Morehead State University. I went back to college in 1987 after I had all my kids. She was more of a friend than a teacher, and she told us that she had never seen so many women with such low self-esteem. She said she would believe it if we were all suffering abuse. It was a clerical class, but she spent an hour every other day just talking to us about us and helping us feel better about ourselves. She taught self-esteem and dress management. She made me look at me. And I wasn't happy, but I said, 'You've got to go on.' And I know, too, that I depended on my kids for my happiness more than I did Rick after the years went on."

Teresa's four children were born between 1982 and 1987, but she lost three other babies, a single child and a set of twins, to miscarriages. Rick, she said, caused her to lose her first baby. He "took his hands and he hit me so hard that it flipped me over," she said. "After we lost the first baby, he never hit me again until I got pregnant with our third child. And then he took the table and slammed it up against my stomach."

But even as Teresa's eyes welled up again and she brushed her wet strands of dark blond, shoulder-length hair from her hollowed face, she said, "You know what? On our honeymoon, he shoved me up against the wall because I wouldn't have oral sex. He had an evil streak in him and he said, 'I'm going to be just like my dad.' But I always felt sorry for Rick because he's got a big family, and nobody ever tried to help him. Rick felt like he was a black sheep." Rick's father, Teresa said, had battered Rick's mother, just as, in various ways, he'd abused Rick and his siblings, too. Experts agree that abuse is a vicious cycle. Rick was abused, he watched his father abuse his mother, and he received the message that battering is somehow "normal." The little boy in the man could not differentiate the good from the bad in his father's behavior. Rick's desire was to emulate his father, to act as he did.

Teresa and Rick's own marital battles increased in frequency and in intensity as his jealousy escalated. According to Teresa, Rick's constant accusations that she was engaging in clandestine affairs alternately caused the couple to quit whatever job each held so that Rick could monitor Teresa twenty-four hours a day. But it was while her back was turned, she said, that Rick's battering began. She recalled, "Rick slapped me across the face once. After that, as far as I can remember, he never hit my face. He always waited 'til my back was turned, and he'd go for my back. Or he'd wait 'til I'd turn back around and he'd go for my front. One time, he picked me up by the rollers in my hair. He went from throwing a lit match down my blouse to throwing hot cups of coffee on me. A glass he threw, one time, went through the wall. A screwdriver he threw, one time, went straight through the wall. When he hit, nine out of ten times your back would be turned. It got to the point that the kids would not leave the room. They were going to come in there and help Mommy." Teresa tried to report the abuse, but her pleas fell on deaf ears. She said, "The law had been called . . . usually because of his behavior [and] his violence, but we were still married, so it was, to [the police, a] domestic [problem] in the household. 'Go to bed, sleep on it; it'll be all right.'"

By January 1991, Teresa had experienced enough. She told us, "My New Year's resolution wasn't to quit smoking, it wasn't to lose weight. It was to divorce Rick. On January eleventh of that year, Rick had a cyst on his back that had to be surgically removed. In February he had his first cataract surgery. In March he had his second cataract surgery. And in April he went for colon cancer testing. We didn't get the results of that test until July, but I told him on May 12 that if all his tests came back all right he wouldn't see me around again, because I was divorcing him. He said, 'Yeah, right. You ain't gonna leave me. You ain't never gonna leave me. Who would have you?' On May 12 I took off my wedding band and I had him to hand me his, and they never went back on."

On July 5, 1991, Teresa learned that Rick did not have colon cancer, and on July 10, 1991, she kept her appointment with an attorney, who drew up her divorce papers. "I wanted to help him," she said, referring to Rick. "I wanted to be with him. But I was so tired. I was so tired. I was tired of the kids having to see it all." Teresa was also weary, she said, of protecting her children from Rick. "If I knew he was going for one of the kids, he'd have to kill me first, 'cause that's when I acted like a maniac. I went for him, [and I said,] 'You ain't touchin' them. You ain't doin' those kids like that.'"

In spite of her qualms, Teresa took action. But because she couldn't gather sufficient cash to file for divorce until July 31, Rick refused to believe that she'd had the papers prepared. Teresa recalled, "Well, on August the first the law came out to our home late one night and asked to see Rick. He was at work. I said, 'Please don't serve him while he's at work.' And the officer said, 'I won't. What's the best time to catch him tomorrow?' But he went straight on down there and served those papers on him. So Rick came home, tearing up havoc. I thought I'd already seen the worst, but that night when I called the law he broke all the windows out of the house and he came at me and our son David."

According to Teresa, between August 1 and October 8, 1991, the day their divorce became final, Rick's constant, alcoholic rampages terrorized her and their children. He alienated their friends from her by telling them that she'd been having an affair with Jimmy Hilterbrand, a mere acquaintance at the time, she swore, but a man she later married. She took out an emergency protective order (EPO) to prevent Rick from contacting her, but according to Teresa, when Rick would appear at her door despite the order, police refused to intervene. "Anybody I'd call at the police station would tell me, 'Teresa, when we get up there, he won't be there.' I'd say, 'I'm telling you, he's here now.' They'd say, 'Well, he'll leave in just a little bit. Just don't open the door.' And I'd say, 'He's already in the house. He comes in here while I'm at work.' They never came again after that EPO. They never came again."

We asked, "Throughout your marriage, when you called the law, did they ever come?"

Teresa replied, "I only called the year of our divorce. They told me, 'It's just a domestic dispute. Sleep on it; it'll be all right.'"

We then asked Teresa if, during her marriage to Rick, she thought family or friends had been aware that she was being battered. "Everyone knew what kind of person he was," she replied, reaching for another cigarette. But both her family and Rick's family, she said, now deny it. "Me and Rick both would go over there and talk to my family about what was going on. My sister would say, 'Teresa, where'd you get that mark on you?' I'd have bruises. Rick would say, 'I done told you I was sorry for that.' I said, 'You're gonna tell me that one of these days, and I'm not gonna believe you no more.' And it wouldn't matter what I had on. Somehow or other, my sister would spot something on me. And when we came back home, Rick said I did that on purpose. 'You wanted her to see that. That's why you wore that.' I said, 'Someday, I'll probably be glad somebody saw it.'"

As it turned out, witnesses didn't matter after all, as they, too, turned their backs.

"Thinking now about your relationship with Rick Gulley, do you believe there's anything you could have done differently that would have changed the situation?" we asked.

"Stay married to him. I would have put up with it. Right now, if he was to walk through that door, I would remarry him, because he'd be alive. If I could do it over again, I would put up with it the rest of my life."

"Did you," we continued, "ever think your life or your children's lives were in danger?"

"I knew they were. It got to the point where Rick would hold me down on the floor and strangle me. The kids would keep pulling at him or hitting him until they got him away from me."

Teresa talked with Jimmy Hilterbrand on August 17, 1991, at a party she described as a "divorce party, a pre-divorce party, a birthday party for Rick, and an anniversary all on the same day." However, she later recalled having met him in 1979 when she had car trouble, and he'd come to her aid. She added, "In a small town, everybody encounters somebody every day."

When asked about her attempts to get help by filing an emergency protective order, Teresa laughed. "I filed for an EPO. That's not worth the paper it's printed on. He was at my house whenever I got back." After taking out that EPO, Teresa recounted Rick's flouting of the law the next day when he appeared on her doorstep: "'You know you got a restraining order against you,' I said. 'You better be getting your ass out of here, . . . and you better be getting it out now.' Rick then damaged the phone and said, 'I'm leaving.' He said, 'I will be back, Bitch.' He said, 'The next time you ain't gonna be able to call the law.' On October 8, 1991, he looked at me and the kids and he said, 'I hate every goddamned one of you all, and I wish I could kill you.'"

Teresa had referred to Rick Gulley's death, the death that she calls an accident, but the death that the courts deemed manslaughter. We asked Teresa to tell us what happened and, still shivering, she said, "It was April 30, 1994. Rick came up a little after ten that night. A little bit after he got there, another guy came up." Rick, it seems, had arrived to visit the children. Teresa had been dating Jimmy, but they'd been estranged for five months, and the man who had come to visit was an acquaintance who knew Rick, Teresa said, better than she did. But according to Teresa, as soon as her visitor arrived, Rick became enraged. Her son David's presence would prevent Rick and the other man from fighting, she thought, but as the evening wore on she asked Rick and her visitor to leave. Rick left, swearing he'd return. Teresa's visitor asked to stay long enough to drink one more beer, and, as he drank, Rick returned. Teresa remembered, "Rick walks right in the house, fussin' and cussin' and everything else. I said, 'I don't know what your problem is, but you'll be getting out of my house, and you'll be getting out now.' I said [to my visitor], 'You need to go, too.' [He] got up and sat back down. I got the gun out and put it on the coffee table, where [he] and Rick both could see it. Rick left again, then he came back, except nobody heard, and he passed straight through the door to the hallway, and he pointed his finger at me and he said, 'I saw you fucking [your friend] right there in front of our kids, and, you fucking bitch, you're not gonna do that and keep our kids.' He said, 'I'll see you in hell first.' I said, 'Rick, I don't know what you're on, but you need to get out of here.' After that remark Rick walked out of the house for the last time, and, as he exited, slammed the front door.

"There's a lot from there on I don't remember," she continued, "except for shooting the gun. I know I shot it at the door. I was sitting on the couch and the door was closed and I shot at the door."

"He was on the other side of the door?"

"I didn't know that."

"What was your point in shooting?"

"To scare the living daylights out of him. He knew the law wasn't going to do anything. . . . I knew that after shootin' that gun Rick wouldn't be back until he was supposed to come get the kids. I knew that it would scare him that much."

"Was he standing right on the other side of the door?"

"I haven't been able to figure that out."

"What happened after that? Who found him? How did they find him?"

"David said, 'Momma! You shot Daddy.' I said, 'Oh, David, I did not.' I said, 'David, I shot at a door, not at a person.' I said, 'There's no earthly way I could have shot anyone.' Plus, I had this little, girlish gun, this little 22, and the farthest it's supposed to carry is nine feet. That's straight, without anything else in its path. So I got up and I went outside. Well, by then, all the kids were up. I said, 'Rick, get your ass up from there. You're scaring the daylights out of these little kids.' I said, 'You stop that, and you stop that now, or I really will call the law.'"

"Where was he?"

"He was on the second step, laying back. And no sign of blood or anything. . . . I heard him breathing. I knew he was breathing. He was just trying to scare the kids, and I thought that was cruel. I said, 'All right, I'm calling the law.' I went back inside and called the law and said, 'I think I shot someone.' They said, 'Who is this?' So I told them. And they asked who did I shoot, and I said, 'My ex-husband.' Anyway, they came and I opened the door, and I said, 'Are you gonna arrest him this time, or what?' And [the police officer] said, 'Teresa, he's dead.' I said, 'You are a liar.' I said, 'You go back out there and check. He's just playin' possum. He's got you all fooled this time.' He said, 'No, Teresa. He *is* dead.'"

Our conversation continued. "Why did you call the police and tell them you thought you shot somebody?"

"I wanted Rick to hear so he'd be gone when they got here."

"So what happened after that? Were you arrested immediately?"

"No. They let me sit there and drink coffee or wine—the law, the state detective, and most of the police. And I got totally plastered." Teresa also indicated that she had been drinking before she fired the shot that killed Rick. "I knew that I would pass out sooner or later and this would be a nightmare. . . . They took me and the kids over to Mommy's to drop the kids off, and then they took me to the courthouse. We got to the courthouse around ten o'clock that morning, and I was arrested around three p.m. . . . Rick was killed around three a.m."

Teresa went to trial a year after Rick's death. She said she was arrested about three in the afternoon, some twelve hours after his death. "[The arresting officer] read my Miranda rights, but I swore under oath that he hadn't [on] the morning of the accident. And [he] took me down to the county jail. Wouldn't set bond until the next Thursday. This was on a Saturday morning; the next Thursday, I went to the courthouse and they set bond the first time [at] $200,000." Eventually, the amount was lowered, and Jimmy Hilterbrand posted bail. He and Teresa were married August 19 in the jail; the next day Teresa was released to him. She would wait a year for her trial.

Teresa was charged with first-degree murder. The prosecutor offered her a deal in which she would plead guilty to manslaughter one and receive a sentence of fifteen years. Teresa stated, "I said, 'No deal. I don't even want to hear it,' I said, ''cause I'm innocent.' I said, 'I did it accidentally, and God knows in my heart I did, and somehow or another I will convince the jury.'. . . I said, 'I'll take my chances going to trial with murder.'" The next deal offered Teresa was manslaughter two and ten years. A later offer included an eight-year prison sentence and a promise not to object to shock probation, a legal mechanism by which a person unlikely to commit additional criminal acts is released from prison after serving a short sentence, such as a month. Finally, Teresa signed a document releasing her lawyers from liability if she were found guilty.

Teresa described a flawed jury system in which persons who were friendly with Rick and other "neighbors" were drawn for the jury pool. A jury that Teresa would ultimately see as hostile was seated. Teresa would not permit her attorney to put her son David on the stand. Men and women who Teresa counted as friends testified against her. Teresa offered testimony but said, "I was honest and stupid enough to say, 'I don't remember.' I think if I'd made up something that would have been better than telling the truth. They came back with manslaughter." The jury was out approximately two hours pondering Teresa's verdict; she was found guilty of second-degree manslaughter.

Before her parole, Teresa served seven months of her ten-year sentence at the Kentucky Correctional Institution for Women in Pee Wee Valley. In some ways, she said, that experience proved more positive than had the three months and three weeks she'd spent in jail, because she could leave her cell, move around, see the sun.

It surprised her, she said, when she was housed in minimum security. But, Teresa added that she, like the other inmates, was strip-searched often, an indignity that she loathed.

Teresa has a heart condition that caused her to be transferred from her first prison job, serving on a public facility cleaning crew, to her second duty, tutoring other inmates to prepare them to take the tests for their GEDs. When asked whether she had been a B.O.S.H. Group member or if she'd helped make the quilt, Teresa replied no to both. She said that she was shy and that she didn't like groups, and she said that she thought that because she'd refused to join the B.O.S.H. Group, its members didn't like her. But she became friends with Sherry Pollard and Sue Melton, with whom she attended church-sponsored meetings that offered spiritual support.

Teresa's story and fate became tied to the lives of the B.O.S.H. Group members in November 1995, though, when prison counselor Chandra McElroy told Teresa that four more names would be added to those of the nine women serving time for killing or for conspiring to kill their abusers, women who McElroy, Marguerite Thomas, and Marsha Weinstein hoped Gov. Brereton Jones would parole.

Theresa recalled, "I said, 'Chandra, don't do this to me.' I was beyond fighting anymore. I said, 'Chandra, if this doesn't work, suicide here I come.

I'm sick to death of tryin' to get out. The harder I fight, the harder they push me back.'"

Teresa believed that her parole package had been sent to the governor and to the parole board and that it had been reviewed with the others, but the first news that she received in early January devastated her. The night before, she'd seen listed on the television news nine of the names of the women who would be paroled. Her name wasn't among them, but when prison officials woke her that morning, she hoped that the broadcast had been wrong. Soon, though, she knew that her sentence had not been commuted. "They took the four of us that didn't get mentioned upstairs and the other nine down. Don't get me wrong. I was happy for the other nine, but I was hurt, humiliated, and slapped in the face again, but this time by the highest power. And I said, 'God, why did you bring me this far? Why did you put me through this again if I was going to get told no?' I said, 'Why are you doin' this to me? I'm mad at you.'"

At this point in our conversation, Teresa's crying almost choked her. But she continued, "Anyway, we were asked if we would agree to be interviewed by TV stations, radio stations, and newspapers. I said, 'Yes, indeed. I am tired of keeping my mouth shut and letting everybody work for me.' So Louisville WAVE-3 reporter, Connie Leonard, said, 'How do you feel about what the governor did for you all?' Well, she didn't know that my name was one of the names that wasn't on there. I said, 'He didn't do anything for any one of us, but he especially didn't for some of us.' And she said, 'What do you mean?' And I said, 'I'm one of the four that didn't even get any mention.' She said, 'Is there anything you'd like to say to the governor?' I said, 'Yeah, I'd like to know why in the world he didn't acknowledge all thirteen of us.' I said, 'I'd like to know how he could have seen and read all this stuff and not even set any one of us out of here.' So Governor Jones called Marsha Weinstein that night after he'd seen me on the news. He said he didn't know about these other four women. So all our packages *weren't* turned in and our videos *weren't* seen."

Governor Jones finally saw Teresa's parole package, and just before the New Year Teresa received a belated Christmas gift—notice that the parole board would review her case.

"I went before the board, handcuffed and chained. I knew I wouldn't make it. I felt like I was tripping on my own tongue. I felt like I said more to hurt me than to help me."

But Teresa's son David and her current husband, Jimmy Hilterbrand, had, the day before, told the parole board what they knew. "David did break down, but he told things I didn't bring up—like that Rick pulled a gun on me several times when we were married. David brought up so much I didn't think he had witnessed."

In a month, on February 5, 1996, Teresa's sentence was commuted and her husband and children arrived at the Kentucky Correctional Institution for Women to drive her home. We asked Teresa what had been the hardest aspect of rebuilding her life.

"The most difficult thing since I've come home is getting my kids not to back-talk, fight, argue. We still don't have our bond back, and I don't know if we ever will, and that hurts. And then, when me and Jimmy get into it, he'll throw Rick's death up to me. He's been my number-one support, but still, he says some really cutting, mean things."

When bail is set for a criminal defendant, a percentage, ranging from 10 to 100 percent of the bail, must be paid to ensure the defendant's presence at the trial. If the person appears for the trial, the money is returned, minus the bail bondsman's fee. What happened to Teresa's money remains a mystery.

We asked whether the battering that Teresa experienced in her first marriage had caused her to be frightened of the prospect of having relationships with other men or of marrying again.

"Jimmy and I, we got married three years and about seven months after my divorce. I knew I loved Jimmy. I loved Jimmy more than myself. As far as me worrying about . . . going into that marriage, I knew what kind of person Jimmy was. I knew he could be abusive, and I married him anyway—on the condition that if he ever laid another hand on me, I don't care what's hangin' over my head, I'm out."

"Did Jimmy abuse you before you married him?"

Teresa nodded.

"Why did you trust him?"

"We came together when we were both at such a low point in our lives. Jimmy's first wife had committed suicide, and I truly needed somebody."

"Has he abused you since your marriage?"

"Yes, since I've been home from prison."

"Physically?"

"He about broke this finger last week. But he doesn't usually abuse me as far as hittin'—just cussin'. I hear my mother in that. I hear her every time I hear somebody cussin'."

When we asked Teresa what she would suggest that women in abusive relationships do, she said, "Get out. I know my advice and my experience are contradictory," she added, "but I'm being honest when I tell you he's treated me better than anybody in my life."

"And what," we asked Teresa, "do you want for your future?"

"To be a writer. I *am* a writer. I want to be published. Jimmy says he's behind me going back to school, but Jimmy's vibes tell me different. I like to look a person in their eyes when I'm talking to them, because their eyes will give them away every time."

Teresa, like some of the other women, has not come to terms with the fact that her sentence was commuted to time served—to the fact that she wasn't pardoned. When asked to describe the difference between commutation and pardon, she said, "[C]ommuted [means] my . . . time served is gonna be shortened. Pardoned [means] off the record. You are forgiven. 'Go home and behave yourself and don't let it happen again.'" Because Teresa wasn't pardoned, reporting to parole officers is now a part of her life. She also has restrictions on where she can go and whom she can see. Teresa declined to appear on the *Donahue Show* with her Sisters in Pain who traveled to New York because she believes that the parole board, not the governor, was responsible for her release from prison and because, had she joined her Sisters in Pain on the show, she'd intended to explain to the television show audience the difference between commutation and pardon. She believed her tenuous freedom would have been threatened had she revealed that her gratitude is also a guise that masks her anger.

Asked about her desire to go back to school, Teresa said, "I only want to go part time for one thing, and it will get me out of the house."

We had a final question. We wondered if Teresa, who had been so abused, was perpetuating that cycle. We asked, "Would you mind telling us how you discipline your own children?"

"Depends on what happens," she replied. "Depends on what they do. Like, if they back-talk me, they're going to their room for fifteen minutes. If they back-talk me going down the stairs because they had to go to their room for fifteen minutes, they're going down there for half an hour. And they can build all the way up to an hour. If they've been fighting, I paddle them. I know people say you shouldn't paddle them, but I don't believe a spanking is going to hurt them. A beating is going to hurt them." Teresa also described using deprivation of privileges as a disciplinary measure. She stressed that she only paddles her children and her stepchildren when they've been fighting. She said that she and Jimmy disagree on how often a paddle should be used. At the time we talked, it appeared that Teresa was trying to distinguish discipline from abuse.

Teresa's own watery eyes with their huge black pupils had revealed plenty as she talked. Rivulets had coursed down the tiny lines and deeper creases that surrounded her eyes, mapped her cheeks, and aged her beyond her years. After we departed that day we learned from Chandra McElroy that Teresa still didn't leave the house much, except to plant and harvest the couple's tobacco fields that ranged down and across the road—that constituted, in fact, the Hilterbrands' horizon. But the dust that layered the furniture and coated every knickknack in the living room, the insects that leapt from the littered carpet to feast on our arms and legs, and Teresa's sagging bathrobe led us to believe that depression and fear still imprisoned her.

Neither of us could resolve Teresa's conundrums. Her high-school education, her single college clerical class notwithstanding, would not gain her a career that could support her and the eight children in her care. And even if it could, too few jobs exist within driving distance to render such an option realistic.

Teresa had told us that, until she'd spent time in prison, she hadn't realized how much she felt she needed to live with a man. Maybe she meant that she required help in raising so many children. Perhaps she'd concluded that she couldn't plant or harvest alone. But, more likely, she meant that her survival, like that of most people, requires a sense of purpose. And without other role models or options, perhaps Teresa's self-worth is subject to any attention, no matter its sort, that her husband, like her mother, will allot her.

Skull-Light

Think of certain inexplicable deaths
As sullied translucent patches on sea,
The sky a stagnant pool. The river
Of women wash down their walls
With milk of lime and household starch
For All Saints sideways on purpose now.

I make my Easter walking between the graves,
Head high in the air, and seem to be losing him
Twice over, though I am far more truly dead,
Fastened like a limpet to this strip of land.

The real look is creeping back into his eyes,
Eyes I feared to read, that nailed or burned
The words to my lips, and made of his death
With their sudden flaming up a perfect end.

The strange current he gave forth,
As though a beloved red from the topmost
Part of the evening, a scarce-born animal
In spices, that frozen light
Too intense for even the smallest shadow —
What morning, like a sleeve too wide,
Without costing much, can be breaking in me?

Mebdh McGuckian

Excerpted from The American Voice Anthology *(Univ. Press of Kentucky, 1998) and re-printed with the permission of the* American Voice, *Mebdh McGuckian, and Peter Fallon of the Gallery Press.*

Sue Melton

It was Sunday, early November, and snowing. The air felt frostier than our typical upper South, midfall weather. We traveled south first on one highway then another for the six-and-a-half hours it took us to drive from Louisville to Albany, Kentucky, a tiny town smack in the center and on the edge of the Tennessee state line. The prospect of the interview we'd set out to conduct worried us some, as Sue Melton, we'd been told by Chandra McElroy and Marsha Weinstein, was not in good shape. As a matter of fact, she'd never have been paroled had her health not almost caused her to collapse. But cancer and emphysema had taken their toll. While incarcerated, she'd had one breast removed (her only sister had died of breast cancer), and at age forty-seven her prognosis remained guarded at best. We expected to encounter an invalid, and we did. But our experience caused us even graver concerns.

Sue's dragging herself downstairs to greet us on the porch of the house where she'd lived since her parole, her brother and sister-in-law's place that we'd found hard to locate on a winding, rural road, constituted, in itself, an event. Sue's doctors had forbidden her to sleep any longer in the makeshift cellar apartment where she'd first stayed until the dampness and mold had infiltrated her fragile lungs and returned her to the hospital. So now she lived with her oxygen tank on the half-completed topmost floor of that dark-timbered house. Even her stair climbing had been restricted to a weekly foray from her two-room enclave to the first-floor kitchen or to the doorstep so a family member could drive her to an appointment with one of her several specialists.

Yet for a person so sick, Sue looked better than good. Only what we'd been told and the awkward oxygen tank, an out-of-place eyesore that squatted in a remote corner of her bedroom, hinted that the girlish woman before us could be ill. But what disarmed us most were the contrasts, the counterpoints, not only between what we saw and what we knew to be true but also between Sue Melton's placid countenance and her volatile conversation. As we gathered in her bedroom, Sue told us her tale. She sat cross-legged at the head of her ruffle-and-pillow-bedecked bed, and as she spoke she clutched to her chest a teddy bear that had *Christmas 1996* emblazoned on its chest. The room held only one chair, so Angie and Linda took turns moving from a makeshift seat at the foot of Sue's bed to the rocker across the room. The irony, though, was that despite the lack of seating space, Sue's bedroom overflowed. Hot pink flounces cascaded from the window, from the bed, from everywhere, it seemed. Photos practically nudged each other off her French provincial dresser and flower-papered walls, colorful images of Sue's only child, April, captured at every stage of her twenty-year life. The most recent pictures revealed an attractive, smiling young woman, a baby girl grown up. Atop every available surface, competing for space with the photos, sat stuffed animals, dolls, and mementos of events that Sue had missed. Sue's haven, a teenage girl's attic retreat, complemented Sue herself, a slight, almost shy, yet earnest woman with her hair in a flip reminiscent of Alice in Wonderland and Mary Tyler Moore. We felt we'd stumbled into the presence of an aging innocent trapped in a fairy tale, into the presence of a woman whose emotional, if not physical, survival depended on reinventing her very existence. The bear, she told us, had been an early gift because her relatives knew how she cherished Christmas. From the adjacent, not-yet-finished living room, an already-decorated artificial tree stood, majestic, its bright lights blinking furiously, a month and a half before the holiday. Although she never said so directly, Sue hinted that Christmas 1996 might be her last. But the picture of Sue sitting on her frilly bed amidst the trappings of a youth she'd never lived contrasted so sharply with the words she spoke that we wondered whether we, like Alice through the looking glass, were facing stark reality or a frightening, poignant reflection of a topsy-turvy world. By the time we left, the chill outdoors had seeped into our bones. Even in Sue's homey, space-heated suite with its sentimental swags and bows, seasonal lights continued to wink and blink in heated frenzy or flash in frantic code, depending on our shifting points of view. Either way, we couldn't be warmed or comforted by signals so contradictory to the story we'd just been told.

If Sue remembers much about her youth she won't admit it. What she recalls, she said, is the rejection she felt from parents who ignored her. She was born the first girl but the third child of a family of four, and she recalls feeling grateful for her small build because, she said, she believed that her size helped protect her from being singled out by a father whose temper rivaled the wrath of God. Anger and God were inevitably linked in Sue's family; the Pentecostal church in which she was raised held to rules clear and absolute: Sue and her sister would wear dresses, not slacks, and would grow their hair long in God's name. Sue recalled how once she wanted bangs so badly that she broke strands of her hair into a jagged strip to frame her forehead. On another occasion a teacher at school took Sue under her wing and treated her to a hairstyling session at a beauty salon. She never forgot that teacher who made her, she said, feel special.

One time Sue's father, too, made her feel significant. One time. That singular event occurred on a family trip to an out-of-town park, and Sue said that her usually grim-faced father smiled that day. But family excursions almost always meant trips to church and back: twice on Sundays, always on Wednesdays, and on other days throughout the week as the spirit moved the preacher to proclaim the gospel truth.

But when Sue reached age thirteen a more powerful event took the place of what would remain her one pleasant memory of a day in a park. Her family had come home from church, and Sue's father scared her by glaring at her while taking off his belt. He beat her with that belt, hitting her harder with each lick. He offered no explanations or apologies after he raised enough welts and heard enough cries to suit him. He simply stalked off, a righteous man of God. That night Sue's mother sneaked into her daughter's room to comfort her. She told Sue that her father had beat her because he had witnessed that day in church a boy named Wayne putting his arms around Sue. Crouched together with her mother in Sue's bed, Sue knew then that her mother feared her father; she knew, too, that her mother had offered the only advice and protection that she could when she commented that Sue's beating would have been less severe if Sue hadn't cried so hard.

"I always felt everything was my fault," she said. At thirteen no child is ever grown up. But at age thirteen Sue learned what, in her family, was sacred. She realized that for some people, women especially, scripture could be bent by a strong man's will. And she learned that the lay of the land that her daddy's beating had promised was not an Eden, but a desert, forever and ever, Amen. So it isn't surprising that Wayne, whom Sue had met when she was twelve and he was fifteen, convinced her to marry him when she turned thirteen.

At this point, Sue's story could be Karen Stout's (Stelzer's), for like Karen's initial reaction to Jim Stout, Sue hadn't cared for Wayne when they'd first met at school. But just as Jim courted Karen by showering her with attention she'd never known, Wayne did the same with Sue, even to the point of restraining her in a locker for speaking to another boy. Like Wayne, Jim had captured Karen for talking to another male student. And just as Karen had misinterpreted Jim's motives, Sue confused Wayne's jealousy and possessiveness with passion. Her father and her minister had taught Sue that love manifested itself as repression, anger, and rage; amidst the din of loud and physical men Sue couldn't hear her mother's meek voice, a voice that, at any rate, had been all but silenced by the need that mother and daughter shared to hide behind attitudes and within bodies both passive and petite.

So, thinking that Wayne loved her, Sue agreed to elope. The two took off to Tennessee, where a minister married them after they lied about their ages and after Sue's aunt acted as witness. But for Sue, romance died early and hard. She and Wayne spent their honeymoon back at his parents' house in Albany, and they started their married life in a house that Wayne's grandparents gave them. But even though Wayne proved himself a financial success from the outset by running an oil company and working on his family's farm, his grandparents treated Wayne and Sue as children, setting curfews and boundaries that the newlyweds fought for eighteen months until they bought a trailer that would equip them, they hoped, for independence.

Sue and Wayne's longing for freedom and the fact that they planted their trailer near a highway went hand in hand in a symbolic sense, but Sue and Wayne had drifted apart. Almost from the start of their marriage, Wayne's roving eye drove a stake between them. His infidelities escalated to the point that he brought his lovers home, paraded them before his wife, and had sex with them in his marriage bed. Of course Sue cried and argued, pleaded and cajoled, but ultimately she lived by Wayne's rules because she'd been taught that wives should obey their husbands, that divorce is a heinous sin.

Worse than the strangers for whom Wayne threw open their trailer door, though, was Wayne's infatuation with Sue's first cousin. Wayne's telling Sue that he'd fallen in love with a woman so close to her own flesh and blood nearly killed her. But Sue finally left home then, she claims, not because of her own pain, but because she felt sorry for Wayne's having to choose between the two women.

Sue packed up, left Wayne and the jobs she'd worked since age sixteen—hemming cuffs in a sewing factory, selling clothes in her mother's store, helping to tend Wayne's family's farm—and moved to Indiana. And Wayne's life worked out just fine, Sue said, until Sue's cousin up and left him, causing Wayne to feel a surge of remorse and to act on an impulse to win back his wife.

It seems that the Melton's separation had caused both sets of in-laws to speculate and to spread rumors regarding Sue and Wayne's relationship, and when Sue's father saw bruises on her body, he stood up to Wayne and ordered him to stop beating his daughter. Sue melted at her father's rare display of affection, but she returned to live with Wayne. She hadn't been a good enough wife, she decided. As far as she knew, Wayne's family had never abused him, so just as Wayne had said, she'd deserved her punishments. And one kind word, one lustful glance from Wayne, could, in Sue's mind, wipe away years of abuse and neglect. In time—and Wayne and Sue stayed married for eighteen years—no one would need to lock up Sue; she learned to imprison herself.

Wayne and Sue had been married for fourteen years when April was born. Sue refers to April as her miracle child because physicians had told Sue that her irregular menstrual cycle meant that she couldn't conceive. Then, when against all odds Sue did become pregnant, her doctor wanted to abort the baby; he feared that, because it never moved in Sue's womb, it would be born severely retarded or dead. The doctor based his prognosis on Wayne's having battered Sue during her pregnancy. Standing outside their church, Wayne had punched Sue hard because, after visiting her father in the hospital, Sue had spoken to an old family friend, a man she'd run into on the hospital steps. Her friendly greeting had sent Wayne into a jealous rage. After he hit her she was taken from the church parking lot back to the hospital where, as a patient now herself, she was given medicine that could, her doctor later told her, have harmed the baby. As is so often the case, no one reported Wayne's abuse. But Sue vowed to give birth to the child that she so desperately wanted, and her gamble paid off when Sue's daughter entered the world a normal, healthy child.

Before April's birth, Sue's natural doubts about her baby's well-being remained overshadowed by Wayne's insistence that he didn't want children, that this child could not be his, and that if the baby were a girl he would give it away. According to Sue, after April was born Wayne reversed his stance and acted the role of proud papa. But increasingly, he viewed Sue as the enemy, as the woman whose attentions to April somehow diminished his own relationship with his wife. According to Sue, within months of April's birth, Wayne's jealousy grew unbearable.

By the time that April turned four, Sue could no longer endure Wayne's abuse. She secretly filed for divorce but postponed having Wayne served with official papers. His constant verbal attacks had caused her to withdraw into herself so completely that her family physician admitted her and her daughter to the local hospital for several days so she could regain her strength and return to her senses.

When Sue left the hospital, she left with a plan. Her plan was to flee with her daughter to someplace safe, because she believed that saving her life depended on leaving Wayne. But on the first night of her release, Sue and April stayed at Sue's mother's house, where Wayne found them and begged Sue's forgiveness. Sue convinced Wayne that she and April would be staying with her mother for a while, but the next morning, after Wayne had left, Sue gathered up April and her ten-year-old niece—a playmate, she hoped, for April—and fled to Cave City with nothing but the clothes on their backs and the cash that Sue had hidden for her long-awaited escape.

As soon as Sue and the children settled into a motel, Sue called her attorney to have him deliver their divorce documents to Wayne. But she also phoned Wayne so he wouldn't worry about April, even as Sue herself worried about April's unhappiness over being separated from her father.

Shortly after Wayne had been served with notice that Sue had filed for divorce, Sue moved back to Albany, bought a trailer where she set up house with April, and permitted Wayne to visit his daughter whenever he pleased. The arrangement proved less than perfect, though; Sue's guilt concerning April's attitudes and well-being caused her to shower the child with presents and to invite company over to entertain April and spend the night. When Wayne got wind of Sue's houseguests, his jealousy raged, and one day, on the pretext of coming over to assemble his daughter's new dollhouse, he beat Sue unconscious. After regaining her senses and finding herself outside, face down, and drenched on the muddy ground, she was taken to the hospital, where she was told that Wayne had kidnapped April.

The next day Sue obtained a restraining order against Wayne, but she drove to Wayne's house hoping to find April and to take her home. Wayne and his family, however, had spent the previous night convincing April that Sue intended to hurt Wayne by putting him in jail, so by the time Sue arrived April had become so physically ill that, to calm her, Sue promised the child that she would never allow Wayne to be imprisoned.

This might have been the end of Sue and Wayne's story, but because they shared a daughter, until Wayne died of cancer in 1996, the couple, though divorced, stayed in touch. Sue said that in recent years their relationship even improved, and she reported that Wayne asked her to visit him in the hospital just before he died. She did go to see him, but because April remained in Wayne's room throughout her stay, her ex-husband's conversation didn't amount to much. Sue said she still wonders whether, with his last breath, Wayne intended to apologize. But to apologize to Sue would have meant to confess to April, something a man desperate to gain self-esteem could not do, Sue realizes, even on his deathbed.

But when April was four, just after Wayne learned that Sue's threat to divorce him was real, Sue met a state park maintenance supervisor named Larry. He treated April well, Sue said, and Larry's son, who lived with him, was only four years older than April. The two children, like their parents, grew to be almost inseparable, and Sue and Larry decided to marry. But the marriage ended after just two years because Larry, who, according to Sue, lived to drink, allowed an endless flow of his drinking buddies into their house to hang out on a regular basis. The drinking didn't bother Sue, but the drunkards' foul language did. April shouldn't be raised around such talk, Sue said, and a penitent Larry would sometimes chastise his friends. But after-the-fact reproaches always came too late to placate Sue, and Sue determined to leave that marriage, too, even though Larry was the kindest man she'd known. He was the only man with whom she'd ever lived, she recalled, who'd never raised a hand to hit her.

It doesn't take much when expectations sink so low that settling for what most people would perceive as a loss appears to be a gain in disguise. And, in fact, it didn't take a lot for Sue to decide that even though she intended to divorce Larry, she also needed to return to him—first just on weekends, then full time—for another two years. Later, while in prison, Sue wrote, "Larry and I were very much in love, but we had no communication skills—none at all between us." This part of Sue's story, perhaps the most cheerful part of her tale, cut more deeply in the listening than did her pointed recollections of pain. Sue remembered love as the absence of abuse, as the space that exists beyond battering but that also hangs, suspended in a realm devoid of expression, in a region absent of words. "Larry and I were very much in love," Sue had written while in prison. And perhaps they were. But what Sue described as love seems more like safety.

After two more years, Sue decided that she had to move out permanently, and she did. Soon thereafter Larry had second thoughts. He phoned her and promised her that he'd give up drinking if she'd return. But she'd begun seeing another man, and she told him that he'd called too late. A couple of weeks later, she phoned him back to say that she'd changed her mind. But then he said that *her* call had come too late. Sue and Larry never lived together again, but Sue says that until the day of her arrest she and Larry still got together from time to time to communicate in the only way they could.

After Sue and April moved out of Larry's house, they headed for a new life in Bowling Green, where Sue's brother lived. Sue's plan was that she and April would stay with her brother until she found a job and could move out on her own. But soon after mother and daughter arrived in the city, Sue treated herself to some rest and relaxation in a restaurant lounge, and that's where she met Herbie Cannon, a sometime-factory worker who spent more time laid off than working. Within a month Sue had agreed to live with him; the intense romance of their courtship proved Herbie's initial appeal. Every day, Sue said, her eyes lit by the memory, Herbie would decorate their house, inside and out, with dazzling love notes. Tucked under Sue's pillow and dangling from trees and banners were Herbie's lavish messages that proclaimed in bold ink to Sue and to the world at large, "I love you" and "I missed you." Because Sue had rarely felt special, Herbie's style struck her as the mark of a Hollywood hero. Their marriage would be a fairy tale. Their family life would be spectacular. Sue would be somebody after all.

But following their marriage Sue realized that the fairy-tale life that she'd believed in had metamorphosed into a gothic myth, into a legal contract drawn up by Dr. Jekyll and witnessed by Mr. Hyde. Instantly, Herbie declared April the enemy. He raged with jealousy over Sue's relationship with her daughter, and he threatened the child so severely that April insisted on keeping a stick by her bedroom door. While in prison Sue wrote about April's nightmares concerning Herbie, about the terror that once caused the child to claw the wall so hard in her sleep that the next morning Sue had to peel paint chips from beneath her daughter's fingernails. Sue also wrote about the time when she left April alone in the house with Herbie and returned to find April hysterical, locked in her room clutching a steak knife. In time Sue took to crawling in bed with April each night and to attaching their nightgowns with safety pins, a precaution against Herbie's attacking her child by surprise.

But Herbie's jealousy of April exemplified only one aspect of a marriage torn asunder. On their wedding night Herbie announced that he wanted his relationship with Sue to be "modern," a euphemism that he employed to inform his wife that he wanted her to participate with him in orgies, just as he wanted to watch her perform sexually with women. Sue's refusal didn't daunt him; Herbie merely substituted the orgies with more private sexual practices that he'd devised to stimulate himself while torturing Sue.

In the brief autobiography that she completed while incarcerated, Sue wrote, "The first time he tied me up he'd put something in my soft drink that knocked me out. When I came to I was tied to a dining room chair and the chair was turned upside down. He had his National Guard uniform on and he was beating me with his belt. He made me tell him that I enjoyed what he was doing and that it felt good. He made me tell him that I was his sex slave and that he was my master. He used his sex toys on me, he used a cucumber, he used frozen and [burning] hot dogs, and this went on for about eight hours.

"The second time he tied me up he tied me to the corner of the bed with broken jars on my wrists. If I tried to move at all, they would cut me. He used the same things on me this time but added a hot curling . . . brush. He had a syringe and jalapeno juice and gave me shots in my vagina with it. He told me he was making me hot enough for him. This went on for two-and-a-half days without bathroom privileges. He kept telling me that I had to do and say what he wanted or he would do this to April. He brought a dog into the house and put a gun to my head and tried to make me have sex with the dog."

Sue added, "In order to cope I would think about labor pains and comfort myself with the fact that when it was over I'd still have April."

But one Christmas vacation April announced her intention to live from then on with her father, Wayne. She felt that she could no longer survive the sexual advances with which Herbie had begun to threaten her, nor could she endure his escalating verbal abuse any longer. Not wanting April to live with Wayne, Sue proposed that she and April find another home together. She shared her plan with Herbie, a decision that almost proved to be fatal. That same week, an enraged Herbie engaged a man to rape Sue, to "sodomize" her, she said, with a broom handle, an act that Herbie hoped would scare Sue into staying. But the rape that sent Sue to the hospital cinched her decision to escape. While Sue was still being treated, Herbie came to visit his wife and forced her to walk with him to another floor, the hospital's mental ward. Should Sue ever dare to tell anyone the truth about her rape, he swore, he would have her committed to that very ward where her confession would be dismissed as evidence of psychosis. Herbie's words *did* terrify her. But instead of freezing her into submission, his threat encouraged her to escape, without bringing charges. Two weeks following her release from the hospital, on the first occasion when her out-of-work husband left her alone in the house, Sue and April fled to an apartment in Burkesville. In an attempt to hide their whereabouts, Sue enrolled April in school in a nearby town. But, as when she first left Wayne, Sue phoned Herbie "to appease him," thinking, she said, that by doing so, he "would not hunt them down." She didn't tell him where they were, but knowing how she would feel if her daughter disappeared, Sue convinced herself that she didn't want Herbie to worry. She also recalled needing to contact Herbie so that she could be certain of his whereabouts. To feel safe, she needed to know that he was as far away as the end of a long-distance phone call, that he was "out there" somewhere instead of anywhere near.

But as a result of her call, Herbie did hunt down Sue. He found her at home; April was at school. Grabbing one of April's Cabbage Patch dolls, Herbie mutilated and severed it to show how he intended to dismember April if Sue failed to return to him.

Sue wrote in her life history, "I just kept promising him that I might come back to him, but when he got the divorce papers he went crazy. He told me that April had to pay with her life because I loved her more than I loved him. He promised me that April's days were short. I begged him not to harm her. I told him to do anything he wanted to do to me, but to leave her alone. He just laughed at me. Then he told me that if I took April to her father and told her that I didn't love her and never wanted to see her again, he'd let her live. Of all the things he'd ever done to me, this hurt me the most. I told him I would do this. April's safety was all that mattered to me. While I was packing April's clothes, he called. He told me that it didn't matter where April was, I'd always love her more, so he'd get her wherever she was. He promised he would do everything to her he'd done to me and more."

For weeks, then, Sue and April remained where they were, Sue frozen in a limbo born of her fear and her failure to see any options. Without warning, Herbie would arrive at their door wielding weapons and threats. One night, though, he called before he came to announce his intention of killing April that night. He warned Sue that he was on his way. Terrified, Sue awakened April, whose girlfriend was spending the night, to tell her that they all had to leave. But April, who refused to run or hide anymore, assumed an I'll-be-damned stance that so scared Sue that, for the first time in her life, she said, she hit her daughter and forced April and her friend to hurry to the friend's house to safety in the friend's mother's care.

Sue wrote, "I went and sat out on the road. Herbie showed up with a gun and went from apartment to apartment asking if we were there."

Eventually, Herbie left and that long night passed. But Sue's story continues: "One day there was an incident where Herbie had just beaten me and the phone rang. Herbie held a gun to my head and made me tell the person I was too busy to talk. Later that same day my friend Arlene came over to visit. She saw how upset and scared I was by the expression on my face. She told me that if I didn't soon do something, Herbie would end up killing me and April. She said she knew someone she could get to teach him a lesson. I was so scared for the lives of myself and my daughter by that time, that it sounded like a good idea to me. I told her to do that."

As Sue told us her story, her Christmas bear clutched to her chest, she swore to us that, when Arlene suggested that Herbie be taught a lesson, she thought Arlene meant a beating that would scare him away from mother and daughter for life. But a week after Sue agreed to Arlene's offer, Arlene brought a man named Frank to Sue's apartment. In front of Sue, Arlene told Frank that Herbie had threatened to kill April, a fact that Sue verified. Frank left, saying he'd contact Arlene later.

A full week passed before Arlene and Frank returned together and, according to Sue, promised that on that very night they would teach Herbie "a good lesson." Coincidentally, perhaps, Herbie phoned that morning to assure Sue that he would come that night to get her. Sue said that Arlene and Frank instructed Sue to tell Herbie, when he called back, that she'd meet him and lead him to an orgy, a party at which an unsuspecting Herbie would tangle with Frank and Arlene.

Sue did as she was told, but she said that while Arlene and Frank were still sitting in her apartment planning that evening's events, she'd stepped into the bathroom. Through her thin walls she'd overheard them discussing the fact that Frank would hurt or kill Herbie before Herbie could hurt or kill them. That conversation, Sue's first inkling, she insisted, that the conspirators who'd promised to teach Herbie a lesson might actually be planning his death, scared her sufficiently for Sue to take Arlene aside and ask her to call off the party. But Arlene laughed and replied that if Sue truly wanted to call a halt to their plans, Sue should confront Frank herself. Knowing that her decision could prove fatal, Sue chose to remain silent.

There's no question that Sue led Herbie to his death that night, not in Sue's mind, nor in the minds of the prosecutor, the attorneys, the judges, or the parole board members. Together, Arlene and Frank drove to Arlene's sister's house, a location that Arlene had borrowed. Sue, in her car, met Herbie on the road, and in his car he followed her to the house where Herbie had been told that he and Sue and Arlene would indulge in marathon sex. But Herbie hadn't expected to encounter Frank, so when he spied him at the house, Herbie first raged at Sue's deception, then said he wanted to go buy a bottle of gin before their orgy began. Everyone in the house piled back into their vehicles and drove off with Herbie to purchase liquor. But according to Sue, after the caravan returned, Sue fled the scene when Herbie entered the bathroom and Arlene began mixing what may well have been the last drink of Herbie's life.

Any woman, or man, for that matter, escaping a scene from which destruction could be the only assurance of salvation—and a damning, soul-shackling salvation at that—would have had to have fled as a bundle of naked nerves. Sue told us that she felt so on edge that she wanted to die. Maybe it was because she felt that way that she attempted to drive straight from Arlene's sister's house to stay with a man she'd met just a month before in Somerset. But in Monticello her car broke down, and local law officers gave Sue a lift to the police station, where she called her new boyfriend to come take her home. He did, and at five o'clock the next morning, Sue's phone rang. It was Arlene calling to say that Herbie "wouldn't be bothering" Sue anymore. After that terse announcement, Arlene, Sue said, hung up.

At noon Sue's phone rang again. This time it was a state trooper who was also Herbie's best friend. He told Sue that Herbie's burned car had been found on the side of the state park's main road. He said that its charred contents included the ashes and bones of a blackened body.

Sue said she then called Arlene, who refused to talk on the phone, but who met Sue at Sue's sister-in-law's house to tell Sue that yes, the body in the car was Herbie's.

In prison Sue wrote, "I asked her why, and she said that she'd drugged Herbie and drove his car. Things had gotten out of hand, and she had to burn the car because her fingerprints were all over it. She burned it with him inside of it. I told Arlene I was going to the police, and she said that, if I did, . . . April's head would be served to me on a silver platter."

Sue gathered from Arlene that the conspirators' scheme had been to drug Herbie so that his death would look like a heart attack. Arlene told Sue that Herbie was dead before his body was burned; the police told Sue that that wasn't the case. But burned dead or alive, even as a splintered skeleton, Herbie had only begun to haunt his widow.

It seems that Sue failed to contact the police for several reasons. One was Arlene's threat, of course, a threat first echoed by Frank and later by a man named Tommy. Apparently, Arlene and Frank hadn't been the sole originators of the scheme to kill Herbie. Tommy, a member of Arlene's extended family, had been the behind-the-scenes man who had contacted Frank for the job. Also, at some point, Sue said, she'd promised to pay Arlene and Frank and Tommy $5,000 to teach Herbie a lesson, an arrangement that most people would think could only be cinched with Sue's full knowledge of the conspirators' intent. Sue began to believe that Arlene, her longtime friend, had slept with Herbie, that they'd had an affair that had gone sour, and that Arlene might have harbored ulterior motives for her mission to help her friend. Finally, Sue said, most of Herbie's friends were local police. He'd met some of them in the National Guard, and, until the night of his death, he'd spent many an evening cruising with his cop friends, thrilling at the power that police held over people and at the fear they could arouse while on patrol. Often, Sue said, Herbie would brag about his police pals and taunt her with the fact that she could never trust the law to rescue her. Once Herbie, tired of what he considered Wayne's interference in his life when he came to collect April for visits, told Sue that he'd discussed with a policeman friend how they could run Wayne and April off the road, kill them both, and plant a gun on Wayne so that their deaths would appear to be a murder followed by a suicide. No, Sue couldn't call the police, she decided. So, instead, she ran.

Sue took April to Dalton, Georgia, a location that Sue's mother selected because the man from whom Sue's mother had bought her Albany clothing store had come from that city. Neither Sue nor her mother had been anyplace near Georgia, but Dalton sounded familiar and therefore safe.

According to Sue, her mother didn't know anything about the circumstances of Herbie's death. Of course she knew he'd died, but Sue's mother thought the cause of her son-in-law's death was what the police at that time thought, too—an inexplicable accident. After all, Sue's whereabouts that night had been verified. She'd even spent part of the evening at a police station waiting for her ride. Sue's story to her mother was that she needed a change of scenery, and Dalton seemed as good a location as any to rebuild two shattered lives.

Because Sue hadn't shared with her mother the truth about Herbie's death, she couldn't tell her that her move was motivated by more than wanderlust. She said that in the days and weeks and first few months following Herbie's murder, Arlene, Frank, and Tommy took turns threatening Sue. They wanted two things from her: assurance of her silence regarding the crime and the $5,000 that she owed them. Knowing Sue's love for her daughter, Arlene and Tommy kept dropping by to share with Sue their stance that it would be a shame if they had to harm April. Frank took a different tack. He suggested that Sue's debt could be paid if she agreed to prostitute for him; Frank's career, she learned, included his role as a pimp.

It is at this point in Sue's story that we found it hard to fathom Sue's thinking. She said that Frank's offer shocked her and that, of course, she turned him down. We asked Sue if she had ever intended to pay Herbie's killers $5,000, and if she did, what the source of those funds would be. Sue said that yes, she would have given them the money were it not for the fact that, in her mind, by burning Herbie, dead or alive, they'd forfeited their right to a reward. In Sue's mind, there was death and then there was *death*, and she couldn't imagine a worse way of dying than to succumb to the heat of fire. To subjugate even the devil himself to the living hell of licking flames couldn't be reconciled in Sue's mind with any deal, no matter what. We wondered whether the fiery preaching of Sue's Pentecostal faith or some deep-seated need to defend her batterer against a violent end caused her to regard one means of death as more or less just or justifiable than another. She didn't know, she said, but she had indeed stood firm in her decision to renege. As to how she would have obtained the $5,000—well, she said, she'd planned to get the money from the insurance settlement on her house that had, she thought, been burned down by men trying to get even with her on a business deal. But Sue's refusal to fight fire with fire is an irony that didn't appear, as she recounted her experience, to have struck her at all.

From the time Herbie died in July 1988 to February of the following year, Sue fended off her coconspirators' threats. But in February she moved to Georgia and found a job as an aide in a nursing home, and April divided her time between living with Sue in Georgia and with Wayne in Albany, Kentucky. Sue recalled that her new life in Georgia was good as long as it lasted, but it didn't, in fact, last long.

Shortly after her move, Sue was arrested in Kentucky at her mother's house. "The state trooper and the sheriff from Albany came down, and the sheriff knocked on the door. I went to the door, and he . . . said, 'We need to talk to you.'. . . It was the local sheriff, and I went out to the car with him, and the state trooper was there. He was from Berksville, I think . . . I think they radioed . . . that they had found me. . . . He said [the detective would] be here in about two hours, and they left." The detective came and took her to the state police station in his car.

Sue said that at the station, "He went through my purse then, and he found my driver's license. My maiden name threw him; I don't know why. I still had a Kentucky driver's license, 'cause I was in the process of moving back."

Sue told us that at the time of her arrest, her daughter did not know of her involvement in Herbie's death; she had told her daughter simply that "somebody killed him."

Sue Melton was charged with murder, arson, and complicity to murder. She believes that someone tipped off the police. Her family provided an attorney, but Sue said that she didn't tell her defender about her sexual abuse. A counselor at the jail told her that she should discuss her battering with her attorney so that a psychiatrist could evaluate her. But Sue said that her lawyer didn't want such information. When asked why, she answered, "My attorney didn't really work for me." She described her attorney as a friend of prominent court officials and declared, "I feel like all they really wanted was a conviction, 'cause when I got out of jail, I [had] stayed there six months. They at first wouldn't set me no bond at all. Then, when they did set it, they set it at a million dollars. [Later, Sue said that Arlene had a better lawyer from Louisville, and so Arlene's bond was set at 10 percent of Sue's, $100,000.] Then, a week later, [the judge] called. [He] wanted me to come to the office, so [the lawyer] and I went, and the judge told me they were seeking the death penalty. The judge told me he would see that [I] fried if [I] didn't take a plea, and [my brother and April] spoke up and said 'You should take [it].' . . . [April] said, 'Your mom's going to have a nervous breakdown, and your brother's going [to] die with a stroke or heart attack with his blood pressure.' And April—you know what she was going through [with their] asking the death penalty for me." Sue still did not tell April the whole story; the truth telling would come later, when Sue was incarcerated at the Kentucky Correctional Institution for Women in Pee Wee Valley.

Sue remembers prison as a place not as bad as she had anticipated, but she recalls her incarceration as, at first, difficult and frightening. She described her initial experiences: "You get your ID. They take a picture and take you down and get your uniforms. For the first few days you have to stay in uniforms while you're in the—they call it the fish tank. I really thought that I was going to a fish tank. I hear these girls in jail have been there, and they're talking about a fish tank. And we went downstairs to get our uniforms and our sheets and stuff they give you there, and there it was. I thought it was a man; he waved and it turned out to be a woman. She got a hold of my hair . . . and I said, 'Sheila [another new inmate], you think I'll get in trouble cause he touched my hair?,' 'cause there were officers there. . . . She just cracked up; he had a beard, [but] she said 'That was a woman.'"

Sue's medical problems made her job assignments difficult to complete. "When I first got [to prison] I went on landscaping [duty]. It was like cleaning up the yard . . . and picking up cigarette butts. That was the worst job I had, 'cause [even when] it got wintertime, you had to stay outside until three o'clock. If it was snowing, raining, whatever, you wasn't allowed to go to the dorm. And I already had breathing problems." Sue spent four-and-a-half years in prison, and while there, her duties changed from custodial to clerical work for the prison chapel and for offices at the University of Louisville's Shelby Campus.

Sue then echoed Sherry Pollard's comments by describing how, with Chandra McElroy's help, she and Sherry had founded the B.O.S.H. Group. Among the benefits that that counseling group provided her, Sue said, was that its members showed her for the first time that she hadn't been the only woman in the world, as she told us that she'd thought was the case, to endure almost unspeakable sexual abuse.

When B.O.S.H. Group members made their quilt, Sue contributed a square that depicts her daughter, April, with the stick that April kept by her door, and a square that outlines a table turned, like Sue's world, upside down. Sue thought, when she spoke with us, that she'd probably drawn another square, too, a picture of herself tied up, but some self-protective lapse caused her to remain unsure. "I helped in [designing] about all of it," she said. "Some of it I didn't, like on the days I'd get my chemo [chemotherapy treatment]. If they worked on it that night, I'd be too sick. I sewed the lace around it and helped make the squares."

While in prison Sue's asthma, a condition that she'd developed while living in Berksville, had worsened until she was diagnosed with emphysema. And it was in prison that Sue was diagnosed with breast cancer, too. She described being taken, wearing shackles and her orange prison jumpsuit, by prison guards to Suburban Hospital in Louisville, where one of her breasts was biopsied. At the very moment following the biopsy that Sue's handcuffs and shackles were locked back in place, the doctor who'd performed her biopsy advised her of her malignancy, announced to Sue, her guards, and all within range of hearing that Sue did, indeed, have cancer.

Shortly thereafter, Sue's journey towards parole began. Sue said of Governor Jones's reaction to the B.O.S.H. Group's quilt, "He made the statement that the tears was rolling down his cheeks, and he made a statement to his wife that they needed to help those women."

Sue explained that she had served one-fourth of her sentence and so was eligible to go before the parole board, which had previously ruled that she must serve an additional four years before she could be paroled. However, Sue received a letter on December 24, 1995, telling her that the board was going to review her case. Like her Sisters in Pain, Sue would have preferred a pardon clearing her record and restoring her civil rights. But she doesn't blame Governor Jones for choosing to parole her and her Sisters instead. Sue indicated her belief that he did what he thought he should. She commented, "He [Jones] seems like such a good man . . . I'm tickled to death he did what he did for me. He had the parole board bring me back up and let me out." Although Sue received clemency at almost the same time as did ten of her Sisters in Pain, she was granted parole based on her health problems instead of on her history of abuse, and her name, although on the list prepared by the Department of Public Advocacy, had not been included on Helen Howard-Hughes's roster of cases eligible for early clemency hearings.

On January 29, 1996, the day that Sue was released from prison, her sister-in-law and niece drove her from Louisville back to Albany. Sue told us, "I wasn't used to being out at night, and it was afternoon when they picked me up. I seen it was going to get dark before we got home, and it scared me. We stopped at a restaurant, and I couldn't even eat. All the way home I kept thinking they was going to come after me, the people from prison, 'cause I felt like I wasn't really out. I'm not as bad as I was, but I still look out sometimes and have the feelin' they're gonna come get me."

When asked about her experiences with her parole officer, Sue replied, "I don't really have no contact with him [except] when I go in [for a scheduled meeting]. For six months, I had to go in twice a month. Now I just have to go in once a month. But . . . I have to get permission to go anywhere. Like, I have permission to go with April to school at Somerset Friday and do some shopping." Sue seems to believe that travel restrictions are the worst part of parole, but that even those strictures are far less severe than those associated with being a convicted felon.

Sue spent the first months of her parole confined to one floor, then another, of her brother and sister-in-law's house, not only because of her fragile health but also because of a clinical depression that gripped her and wouldn't let go. "I wasn't getting dressed and I wasn't really getting out of bed because I didn't feel like I had no reason," she said.

One day Sue's niece arrived home to find Sue on the floor, unconscious. Sue was rushed to the hospital for a stay she barely recalls. But her doctor prescribed counseling as vital for Sue's recovery, so when Sue was too physically ill to travel to her counselor's office in town, as she still was when we saw her, the counselor came to her, she said. Was she feeling any better? we asked. "Well, yes," she said, if feeling better meant getting dressed most mornings.

But Sue spoke of other plans and projects that caused us hope for her emotional health. She'd helped to start a battered women's support group in Albany, she said. Only four women had joined so far, but that meant that four women who hadn't had help before were finally able to share their stories and, in time, perhaps with the help of one another and professional counselors, might resolve their situations. And Sue was also fighting the Department of Housing and Urban Development, taking on its policy makers and managers concerning the need for equity in allowing convicted felons to rent low-income housing.

The cost of living has always proved higher for Sue Melton than for most people. When we asked her why, throughout her life, she'd run, almost, from one abusive relationship to the next, she said, "I don't think I really stopped and thought about it. I think I had more fear of not having a home and of not being able to afford living on my own than I had of the men who always told me I could never survive on my own."

Sue noted that the hardest part of living now is knowing that she is responsible for Herbie's death. "I hated him, but I still loved him," she said. She hated him for what he did to April, but she'd forgiven him for how he'd treated her.

Among Sue's first visitors in Albany, following her parole, were a flock of female parishioners from Sue's mother's Pentecostal church. They informed Sue, before they took their leave, that she would "burn in the hottest part of hell," not, it seemed, for conspiring to murder, but for painting her nails.

So even though Sue acquiesced to her abusive husband's death by staying silent when she should have screamed for help, we knew, as had Sue, that such women as those in Sue's mother's church would not have helped her. They would not have even recognized as evil the battering that they believe to be all men's prerogatives and most dutiful women's fates.

Sue had been well enough to travel to Manhattan with a few of her B.O.S.H. Group friends to appear on the *Donahue Show*. She commented little on that experience except to say that she wished that all of the battered women who had been together in prison could have shared the trip to New York and could have shared, particularly, the women's visit to the Statue of Liberty. "Governor Jones reminded me of my second husband, Larry," Sue said. "When Governor Jones met me on the *Donahue Show* he said he knew exactly who I was, and he cried. Larry, too, was kind that way."

Angie asked Sue if there was anything about her case or about domestic violence that we hadn't discussed but that she would like to mention. Sue answered, "I think it is important that my lawyer scared me into a plea. . . . I was heavily sedated while I was in jail, and I came home on antidepressants." Sue believes that she could have been found innocent had she had a different attorney, but faced with the possibility of the electric chair, she chose to plead guilty.

We left Sue long after the sun had set and after the wet, heavy flakes of snow had begun to stick to her bedroom window, their slide down the frosted glass forming patterns reminiscent of a pioneer crazy quilt. As we departed, Sue's makeshift living quarters, though small, seemed even cozier by lamplight than they had by the pale light of day. The nighttime shadows of pictures and knickknacks multiplied the photos and memorabilia, creating a haven of nostalgic comfort backlit by reflections of the Christmas tree's still-blinking lights shimmering in the dresser's gilt mirror.

As women who'd been raised in loving families and as academics, we'd been sure that we could not only distinguish appearance from reality, but that we could also analyze the difference. Yet on that cold, black night as Angie's sturdy Ford Tempo sped us back to Louisville, neither of us felt savvy enough in the face of Sue's sad story to identify her as the heroine, the victim, or the culprit of her tale. She was each of these, and she was all of these. Sue had paid for her deed perhaps too dearly, perhaps not dearly enough. And possibly, unofficially, her private need to pay would never end. In the car, our conversation turned to our concern about men who tell women that any abuse they endure is the women's own fault and to our concern about those women's mothers who, by teaching their daughters to hide, tacitly enable abuse to continue. We talked about religious denominations who teach their female parishioners to feel small and helpless in the hands of an angry God and who teach their male parishioners that they are the manifestations, the very images on earth, of that pompous deity. We railed at the irony of any religion, of any conduit to salvation, condoning and even encouraging attitudes both outdated and evil. And we bemoaned the fact that so many families, communities, and cultures within Kentucky and beyond place so little value on the formal education that would teach men and women to value themselves and each other and that would offer them opportunities to sustain themselves financially, intellectually, and emotionally without having to subjugate themselves or succumb to others to survive.

Even though the drive from Albany to Louisville is long, by the time we reached the city limits, our conversation had barely encompassed the gist of what we needed to say. We'd agreed, though, that appearances and reality are often confusing—frighteningly so—especially in a society bent on identifying people as good or bad, as innocent or guilty, as psychotic or sane, as polar opposites who, for simplicity's sake, are rarely referenced as multifaceted individuals, each subject to a complex heritage. Despite her sweet smile and her holiday sentiment turned sentimental, we knew that Sue Melton was no longer young or naïve. Yet we knew, too, that her role as a convicted felon masked truths about everyone else in Sue Melton's life who had failed to come to her rescue.

If I Could I Would

exorcise what birthed your pain. Early you cringed
then fought, conditions still moving to cancel
each other out. One day you remembered what he did
to you. Portrait of the artist whose father wanted her
pacified, or dead.

Learning to feel the edges of yourself, where you begin
and end, how tall you stand and where. Your flesh
curls back, muscle and organs to the highest bidder,
fluids raging through channels clogged by fear. Fresh
air of morning turns you raw.

Now a chorus of numbness and pain says stop. Wait for
your after-image. Savor the power held in a young
girl's skin: small drum and shield against his
hammer of hate. Remember to breathe. Remember
to breathe.

Now he is gone to age, a broken thing who cannot know your name. You have
grown beyond his power, a woman
he'll never catch, comrade to those he shattered
in your path. You who survived have only to greet
yourself.

Margaret Randall

Excerpted from The American Voice Anthology *(Univ. Press of Kentucky, 1998) and re-printed with the permission of the* American Voice *and Margaret Randall.*

Margie Marcum

It's a fact that the stories behind the stories that shape the lives of the Sisters in Pain could be traced straight back to Eve. But a saga that stands apart from the rest is the story of how Helen Bowen, a caseworker at the Big Sandy Family Abuse Center in Floyd County, Kentucky, took up Margie Marcum's cause and acted as the advocate for the Sister in Pain subjugated, almost, beyond speech. Helen's fight to reclaim Margie's life is a tale that we first heard upon attempting to contact Margie. "Oh, no. Call Helen; Margie won't say much to anyone else," a half dozen people advised us. So we did phone Helen Bowen, a woman willing to meet us anyplace, anytime, to discuss the abuse survivor whose case she'd taken to heart. Would she bring Margie with her? She would if she could, she assured us, but she wouldn't know if she could until the day of the meeting itself, as Margie almost always stays in her house; speaks only to her children, her grandchildren, and Helen; and trusts no one else. Since Margie Marcum was paroled she's lived like a recluse on permanent retreat—like a woman resigned to paying perpetual penance. We spoke to her by phone, but she said no to being interviewed by saying "yes" and "maybe" repeatedly until her hollow voice, which refused to commit to any firm date, wore us down. Ironically, that very lack of affect is what inspired Helen Bowen to become Margie Marcum's crusader. And when Helen met with us alone, in Louisville, she told us Margie's story.

"I was the [Center's] caseworker, . . . and on July tenth [the Big Sandy Family Abuse Center] received a phone call from [Margie's] daughter, Freda Maynard, and Freda just wanted to know if someone could go to the jail to visit with her mom just for moral support. That's how I got to know her. I went to the jail and got no response from her—nothing at all. . . . I didn't know her. She just gave me the chance. I knew that there was resources out there that was available to her, and she had just given up totally. And I just thought, 'We're gonna fight!' so I brought in [a counselor with] . . . Family Life Services, and he began to see Margie twice a week. And then I visited her anywhere from three to four times a week, and we kind of seen the light at the end of the tunnel. She began to talk with us, but she would not tell us in detail what had happened to her. She would talk about her children and how she missed them. It took us several months to get from A to B with her. . . . She was just . . . fragile, . . . broken down. She always stared at the floor, her hair down in her eyes."

When Helen Bowen first met Margie Marcum in midsummer of 1992, forty-year-old Margie, said Helen, looked twice her age. On May 21, 1987, Martin Circuit Court had convicted her of manslaughter in the first degree for the death of her husband, Marion Marcum. Classified as a violent offender, she had been sentenced to fifteen years in the Kentucky Correctional Institution for Women in Pee Wee Valley, Kentucky, but between May of 1987 and mid-February of 1992, her attorney had kept her out of jail on appeals bond. After her appeals bond expired, Margie was first incarcerated in the Pike County Jail in Pikeville, Kentucky, and then she was transferred to the Regional Detention Center in Johnson County before being relocated to the state women's prison. Helen, who counsels as many as seventy abuse victims each month, said she saw in Margie how close a person could come to being dead without actually dying.

Helen noted that Margie's sexual abuse started at age six. That's how old she was when she claims her father began to molest her. He didn't stop until she turned thirteen; her physical and psychological abuse had started much earlier. From time to time, as Margie grew up, her mother headed for Chicago with a few of her eleven children and left the rest at home on Rockcastle Road in Martin County to be cared for by their father. Almost always, Margie, the seventh child, was left behind. Helen said that Margie told her mother about her father's abuse and that Margie's mother ignored her. Years later, Margie learned that at least one of her sisters had also been molested by their father. Until then, she'd thought he'd considered Margie, alone, to have been worthless.

Margie left school after the fifth grade and, at age fifteen, she married Lonnie Mills. But soon Lonnie left for Vietnam, and Margie, in his absence, had a son by a man she didn't marry. Then she met Marion Marcum. Margie and Marion dated; in four years, Margie, pregnant by Marion, divorced Lonnie and married Marion. Six months into their marriage, the battering began. Margie now recalls Marion's abuse in memory shards that kaleidoscope into vivid images that fade as quickly as they form. Since her childhood, she's practiced forgetting so well that it's hard for her to reverse her survival technique in order to detail old wounds for the record. But among the batterings Margie reconstructed for Helen are these. Marion's drunken response to Margie's asking him where he had been one night six months after their wedding day was to slap his wife and to shoot his gun at the sky. That evening, Margie attempted to take her two children and run, but as they started across a creek, she and her infants heard Marion stalking them. They had no place to turn but to a neighbor's house, where they hid for the night.

From that time on, the violence escalated. Regular beatings split Margie's lips, blackened her eyes, and caused red welts and purple bruises to render her body a battleground—a cross-hatching of scars raised by repeated skirmishes. Sometimes, wanting to fix herself up, Margie would put on makeup. For that, Marion would blacken her eyes with his fists, call her a whore, and accuse her of painting her face to lure other men. Marion's rules expanded with his mounting jealousy. Margie was not to use birth control, so she didn't. As a result, she bore four children during their marriage. But despite the living proof of Margie's adherence to her husband's commands, Marion once raged so in his random searches for hidden contraceptives that he tore the fabric from their couch, sure that Margie had stashed birth control pills in the furniture. And one of the sons who Margie gave birth to during their marriage could not, Marion claimed, be his. According to Margie, the child's father was indeed Marion and could have been no other.

The Marcum's children witnessed Marion holding knives to their mother's throat and guns to her head. They watched as Marion threw all of Margie's clothes out of the house, and when Marion beat their mother, the children begged him to stop before he killed her.

On several occasions Margie called the police, but when they arrived at the Marcum's rural, isolated Appalachian property, they refused to advance beyond the bottom of the hill that led to the trailer where Marion held Margie hostage. Margie and her now-adult children later told Helen that Marion terrified the entire community. If Margie wanted protection, she could drive into town and swear out warrants against her husband. This, said Margie, is what the police would shout from a distance.

But Marion kept Margie his prisoner. She had no money, she had no car, and the friends and family whom her husband permitted her to see she kept, for their sakes, away. She feared that anyone who came too close would also get hurt by Marion. And because, years before, Margie's own mother had ignored Margie's molestation, Margie saw little point in asking anyone for help.

If the family needed groceries, Marion would drive his wife to the store. If she lingered too long, he would accuse her of soliciting men. In an attempt to make peace with the man from whom she could not escape, Margie put what trust she had left in Marion's hands, hands that, her children recall, left fingerprints on their mother's throat each time Marion tried to choke her. In an attempt to increase their intimacy, Margie confided in Marion that her father had molested her. But Marion's response to Margie's confession was to betray her. He drank more and more, and when he drank he joked with his friends about Margie's childhood abuse. He also, when friends or family assembled, grabbed Margie's breasts and encouraged Margie's son, Steve, to do the same. Helen said that Margie and Margie's sister, Rhonda, both stressed how Marion raped Margie night after night by forcing her to have sex against her will. Not only did Marion circumvent Margie's literal escape but he also prevented any psychological relief she might have gained from reading. He banned all books from the house on the grounds that women shouldn't read because reading taught women "how to chase men."

Just as Marion forced their children to watch as he tortured their mother, he forced Margie to witness his physical abuse of their children, especially of their daughter Freda. Family and neighbors grew accustomed to Margie and her children knocking on their doors in search of refuge. They also grew used to Marion's sheepish courting and to his coming to retrieve his wife and children. He attempted to woo Margie by mouthing the empty promises that deluded no one, but that everyone within hearing remained desperate to believe. Marion threatened to kill any member of Margie's family who tried to protect her from him. He shot at one of Margie's sisters, just as he shot Margie through a car window. Eventually, Margie found some relief from Marion's abuse in the same drugs that intensified Marion's cruel and erratic behavior. She began to self-medicate and to escape into sleep through swallowing sedatives with alcohol.

Like Margie's, Marion's childhood had been rough. He'd been raised in orphanages and foster homes, and he told Margie that he blamed his mother for abandoning him. He rationalized that his mother had left him to be with other men. As an adult, he struck out at those closest to him, holding them captive with his anger and abandoning them by squandering grocery money and rent on alcohol. Once the family's new trailer was repossessed because Marion had neglected the payments. Many times, Margie told Helen, the family went hungry. More than once Marion was arrested for driving while intoxicated. But when it came to Marion's continuing to batter his wife, law officers continued to ignore what they termed the Marcums' domestic disputes.

Margie and Marion Marcum had been married seventeen years when, one October evening in 1986, a party at their mobile home broke up because Marion became abusive to one of his guests and turned on him with a knife. Marion accused the man of having an affair with Margie. According to Helen, Bobby, Margie's son and Marion's stepson, grabbed Marion's knife and separated the brawlers. After the guests left, Bobby backed his car down the hill to head home. But just as he reached the bottom of the drive, he heard a gunshot and drove back up the hill to find his stepfather dead beside his truck. Later an eyewitness at Margie Marcum's trial eliminated Bobby as a suspect by swearing that he saw Bobby Marcum in his car, backing down the hill, as the gun that shot Marion Marcum exploded in the night.

At the time of Marion's death, Margie had a blood alcohol level of 0.25, more than twice the legal limit. As she was the only person in the vicinity of the crime other than Marion himself, Margie was charged with murder. The coroner, who could have evaluated the case as a possible accidental death or as a suicide, had left town the previous day and could not be reached. The required postmortem was never performed, or at least the coroner produced no report. Marion always carried a knife; in addition to having been shot, Marion died with a knife wound at the base of his neck.

When Bobby Marcum found his stepfather's body, he also found Margie Marcum thirty-five feet away in the couple's trailer. Could she, he wondered— as others still wonder—have committed the crime and fled the scene so quickly, given her level of intoxication? After the police arrived, Margie was arrested, but her clothes were never tested for residue from Marion's gun, and the gun that fired the fatal shot had already been destroyed. Upon seeing the weapon, Bobby had smashed it to pieces and had hurled it down the hill. Helen wonders whether someone who knew Marion's habit of carrying a knife hid after the party, knife in hand, killed Marion, and then fled, using the gunshot as a diversion. She noted that in Margie's trial few people alluded to Marion Marcum's knife wound, and she emphasized that Margie has always sworn that she can't recall specifics regarding that evening. The three guests who'd left the Marcums' party fled the community, and they were never tracked down or questioned. In court, Margie Marcum pled not guilty, but she was convicted of manslaughter in the first degree for the shooting death of her husband. Neither Margie nor her lawyer alluded to the fact that she had been battered almost daily during the seventeen years of her marriage.

Although Margie had a dated record of the abuse that she sustained at Marion's hands, it was not entered into evidence. The decision to not use the abuse as a mitigating factor or as evidence of self-defense proved costly for Margie. In 1992 an attorney named Keith Bartley volunteered to work to obtain a new trial for Margie. He subsequently filed a motion asking the Martin Circuit Court to grant Margie Marcum a new trial.

Geoffrey D. Marsh, an assistant commonwealth's attorney, responded to the motion for exemption from violent offender status. The response stated that the defendant's failure to raise a particular defense at trial does not constitute grounds for a new trial unless the defendant alleges her attorney to be ineffective, a position that Margie never took.

The legal principal of *res judicata* (the thing has been judged) means that once a ruling has been made, it cannot be debated and decided again without an extraordinary reason. If new evidence that could not reasonably be known at trial surfaces later, a court can grant a new trial. But Margie Marcum's abuse was known to her and to her attorney as well as to many others at the time of her trial. The legal system cannot lightly permit new trials, as, theoretically, convicted defendants could file endless motions. Sometimes, as Margie learned, the legal system can't or doesn't work for an individual defendant.

In the Kentucky Correctional Institution for Women, Margie kept to herself. During the two years and eleven months of her incarceration, she worked in the prison yard and in the mail room. She also attended classes in preparation for obtaining her GED. Although eligible to join the B.O.S.H. Group, she did not. Neither did she contribute to the Sisters in Pain quilt. Chandra McElroy, the prison counselor, and Chandra's predecessor conducted one-on-one sessions with Margie, but Margie kept her distance, even from herself. She'd forgotten, she'd say, when asked questions concerning her case. It was as though she'd buried her memories and her feelings with the body of Marion Marcum.

Helen Bowen spent most of her spare time for several years fighting for Margie by forcing the judicial system to recognize a survivor who could barely recognize herself. Like Chandra McElroy, Helen was also familiar with abuse. So Helen's empathy and sense of justice fueled her twofold mission to become Margie's friend and to have her case retried. During Margie's stay at the Johnson County Detention Center, Helen visited Margie several times a week. After Margie transferred to KCIW, outside Louisville, Helen made the several-hundred-dred-mile round-trip from Eastern Kentucky to visit Margie two or three times each month. Also, Helen said, Margie "would call me on the 800 number at the spouse abuse center, and then sometimes she would call me at home. On my days off from the center, she would call me at home, collect."

Throughout Margie's incarceration, her daughter Freda retained custody of Margie's two youngest children. Helen befriended and helped Freda, too, and she spent hours interviewing Freda and Margie's eldest sons about their mother's abuse.

On the legal front, Helen confronted anyone who would listen. "I had one hellacious time," she said. "I'll admit that. I remember going to the courthouse and saying, 'I need an attorney!' Just yelling it out in the courthouse."

We asked, "[Didn't you get] an attorney interested in [Margie's] case that did exceptional work for her, free of charge?"

She responded, "Henry Piper. He was from Appalachian Research Defense Fund. . . . I had known Henry from working on other cases at the spouse abuse center. In talking with Margie, I never once promised her that she would ever get out [of prison]. But I did tell her that I would take [her case] to an attorney. I went to Henry and basically sat in his office and cried. He said,

'What is wrong with you now? This woman is in jail and she needs your help!' Take it in mind, I [also] went to another attorney. His name is Keith Bartley, [and he] is now the county attorney for Floyd County. Keith is a criminal attorney. He said he would take the case. But I had known Henry, and after everybody got the word of what was going on, . . . I got telephone calls from several other lawyers saying, 'Well, if you need help, I'll help.' But Keith helped Henry by giving him advice. Henry read the [trial] transcript, . . . [and] about a week after that I went back and he said, 'Okay, we'll give it a try.' He made the statement to me, 'I give you no promise'—maybe the same statement I'd given Margie."

According to Helen, Henry Piper believes that Margie Marcum suffers from battered woman syndrome, a condition that, like post-traumatic stress disorder, causes abused women reminded of their abuse to reexperience the anxiety and the hostility caused by that abuse and to lash out in self-defense, as though in battle. This condition, controversial as a legal defense because it perpetuates the view that abuse survivors remain victims, is a condition, Piper argued, that could have caused Margie to shoot her batterer. Helen and Henry learned that Anna Victoria Wilson, an educator recognized as a national expert on battered woman syndrome, was teaching at Eastern Kentucky University at the time that Henry reviewed Margie's case. Helen phoned Wilson, who agreed, after reading the transcript of Margie's trial, to visit Margie in prison. Helen said, "She went out and had one session [with Margie] and called me back and said, 'She's clearly a battered woman and she suffers from the syndrome.' Margie was not too friendly with her, but that was typical. She didn't trust her. She didn't know who she was. Anna went out for a second visit, and Margie was more up-front with her." Even though Wilson had started teaching at the University of Texas at Austin at the time of Margie Marcum's trial, she flew back to Kentucky to testify on Margie's behalf.

Margie filed another motion for a new trial. The court allowed an evidentiary hearing but then reversed itself. In its judicial order, the court declared, "The Court relying upon its experience with the actual trial of this action and the July 13, 1994 Evidentiary Hearing, finds that the Defendant was not a victim of domestic violence and abuse such as to bring her within the statutory requirements of KRS503.050 [the statute that defines justifiable use of force in self-protection and that delineates the conditions under which the experience of prior acts of domestic violence and abuse constitute admissible evidence] and 553.060 [the statute that details improper use of physical force in self-protection]." The court continued, "An issue [abuse] should be determined as soon as possible after a defendant is convicted, and to allow such a hearing to take place over seven years post-conviction is to unduly prejudice both the

Commonwealth's ability to adequately prepare its defense and the rights of its citizens to know that their justice system portrays some semblance of finality." Ultimately, the court's decision was virtually identical to the one given in response to the earlier motion. Although the doctrine of *res judicata* is not specifically mentioned in the later order, it is clearly the doctrine that underlies their opinion. As Margie Marcum learned, a defendant must play all her cards in court; to withhold a card is to lose the right to use it to seek a new trial.

After Governor Jones indicated that he was willing to consider reopening the cases of the battered offenders, Margie submitted a petition for an executive pardon. In it, she stated that although her attorney knew of her abuse, he offered no evidence of it. This time, although she didn't get the pardon, Governor Jones made her eligible for parole.

To help ensure her friend's parole, while Margie was still in prison, Helen found a therapist who would counsel Margie once a week free of charge. Helen saw to it that Margie would be exempted from having to work outside her home "because of her disability, her nerves, and [her lack of] education." Helen commented, "She's continuing to work on her GED, but it's at her pace. We're in no rush. She's got the rest of her life to get it."

"Does she leave her home very much?" we asked.

"Not too much."

"[Did] she [live] under such repression for so long that she [now inflicts it] on herself? Does she . . . stay within the boundaries that she [once was] permitted, [because] she hasn't gone out and done . . . things she once was prohibited from doing?"

"Yes, basically. She's still in the same routine."

"Does she have problems making decisions now?"

"A little. And one of them was to make a decision to come here today. She said she was sick. . . . She sounded sick, but I think she's . . . hesitant about making a decision, and if she does make a decision, [she wonders] if it's the right thing. That's where [her counselor] has come in—helping her to rebuild that self-esteem and trust."

"[She] had her trip to the *Donahue Show* paid for, and then she decided not to go?"

"Montel Williams contacted me as well, and [she said] no [to both appearances]."

"She obviously doesn't enjoy discussing anything about her case. Why do you think this is?"

"Fear."

"Of what?"

"Fear that she's always lived. But, *enough* about her being a battered woman and living that type of fear. Unless you have walked in those shoes, no one knows what it's like. She's afraid maybe she'll say the wrong thing and be forced to go back to prison."

If every abuse survivor had a proponent like Helen Bowen who, in turn, attracted other selfless professionals—attorneys, counselors, and scholars, among others—to work for her cause, the world would, indeed, be a better place. But Helen Bowen, Keith Bartley, Henry Piper, and Anna Victoria Wilson and their ilk remain all too scarce. Because of their advocacy, Margie Marcum was paroled and still gets counseling. Because of their affection, Margie Marcum is learning to trust. Most battered women remain far less fortunate. Most battered women stand alone.

The Key

Had there not been guns in her father's house,
She would never have shot him.

I'm gonna kill you, you little bitch.
He's home, drunk again,
Screaming, throwing things at her—
Shoes, dishes, a heavy ashtray.

Instead of hitting her with brutal words,
Blacking her eye, kicking her dog to death,
Beating her so bad she prays to die,
This time he comes with a hang-dog look,
Says he's sorry, hugs her, rubs up and down her back.
At the end of her rope, she pushes him away.
He grabs, throws her to the floor, rips her nightgown.
She runs. He traps her at his dead-bolted back door,

Drags her through the hall by her hair.
She twists away, hides, searches in drawers
For the key—a last-ditch effort to escape—
In every drawer a gun. She picks a small hand-gun up
It goes off.

Silent as his hundred and nine guns,
He won't go off on her. Ever again.

Sue Terry Driskell

Tracie English

If the collective story of the Sisters in Pain were cast for the silver screen, Tracie English, the youngest of the lot, would be played by the likes of Kate Winslet, or, fifty years ago, by the same ingenuous Judy Garland that starred in *Meet Me in St. Louis*. For Tracie has proved the media's darling not only for her youth but also for the fact that, instead of actually or allegedly killing or conspiring to kill a boyfriend or a spouse, she shot her father, a man who, she says, battered her for years; a man who, right in front of her, kicked and killed her most loyal and loving confidante, her German shepherd Danny. By the time the Sisters in Pain were paroled, Kentuckians had seen Tracie again and again on their local television news. The cameras that turned away from the older, more battle-scarred Sisters in Pain after flashing quick mug shots beneath their names focused day after day and night after night on Tracie's anguished, innocent face. Tears streamed from her huge doe eyes, accompanied by broken sobs, and she looked for all the world like a deer trapped in headlights. That frozen cliché is the image that perhaps more than any other traveled via broadcast waves of sound and light well beyond Kentucky.

In addition to speaking out with her cohorts on the *Donahue Show*, Tracie appeared, after her parole, on the *Maury Povich* and *Montel Williams Shows*, too. Over and over, on hard news programs and on the talk show circuit alike, the sight of Tracie reliving her favorite dog's death caused audiences from Alabama to Alaska to take a closer look at abusers and abuse.

Of course we, too, had seen those satellite-sent tapes of Tracie, that picture and those sound bites worth at least a thousand words, at least a thousand times before we met her at her mother's home in Louisville in southern Jefferson County on a muggy May night in 1997. The truth is that we brought to that, one of our last interviews, more than a poignant, clichéd picture of the youngest Sister in Pain. We carried to that house on Powderhorn Drive (a street name that, were we writing fiction, any editor alert to life's ironies would have insisted on changing) baggage from previous interviews. While in prison, according to the other women, Tracie hadn't bonded with the B.O.S.H. Group.

And after the women's parole, during their trip to appear on the *Donahue Show*, Tracie had alienated others in the group. Instead of renewing her bond with her former prison mates during their all-night talk fest in the South Gate Tower suite of the Seventh Avenue Hotel, she chose to tour the Big Apple. The other women's explicit and implicit messages to us had been that Tracie, a self-centered opportunist, was cashing in on her newfound fame, even at her Sisters' expense. Chandra McElroy, the women's prison counselor, and Marguerite Thomas, the assistant public advocate who'd worked on the women's behalf, had been kinder. "Tracie's still a kid," each of them had said in separate conversations. But we'd been warned that Tracie, influenced by money-hungry relatives and a slick new attorney, might not, without a fee, be willing to discuss her case. On ethical grounds our information-gathering policy prohibited any financial exchange, so we were prepared to eliminate Tracie from our list of interviewees when we decided that, before assuming anything, we would talk with Tracie herself. Of course we could interview her, she said, when we finally called. Of course she would loan us any material in her possession pertaining to her case. Of course we could come to her mother's house the next week, the suburban ranch that Tracie had shared since her parole. And contrary to what we were led to expect, never during our phone conversations or during our interview with Tracie did she or her mother mention money.

As has always been true with the famous and the infamous, the burden of having become a public figure included, for Tracie English, myths that, even if based on kernels of truth, made her appear at once heroic and hedonistic, more as well as less than the still-sheltered, once-battered, then-twenty-five-year-old human she was. Prepared to meet a manipulating, manipulated young woman, we instead encountered a survivor whose straightforward responses struck us, at times, as naïve. We also met her pleasant, if salty, mother, a woman who hovered until she entered the conversation, a woman whose chain-smoking, insistent engagement in her daughter's tale—which is also, in part, her own—mimicked the sort of nervous sentry found less often in a media sophisticate than in a mother hen.

Upon our arrival Tracie invited us to sit at a rectangular table in her 1950s-style front room, in the combined living and dining area entered from her mother's, Sharon Bell's, front door. As we arranged our notes and recording equipment, a shorts-and-T-shirt-clad Sharon greeted us, excused herself to bustle about the kitchen, then returned to the brightly lit room where we were starting to tape Tracie's interview. For ten minutes or so Sharon hovered by the archway to the kitchen. Then, as though unsure of her place, she pulled up a chair and placed it on an imaginary line on the wall-to-wall carpet, on some respectable and respectful boundary about four feet away from our interview, midway on the invisible border between our conversational triangle and the kitchen. During most of the interview Sharon studied us as she might watch TV: bent forward, intent, inhaling the cigarettes she then ground into the ash-tray that she balanced on one knee. But like a sports fan focused on a football match, from time to time Sharon broke her silence and inserted into her daughter's story commentary that she deemed crucial. Dusk turned into twilight and twilight turned into lamp-lit night during our four-hour, four-way exchange.

According to Tracie Rae English, who was born in Louisville on June 16, 1973, her earliest memories include visions of her father, Bill English, beating her mother. "Mom said that before I was born, or before she started showing, she didn't have any problems out of Daddy at all. When she got pregnant and started showing was when the abuse started," Tracie said.

Sharon nodded. "It seemed like six weeks after I got pregnant with Tracie—well, you know how you start to get big. He'd call me a fat pig, a fat whore, a fat slob, and a bitch. And he didn't want me to buy any maternity clothes; he wanted me to buy clothes that could be worn later. It seemed every six weeks it ended up that I was walking down Whispering Hills Boulevard, going to my mother's, or calling her to come pick me up, 'cause he either beat me or locked me out of the house. He'd come in and flip the table over. I don't care what kind of food I had on it. He'd flip it over and it was all my fault.

"Tracie is my fourth child. My other three children are from a previous marriage. Before I married [Bill English], he promised that we'd have [my] boys living with us and we'd fix rooms up. It never happened. I was out of the house more than in. He'd do all these things. He'd park the car where I couldn't get out or lock me in the basement."

When Tracie was six, her parents divorced. "Before that, I went to ice skating, dancing, cheerleading, gymnastics, all that stuff," said Tracie. "That kind of stopped about a year after Mom and Dad was divorced because he wouldn't pay for it anymore. Mom couldn't afford it. We were on food stamps. Then Mom was going to school to get her diploma and all that stuff. Dad, I would go visit him on the weekends. I never wanted to go, but I *would* go. At first he never really hit on me. He would just yell at me. But one night he threw an ashtray, and I called Mom to come and get me. He also beat up my brother and made him leave. [Sharon's son by a previous marriage] was living with [Bill English] after Mom and Dad got divorced. Then [Dad] kidnapped me one time."

"You were how old when he kidnapped you?"

"I was either in first or second grade."

"He had her for two weeks, and his attorney kept calling and telling him he better get her back there. And then he did it again. He did it twice, and both times I dropped the charges on him," added Sharon.

"Why did you drop the charges?"

"Well, he brought her back, and she was safe, and everything was okay, and I just didn't follow through with any of it," Sharon said.

Difficult as it is to comprehend a woman's decision to drop charges against a man who had abused her and who had kidnapped her daughter, every day in virtually every town and city in the United States, battered women in similar situations refuse to press charges. And there is nothing that anyone—police, family members, or friends—can do to keep abusers in custody if their batterers refuse to cooperate. Often, battered women decide to drop charges against their abusive partners after those women have alerted police to their battering and after police have registered reports of the crimes. Also, in most cases, law officers cannot arrest abusers unless the officers witness offenses or unless the abused swear out warrants for their abusers' arrests or take out restraining orders to prohibit the alleged offenders from contacting their accusers. Residual affection for their abusers, the belief that—as their batterers have convinced them—survivors have caused and deserve their torture, and the terror engendered by the thought that angered batterers temporarily restrained will be released to retaliate with greater force cause abuse survivors to fear holding their batterers accountable. While such attitudes appear alien and illogical, such philosophies shape the psyches of individuals whose survival depends on enduring and transcending each moment. Battered women, like men in combat, can concentrate only on executing their next breaths and their next steps. Women who have been abandoned again and again to their fates by people familiar with their situations and who have also been abandoned by the law regard professionals' promises as remote fantasies that they cannot envision or afford to trust.

When Tracie was eight, she and her teenage relative, Tonya, moved in with Bill English, to whom the courts had given custody of both children because Sharon had married again and her current husband, Sharon said, had started to physically abuse them.

"When and how did your own father begin battering you?" we asked.

Tracie said, "He always screamed at me. Throwing things and hitting started about a couple of months after me and my sister moved in with him. He didn't get real violent in front of Tonya. He'd never hit me in front of her, I guess 'cause she wasn't his child. He would take her car keys from her if she was out spending the night with a friend [and] he didn't want her to. He'd go take the license plate off her car. He kicked the grill in on her car. He flattened her tires. He'd do everything, and Tonya moved out when she was about sixteen. She moved in with Grandma [Sharon's mother]. Now I was back and forth. I'd be at Grandma's, then I'd be at [another brother's house]. But [that brother] would get real rough, and I'd get aggravated and agitated with him, so I'd leave there and go here [Sharon's house]. Then [Sharon's husband] would get in his moods, and I'd leave and go to Dad's. I was just back and forth all the time. Then my sister got custody of me and I did really good in school and everything, but they [Tonya and her husband] were trying to save money to buy a house, and they moved to Brandenburg. I could have went with them, but it was such a far distance and everything, so I moved in with Mom. I was fifteen when all this happened."

"How old were you when you started going back and forth [between different relatives' homes]?"

"I was in the sixth grade. And the Social Services Department [*sic*] got into the picture when I was in sixth grade because Dad came up to school and threatened to kill me, right in front of the guidance counselor."

"Do you remember what the reason was?"

"Well, he had to come [to my school] to sign a paper because I was supposed to go on a field trip or something. He had to sign a paper so I could go, and I made him late for work. . . . As he was walking out, he was standing there, and the guidance counselor was to the side, and I guess he didn't see him, and [my dad] said, 'I'm going to kill you, you little bitch.' So [school officials] called the Social Services Department [*sic*]."

"That was the first time there was any kind of report against your father?"

"Well, I'd called 911 before, and my neighbors had called 911 before to report a disturbance. I was in the fourth grade, I think, the first time."

"So you were about nine or ten years old?"

"Yeah."

"And you called?"

"I did a couple of times."

"Do you remember what caused you to call?"

"I was scared."

"What had he done?"

"What *hadn't* he done? He either hit me or he had something he was going to hit me with."

"He didn't know you called?"

"No, [not] until the police would come."

"And then what happened?"

"[The police would ask] 'Did you hit her? What's wrong here? Sorry, but we didn't *see* him hit you.' I'd be bleeding. 'We didn't *see* him hit you. We can't do nothing.' [Then Dad would say,] 'You called the police on me.' [Then I'd] get it twice as bad. I'd get beat so bad I'd pray to die."

"I had warrant after warrant on that man, and I just absolutely couldn't get him to jail," Sharon interjected. "I even had two police officers go out to the salvage yard [Bill English's workplace]."

"When you [and Bill English] were still married?" we asked Sharon.

"Yeah," Sharon said. "I still had to call the police on him [after our divorce], but I couldn't get him served. Every time that would happen [the papers] would be recalled, and I couldn't get him in jail. By then it would be like two or three weeks, or maybe a month, before we'd go to court, and he'd end up buying me diamond rings, new cars—filling the house up with flowers. It was unreal."

"It looked like a funeral home, there were so many flowers," added Tracie.

Although Sharon said she had filed warrants, her statement that the warrants couldn't be served indicates that Bill English never received them. According to Sharon, people with some relationship to Bill English or to his family intercepted them. So long after the event, it is almost impossible to verify Sharon's statement. But failure to deliver a warrant, although possible, remains rare.

We asked Tracie what implements her father used to beat her.

"Everything. He had this great, huge ashtray. I mean, it had to be made out of cement. I don't know how many times I got clobbered with that. That was the first thing that he hit me with that I can remember. Oh, he'd throw shoes, glasses, dishes—it didn't matter. Anything he'd get his hands on, he'd pick. If he didn't have nothing, he'd go at you with his fist. It felt like something could hit you before he would [throw it]."

"Was he employed during this time?"

"Self-employed. When [he and Mom] got married, he owned a plumbing business that did really well. Then he got into the used car business. It was a salvage yard. And he sold football cards. He even sold them to the police. He was in partnership with another gentleman, but [that man] split when I got arrested. The next thing you know, we drove by his house and everything was gone. He'd seen Dad beat the daylight out of me one time, and I thought, well, Mom could go talk to him. [He could] be a witness or something. But he was gone with no curtains, even, hanging in [his] house. It was cleared out."

"They used to have people that would steal things from Service Merchandise or Sears," Sharon said.

"They'd go to work in the warehouse for about two days and get all this stuff," Tracie added. "Dad would pay them. This other guy would pay them, then resell [the merchandise] for half price."

"What was your reaction to your father's abuse, or how did you handle it when it started?"

"I'd run away, that was how, to my mom's or my grandma's or my sister's. Eventually, [wherever I went,] I would answer the phone, 'cause they didn't have Caller ID back then. I'd be [somewhere] for about three or four days, and everything's cool. He'd come looking for me, and I'd hide. When I'd answer the phone, he'd be, like, 'I'm coming to get you,' and he'd come and break the door down and take me out by my hair. Or he would come and Grandma would let him in because she was scared 'cause he'd smacked her before, spit in her face, kicked her car door in, ripped her door off the house."

"When he [brought you back to his house], was he any better to you, or was he worse to you, than he'd been before you left?"

"Sometimes he was worse, but when he was sober and he came to get me and I would agree to go with him, he'd take me on a shopping spree. . . . It was nothing for him to go to Fashion Shop and buy me a hundred shirts."

"So he would either feel guilty or punish you more?"

"Yeah."

"Did you ever feel that you had done something to cause this?"

"Oh, I felt it all the time."

"And you would feel that he was right?"

"Yeah. 'Oh, I'm sorry, Daddy. Let me fix it.' I still feel that way to this day. If somebody comes up behind me and just pats me on the shoulder, and if it's real quiet in the room and I'm, like, really into reading or something, or, like, earlier [today] I was on the phone and Mom just came in and said, 'Tracie,' I know I jumped a foot off my bed."

"We understand that the fact that your father abused you was reported to officials on at least four occasions during your adolescence. Who made the reports, and what, if anything, were the officials' responses to those reports?"

"It was teachers, most of the time, reported it. I know one time Social Services was calling my house every day because I had missed sixty days of school in a row, 'cause he hit me so hard on this side [of my face] here that you can still feel the scar, and 'cause my eye was black. All of it was black, and it took two months for everything to heal up, 'cause I had to get two stitches. While there was any kind of scratch there, he wouldn't let me go to school."

"At least four of your teachers made reports [about your abuse by your father] on separate occasions?"

"More than that."

"Did you know they were making reports?"

"No. They would see me on crutches or with a black eye two or three times a month. They'd see me on crutches where he'd taken a bat to my knees, and my knees are still bad to this day because of it. If I just turn my left knee a certain way, it pops right out of place."

"And on *no* occasion did police come to interview you?"

"No, but this was back in the late seventies and early eighties. I think, if it had been then like it is today, my dad would still be alive because somebody back then thought that, no matter what, you should always keep a parent and child together."

"Do you think [the police] believed your teachers' reports?"

"Well, I think the point of it was, 'Did you *see* Tracie's dad hit her?' And they would be, like, 'No.'"

"So, if there was no witness, [your abuse] didn't happen or didn't matter?"

"Most of my friends at my trial were so young. They were in eighth, ninth, tenth grade. Some of them may have been in eleventh, 'cause I had failed the sixth grade three times. *Three* times. It was because of tardies and absences that I fell back."

Child abuse laws are relatively recent. Before 1970, few laws required anyone to report suspected child abuse or neglect. Kentucky's statutes, in effect while Tracie was in school, required teachers to report such suspicions. Only in recent years have courts enacted statutes requiring teachers and counselors to report presumed child abuse. But now, as in the past, such laws remain difficult to enforce, as the standard of reasonable suspicion is subjective. What one person considers abuse another person may not. For example, children sometimes report such wildly improbable happenings as having been boiled in tubs of water or having been hung by their thumbs from rafters, reports unsubstantiated by apparent injuries or claims to such. Some people would routinely relay such accusations, while others would dismiss the stories as fantasies. Historical and cultural precedents continue to render child abuse laws difficult to enact and enforce.

We asked Tracie to tell us what transpired on the night when she shot her father.

"He had come home and he was mad because I hadn't cooked anything for dinner."

"And you were supposed to be the one who [cooked] every night?"

"When I got to be thirteen or fourteen."

"Was it only the two of you [living] in the house?"

"At this point, yeah. It wasn't nothing for him to go [to the store]. He had lots of money, but he just didn't want to go over to the store because it took up his bookie time. He came home [that night], there was nothing to eat, [and] the basement door was frozen shut. [In the basement] was one of those great big freezers that he put deer meat in and chicken and steak, and I couldn't get in there. That's how it started. He came home [and started] screaming and throwing stuff at me."

"How old were you then?"

"I had just turned sixteen. And I went back to my bedroom trying to find somebody, anybody, to come pick me up, and nobody would come because they had been so scared of Dad. My Grandma wouldn't come get me, Mom wasn't there, Tonya wouldn't come get me. He had threatened to kill anyone who came [to the house]. Literally kill us. So he came back to my room. He was, like, 'Come here.' I was, like, 'Okay.' He was, like, 'I'm sorry.' And I was like, you know, feeling really weird. So when I stood up, he hugged me, and, when he did, he was rubbing [his body] up and down my back. And I was, like, I don't *think* so. You know, getting a hug from your father [should be], like, 'Oh, that's my *baby*'—patting you on your back, not rubbing up and down your back. So, I pushed him away, and he got hold of me again, and he threw me on the floor and he ripped my nightgown all the way up the side. I got him off me and I got to the back door. All the windows in the house was nailed shut, and the doors had deadbolt locks."

"He had done that?"

"Yeah, so he could leave me in the house any time he wanted to, 'cause there was no way out. He used the excuse that we had too many break-ins when people asked why the house was like that. It was like I was a prisoner in my own home. At nine years old he was leaving me by myself until the wee hours of the morning. [But, that night,] I got away from him, and I ran to the back door, and I couldn't get out, 'cause it was locked, and I just felt like I was in a Jason movie, 'cause I'd shaken the door [and screamed] 'Please come open!' [But] he came and dragged me by my hair down the hallway. I had carpet burns all over my butt. You know, [later that night], the whole time the officer interviewed me, I was wrapped up in a blanket, and he was, like, 'You're okay.' [But after my father dragged me down the hall,] I was in shock, but I got away from him again. I hid from him for a few minutes. It was probably one minute. It seemed like a long time. It was probably just a few seconds. I got out and was looking for the keys, and I couldn't find them, and I seen the gun. I mean, every drawer you pulled out, there was a gun in my house. There was over 109 guns when [the police later] came and did their investigation in my house. So I . . . [tried] to get the keys. I just wanted to get out of there. If I'd thought about it, I would have busted out a window and ran. [Then] he moved or something. I was scared to death. You know, when you're in an abusive relationship with anybody, it's like being around a volcano; you never know when it's going to erupt. And the gun went off and I grabbed the keys and left. I had no idea that I had shot him."

"Do you remember picking up the gun?"

"Yes, I remember having the gun in my hand."

"What kind of gun was it?"

"I don't know."

"It wasn't a rifle, but a small handgun?"

"Yeah."

"But you don't remember actually shooting him?"

"No."

"And then what happened?"

"I ran to my neighbor's house when I couldn't find anybody to come get me. He'd let me stay at his house before. It was no surprise [for him] to see me standing there knocking on the door with black eyes or bruises."

"Do you remember anything more about the actual shooting?"

"No, I can just remember hearing [the gun] go off. I guess a part of me won't let me remember it consciously, because, regardless, that was my *dad*, and it took me a long time to be able to remember [any aspect of that event]. When you're in denial . . . you won't remember until you come to terms where you can handle it."

"On that night, what happened after you ran to your neighbor?"

"The [man, the neighbor] I went to every time [I escaped], he said I was hysterical [that night]. I remember shaking a lot. I remember being there. But, you know how you can look and see, in your head, a movie with no sound? That's how it feels, and I remember I couldn't dial the phone because my hands were shaking so bad. [My neighbor] would dial the numbers for me. I called my grandma. Grandma wouldn't come. My sister wouldn't answer the phone. My mom wouldn't answer the phone. 'Okay, Tracie,' [my neighbor said,] 'I'll take you wherever you need to go.' I said, 'Take me to my Mom's, please.' When he pulled out of his garage, I flew to the floorboard, crying and screaming, 'My Dad's gonna kill me! My Dad's gonna kill me! You've got to get me away!' 'Cause, see, in my mind, he was coming after me. I wasn't aware of what happened. I wasn't aware he was injured. I was frantic. I was scared to death. [When we got to Mom's house] I remember I didn't even close the car door. I just took off running. I opened the door and split. Mom changed my clothes because my nightgown was ripped all the way up the side. I told Mom, 'I don't know what happened.' She called the EMS [Emergency Medical Services], the police intervened, and I looked out front, and I remember seeing red and blue lights. I mean, there was cops pulled up in the yard, down the street—all the way down the street. [Mom] called everybody, and then it took [law enforcement and medical personnel] so long to find Dad's house. Then my step-dad had to leave and show them where my dad lived, 'cause we lived up on this hill and they kept passing it up."

"We didn't know if she shot him or not," said Sharon. "Our idea was to just find out if he was okay."

"You didn't know if he was shot. Why would you think he had been?" we asked.

Sharon replied, "[Tracie] came in here and said she had shot the gun. Hysterical, she said she fired the gun. She didn't know if she shot him or not, so if he was shot, I wanted medical attention [for him]. I wanted him taken care of. And then I called his brother and talked to him and told him that there had been an accident. And then I called the police and they came over here and took Tracie, and I never seen her again until we went to court."

We asked about Tracie's arrest, interrogation, and incarceration. Sharon said that Tracie was arrested the night of her father's death. Sharon also reported that Tracie was questioned without anyone other than police officers present.

"I was in the room by myself. A juvenile," said Tracie. "At the police station, they asked me [how old I was]. I said 'sixteen,' and they . . . sat down on one side of the desk and sat me down on the other. I was wrapped up in my blanket. I was scared to death. I didn't know what happened. I just kept saying, 'I want my mom.'"

"You weren't given the Miranda [warning]?"

"No. I don't remember."

"They didn't [read Tracie her rights before] she left this house," Sharon said. "I said, 'Tracie, when you get down there, don't say anything,' because I didn't know what she might come out with. . . . By the time I had gotten down there . . . she had already said something, and they had already arrested her for manslaughter or murder."

"They arrested me for murder," insisted Tracie. "I was indicted under murder."

"Nobody told you [that] you could have a lawyer present?"

"It was like I remember hearing the Miranda rights big speech on TV—like when you watch *LA Law*. But, I mean, I was sixteen years old. What sixteen year old understands, [who's] been through what I've been through? I was in the seventh grade when I was sixteen."

"But, as far as you can remember, nobody told you [that] you could have a lawyer present and that you had the right to remain silent?"

"I don't know. He probably did. . . . I was sixteen with a seventh grade level—how am I supposed to understand that great big speech? And then he was, like, 'We need you to sign this paper for your house to be investigated. I can get a court order, but it would look better if you signed.' So sure, I'm signing my life away, and all these papers—I have no idea what they are. So then, he says, 'Okay, do you want to tell me what happened, or do you want to look bad?'"

"He also told [Tracie] that if she didn't sign the paper, she wouldn't get to see me," Sharon added. "I didn't get to see her, anyway."

"He told me that I couldn't see Mom unless I talked to him and told him what happened and if I didn't sign these papers," said Tracie. "So he's, like, 'Are you hiding something, or do you want to tell me what happened?' So I'm sitting there thinking, 'Oh, great, I'm gonna lose my mom.'"

"Did you remember more of what happened then?"

"No. I started over. I had no idea what I said. To this day, I don't remember what I said."

"Have you ever seen the transcript of what you said?"

"[Someone] had [my transcript], and, he said, 'There's one here, English. Sign here. First of all, Tracie, I'd like to advise you that you have rights again. See, it says that. It says this. If [it] says it, I guess you have . . . You have the right to talk to a lawyer prior to questioning or [voicing] any desire.' And I say, 'Okay.' [The officer] says, 'I've got a form here from the LPD [Louisville Police Department], and this is yours. Sign here, English.' It's, like, 'Okay, I need you to talk up.' 'Yes?' 'What's your address?' 'One hundred Possum Path.' 'Okay.' 'Your birthday?' 'June 16, 1972.' My birthday ain't in '72; it's in '73. See, I didn't even [get born] on June 16, 1972. This is written in. [He asked], 'What school do you go to?' 'Iroquois Middle.'"

"That paper convicted her," said Sharon.

Tracie and her mother discussed the process of procuring an attorney's services. According to Sharon, the attorney required a retainer of $7,500, for which she took out a loan. Sharon's comment regarding the attorney's work was, "He did nothing."

"You went to jail that very night?" we asked Tracie.

"Yeah."

"How long were you there?"

"From the last day of June, [but] they got it down as July first."

Sharon and Tracie discussed those aspects of Tracie's trial that they think particularly unfair. They blamed the prosecutor for what they perceived to be a poor trial.

"[The prosecutor] intimidated all of them [Tracie's young friends who were witnesses]," said Sharon. "They were so young they couldn't hold up."

"[My friends] would start crying, saying 'I don't know, I don't know,'" said Tracie.

"'Well, did you see Tracie's dad actually kick her?' the prosecutor asked. 'No,' my friends would say. 'But you've seen her with a black eye?' he asked. 'Yes,' they said. 'So you're telling me that Tracie could have hit herself and you wouldn't have known it?'"

"How long," we asked, "were you in jail before you went to trial?"

"I made bond."

"[The] attorney's advice was [that] the only way to get her out of there was to take [the trial], and when we got to adult court we just put a bond on her," said Sharon. "[That's] what we did, and we had her out for two years. . . . After she had a job, she was going to school, she was in high school, . . . her job was downtown, and they just grabbed her up and threw her back in jail again, and they kept her in the Children's Center until she turned eighteen. And then, the day she turned eighteen, Buddy, they shipped [her] right over to the police station and put her in the jail. And the next day they sent her to Pee Wee Valley. That was the only time we ever saw her."

In response to our questions, Tracie outlined the activities that kept her occupied during the two years before she went to trial: She attended Jefferson County High School; she worked in a phone store; she received no counseling.

"We had been [in counseling] when we started," Sharon pointed out. "We were going to AA [Alcoholics Anonymous] meetings—Alateen. We was making at least three meetings a week. We had verification slips to put to the attorney's office. He said, 'This ain't nothing, you don't need to do this.'" Sharon indicated that much of the reason for attending meetings was a desire to learn what motivated Bill English. We asked if Tracie's father had had a drinking problem.

"Oh, yeah," said Tracie. "He was court-ordered to go to AA meetings, [but] I got it in here [binder of documents] where it says 'Bill refuses to go to alcohol meetings.'"

"He was drunk all the time after I divorced him," said Sharon.

"[Tell us] your feelings [regarding] how the police treated you the night they arrested you," we asked Tracie.

"I think it was unfair. And, you know, to this day I still hold a little grudge."

"Can you tell us how they were unfair?"

"I feel like they were one-sided, like they gave my dad's people . . . control, . . . and I didn't feel like they took anything into consideration of what happened to me."

"You've told us about the questioning. You were fingerprinted, I presume. . . . Did you spend the night in a holding cell?"

"Yeah. They took me upstairs in the morning, and I did not eat for the first week and a half that I was there. . . . They took me in the dining room, and I couldn't eat. My stomach, I was so tore up thinking what I went through."

"So you stayed in the old [city] jail."

"Yeah. They kept telling me, 'Oh, we'll let you see your mom,' and I kept asking for my mom. . . . When I asked to see my mom or I asked to see anybody, [the answer was], 'No, after you do this, after you do this.'"

We asked Sharon, 'What did they [the police] say [when they took her away?] 'Tracie, you have to go with us?'"

"Yeah."

"Tracie, did they handcuff you?" we asked.

"No."

"So they took [you] out for questioning . . . and then arrested you once you got down there?"

Sharon responded, "Well, once they found out that [Bill] had been shot, they just took her down, no questions. I couldn't take her down there; they took her. They had already made their minds up when they left here, about what they were going to do."

"At some point, [Tracie,] you ended up in the juvenile detention center?"

"Yeah."

"You did not go to the adult prison until you came back to trial?"

"Right."

Although Tracie's accusations concerning her prosecuting attorney can't be interpreted as confirmation of her charges, her continuing confusion concerning her defense illustrates the inadequacy of the judicial system's ability to communicate with people who find themselves trapped within it. Citing her dissatisfaction with the prosecutor, Tracie said, "We really didn't talk about anything until he would come and see me and tell me I'm having a bond hearing. 'I'm gonna get you out on bond, blah, blah, blah.' And then, when I was out, I didn't see [him] until two weeks before I went to trial. And that's when he started preparing . . . my case."

Sharon's voice shook with anger when she said that Tracie's lawyer told her daughter to go into court dressed up, with her hair dyed. According to Sharon, he told Tracie to "look as old as you can."

"He told me," said Tracie. "'It happened like this. Tracie didn't [do] it.' And then he'd say something. 'And if it didn't happen like that, I need to call the prosecutor and cut you a deal so you don't end up in the electric chair. Maybe you can get life.'"

"Were you ever afraid of going to the electric chair?"

"Oh, yeah. [There were reports from many people,] judges from years ago, social workers from years ago, teachers from years ago—way before this happened. But it didn't matter."

It was two years before Tracie's case would come to trial, due to, in Tracie's words, the fact that "they kept laying it over."

"What kind of contact did you have with your attorney [before you went to court?]"

"We went up to see some psychologist," said Sharon.

"Holding up ink blots," added Tracie.

"Did he ever discuss defense strategy with you?"

"No."

"It sounds like you feel you were largely unprepared to take the stand."

"Right."

"And you were the lead-off witness?"

"Yeah."

"Were there any other witnesses called on your behalf?"

"Mom and my sister."

"And we were very discredited," said Sharon. "Nothing we said meant anything. [The neighbor to whose house Tracie fled] was there. He had seen what Tracie looked like after [Bill had] beat her up. [The prosecutor] would say, 'Did you see with your own eyes Bill English try to kill Tracie?' [I had to answer,] 'No.'"

"Dad's sisters could get up there and give hearsay, but my witnesses couldn't," said Tracie.

"So [after the] trial [was] basically over and the jury filed back in, what did you expect the verdict to be?"

"I didn't expect twenty years."

"Did the [attorney or judge] give instructions to the jury in your presence?"

"Yeah."

"What were the possible verdicts the jury could have come up with?"

"Not guilty; reckless homicide, I believe; manslaughter; or murder."

"Were you found guilty of voluntary or involuntary [murder]?"

"What's first-degree?"

"Voluntary. So, tell us how you felt when the jury said, 'Guilty.'"

"I was shocked."

"Then . . . they didn't [sentence you] right away, did they?"

"No, they waited until I turned eighteen."

"They kept her, though," said Sharon.

"They kept me and made me wait until I was eighteen," added Tracie. "[After the sentencing], they took me that day when they said twenty years."

"So, how long were you actually in prison?"

"From June of '91 until February of '96."

"So, you were there almost five years. . . . You were twenty-three when you got out of prison?"

"I turned twenty-three."

"And you had these parole hearings, and your father's relatives opposed your parole?"

"I thought I did not have a shot. I'm not kidding you."

"Correct us if we're wrong, but is it fair to say that you don't feel you were treated fairly by the legal system?"

"No, not at all. [But] now I do, with what the governor and the parole board did for me."

"What about the fact that [the governor] could have pardoned you? He could have wiped away [your] convicted felon [record]. Do you have any feelings about that?"

"There's a reason for that. Maybe he feels . . . that we're protected this way, because we are still in the system some way. There's a number of reasons why."

"Tracie, it sounds as though [when you shot your father] he'd been starting to sexually abuse you. Had he abused you, sexually, before?"

"Yeah. He'd molested me before. I think I was thirteen. He didn't penetrate me, but he fondled me."

"He used to beat her with a sock that had a bar of soap in it and walk in when she was taking a shower," said Sharon. "And see, I didn't know any of this was going on. Tracie will tell you how I found out about it."

Tracie said, "One time I was on my way [to Grandma's]. Dad knew where I was going. He knew that my mom was at my grandma's and that I was going up there. Well, he got there before I did, and everybody remembers this, 'cause the whole neighborhood remembers hearing me cry and scream in the middle of the street. When I got there, he had my mom in the middle of the street, beating her. This was two or three years after they were divorced, and she thought [her beating] was over a car he gave her, but it was 'cause I was gonna tell her what was happening to me, and I wanted to come stay with her forever. And I got there, and he was beating my mom up, and I didn't know what to do. He was gonna grab me, so I ran into this lady's house that lived there for years, and she was in bed, and I jumped in bed with her, screaming and crying. I told her, 'Ruth, Dad's beating Mom in the middle of the street.' She said, 'Well, come with me. I'm gonna go check it out.' So she went out there, and there was Mom with Dad on top of her, beating her."

"[Bill English] was drunk all the time after I divorced him," said Sharon. "He would ride Tonya and [Tracie's friend] over to Doss High School, and Tonya was mixing whiskey into his coffee on their way to school. That's how early [in the day] he started."

"Tracie, about your father's drinking, do you think that was a cause or a contributor to his abuse?"

"Well, I believe in my heart that my daddy never intended to hurt me, and I feel that my grandpa must have mistreated him. He had to have."

"Did you know your grandparents on that side of the family?"

"Well, I knew my grandmother. My Grandmother English was the sweetest woman that ever walked on this earth. I mean, for years Dad would not tell her that Mom and Dad were divorced. She didn't know, until, I think, Dad kidnapped me."

"Did you ever know [your Grandfather English]?"

"Yeah. I don't know why, but I was scared of him. I didn't like my grandpa."

Sharon said, "His youngest daughter wouldn't even stay in the same room with him by herself. I believe that his daddy must have abused him sexually, too, because that's why he treated their mother the way he did. Because she let it happen. Not *let* it happen, but knew it was going on, because you *always* know. The mother knows when this is going on in her house. [During Tracie's] whole trial, [the entire English family kept saying,] no, that didn't happen and this didn't happen [in their family], but I believe [they denied the truth of their own abuse] because they had been through it and nobody did anything about it. . . . [Bill English] belted me the same way he did Tracie, and I believe his daddy did his own family that way. [Tracie's Grandfather English] would give [his wife] ten dollars and tell her to go to the grocery and buy food for all their kids, and he'd want receipts."

"The only time I seen [my father's brothers and sisters]," said Tracie, "was when I would go there for holidays. Dad would drop me off and he would leave. He'd give me presents to give them and [he'd] leave."

"He never saw [his family members] himself?"

"Not unless they came to get a part for their car or to borrow money or something to that effect. He would pick tomatoes and send them down to Grandma."

"But you never heard from your father what happened [to him] when he was a kid? He never talked about it?"

"No."

"He did to me," said Sharon. "He'd talk to me about how his daddy would get drunk and rip his [own] clothes off. [Bill's dad] would do that in the middle of Kroger. And Bill would do the same thing. Fifty-dollar shirts he'd take and rip the buttons right off."

"Now, looking back on it, you can laugh and say, 'Oh, he really thought he was The Incredible Hunk,'" added Tracie. "But, back then, when it was happening, you were scared to death. One time, I was over at his girlfriend's house. She was babysitting me, and I was using the restroom, 'cause you never knew what time [my father] was gonna get there—anywhere from 5:30 until 11:30 or 12:30 at night. I was using the bathroom, and I was coming out, and he said I was making him late for his bets to be called in. He started yanking the storm door. I thought he was going to pull it off. The next thing I knew, he grabbed the rearview mirror off the window and started smashing it, saying, 'You always cause me to be late; I don't know why I fool with you!'"

"When you speak in public about your father's abusiveness, you talk about your father having killed your favorite dog. When was that in relation to [your father's] death? How long before his death had he killed your dog?"

"I was probably about thirteen."

"Why did he kill your dog?"

"Because my dog started barking and growling at him when [my dad] went to hit me. My dad's, like, 'I'll show you!' and he started kicking him and jumping on [my dog before he shot him]. [Dad] made me carry [my dog's body] down to his truck. I was all covered in blood. I just went to my bathroom. I don't know how many showers I took in a week's time."

"What was the dog's name?"

"Danny. He was really some neat dog."

"Was that just another terrible event amidst the things your father did to you, or was that a turning point in terms of your relationship with your father?"

"Oh, sure, it was [a turning point]. I really didn't talk to him after that, you know, for several weeks. If he asked me something, I'd say, 'No' [or] 'yes,' and go on my way. I think the sexual abuse, the hitting—it's all gonna scar me, but [Danny's death] is something that really stands out."

"If you could tell women who were being battered by their fathers or by their husbands or by anyone else one thing, what would that be?"

"Self-esteem."

"What about self-esteem?"

"Well, it's, like, when you're abused, you don't have it. You think you're the bottom of somebody's shoe. Get out of [your abusive relationship]. Break the cycle, because it's gonna continue, over and over. A smack across the face could easily become a busted rib."

"Who or what, if anyone or anything, could have prevented you from killing your father?"

"For him to have gotten the proper counseling and [for him] to have stopped drinking and [to] have moved me permanently out of the house instead of letting me leave and go back and leave and go back. The justice system failed me when they should have been protecting me."

"What do you think they should have done, and at what point should they have done it?"

"From the get-go. From the first report. That's when I was in sixth grade and he threatened to kill me."

"I think," said Sharon, "if I could have done anything about it, it should have started there. It should never have gotten to her. If I could have put him in jail, maybe just one night in jail would have made him stop and listen. But he never spent that one night."

"Then, Sharon," we asked, "as Tracie's mother, do you blame yourself, too, for not having intervened earlier?"

"I blame myself," she said. "I blame the connections [Bill English] had downtown. They were too strong. I feel like [things might have been different] if the state could have just made him do one thing. Just one. I wouldn't care if it was just making sure he went to AA meetings. You could not touch him. He was like The Godfather."

"How are you," we asked Tracie, "dealing with the stigma of being labeled a felon, or how do you think people who don't know you perceive you?"

"Well, from every person that I've come in contact with, I've never heard a negative comment. Sometimes the statement is, 'Well, I would have done the same thing. He deserved it.' And I feel, in [my dad's] defense, 'Hey, wait a minute! That's my *dad*, regardless, and nobody deserves to die like that. Nobody deserves to die, especially by the hands of their own child. And I just hate that the circumstances escalated to that degree. If they would have been there to intervene."

"Would you advise [a battered woman] to avail herself of the legal system?"

"What do you mean, *advise*?"

"Call the police."

"Now, I think things are different. The eighties was definitely different from the nineties. I think [now] they at least make the men go to jail for the night and make them leave their property or something."

Sharon added, "They've got the laws, but they don't enforce them. They need to start enforcing what they have."

"You've sought or received more publicity than most of the other women who were paroled when you were," we said to Tracie. "Why is that?"

"It's because I want to help. The more I get my story out, the more it's gonna reach out and touch somebody."

"Have you watched the talk shows you've been on?"

"Yes."

"Have you felt that they have achieved what you hoped they would?"

"Well, there was this one person on Maury [the *Maury Povich Show*] who said abuse doesn't justify killing somebody. I wasn't saying that it *justified* what I did. I was trying to explain why, to help and prevent. . . . Because I know there are still Tracie Englishes out there. They might be white, black, or Chinese, but there *are* Tracie Englishes out there."

As openly and honestly as the Tracie English who sat before us spoke, even she failed to recall during our interview all that she had suffered at the hands of her father. The handwritten life history that she composed while in prison details additional, specific incidents of her psychological, physical, and sexual abuse.

In that document she states, "I never told anybody [about my battering] because I thought it was my fault. This was my father, and, if *he* did these things to me, what was somebody that *didn't* love me gonna do?"

What indeed.

Gravity

The outer petals of the champagne rose
brown, stiffen, and retreat from the bud's softness.
The sky is more bitter than bright;
sister, it is our one acrid reminder:
the blood under our skin
blue above our heads.

Permeable, the tongue searches for its likeness;
flammable, the heart attempts the same but knows better.
This is not a game of evasion or invention
or even passion.
It is the arch digging for a nesting place.
It is the importance of the roof.
It is the catechism of balance versus the catechism
    of imbalance.
It is the posture necessary to right myself,
the sentient knowledge of fingertips.
It is the mother of light
and the daughter of darkness.

This room is a fossil equipped to steal imprints:
breasts, thighs, mouth, arms, neck.
Voices of escapees cool my palms.
I am the pitiful woman whose silence is stronger
than the walls of any house,
whose mind and body battle each other to impotence.

I am not a marrying ground.
I am not a nursing ground.
Do not call me miss.
Do not call me mama.
Do not beg for blessings.
I am like and unlike.

My mouth shuts easily,
but I have a word for every opening and every open space.

Lift the door and the way out alters the body's
    comprehension.
Thorns try to trap;
offspring sink to the bottom of the weeping wells;
but here we have dropped our own spirits into a pot,
here they have been clarified.
The bone rooms on the other side remain constantly
    jammed;
but in this small space even the unnamed and the
    unknown are protected.
Here we are as safe as the serpent used to be.

The language reaches far past absence,
past the fossils and the silence,
back to the sack and the spill,
to the moment of water,
to the time of the palm and the roof.
The fists forget themselves.
There is only the spray, the sticks, the hands, the scent of
    the sea at night;
The beautiful body stretches open, tunnels far into dark-
    ness, and then rises
to cut plainly the shoreline and the skyline.

Here the dead petals split from the heart are wings.
Our bodies provide balance:
we are flight;
we are our own grounding.
We have come to the place without the serpent.
The hands wrung tight as linen open.
Stand quiet for a moment.
Listen as the words of the bone rooms
gasp on the cold stone floor.

Listen as a few of the stubborn hearts alter.
Listen to the fear run out;
soon it will only be memory.

Jan Freeman

Excerpted from The American Voice Anthology *(Univ. Press of Kentucky, 1998) and reprinted with the permission of the* American Voice *and Jan Freeman.*

Montilla Seewright

It was a muggy May morning in 1998 before we finally met Montilla Seewright. We had talked with her half a dozen times or more the year before to schedule, confirm, then reschedule interview dates, but as each appointment arose some catastrophe had caused her to cancel or simply to not show. The fact that Montilla couldn't claim more than transient addresses, and so not even a phone of her own, hadn't helped, and she swore that at least one public housing official hadn't wanted us to interview her and had failed to return our phone messages or to deliver our mail. The accuracy of Montilla's assumptions mattered little in the long run, though, as once a subsidized apartment in Louisville's Newburg neighborhood became available, Montilla moved again. It was in that first-floor, red-brick residence facing southeast Louisville's Rangeland Road that, thanks to Marsha Weinstein's intervention, we finally met Montilla. Acting as our go-between, Marsha, to whom a fond Montilla continued to send occasional notes, had driven across town to tack a memo to Montilla's door. The message alerted her to our impending visit, and when we arrived that Monday morning after more than a year of thwarted meeting dates, Montilla was at last living in a place that she called home.

She'd covered her walls with colorful artwork, and she'd decorated her refrigerator door with plump and sassy pig magnets. The three of us pulled up chairs to Montilla's kitchen table and talked for an hour or so before sharp, staccato cries from her bedroom alerted us to Yasmine's, Montilla's almost-two-year-old daughter's, awakening. After Yasmine joined us, her rhythmic, raucous demands for attention interrupted her mother's recollections. In fact, the baby's exuberant crying and crawling, her stretching to reach our recording equipment and to grab our pens and to grasp what she could of the adult world gathered before her, constituted a surreal counterpoint to Montilla's accounts of abuse, abandonment, and addiction. Plunged into that vortex and trapped in a vicious spiral of decline, Montilla had made, by her own admission, error upon error, mistake after mistake. Yasmine, she said, had resulted from her last miscalculation in judgment, a short-lived romance initiated after Montilla's 1996 parole from prison. Yet Montilla said that she considered her youngest child not a cipher or a problem, but a fat and feisty prize.

At the time of our interview, Montilla, a willowy African American woman, was still a few years away from her fortieth birthday. She'd been born in Louisville in 1962, the third in a family of four children sired by three different fathers. Montilla's mother's only marriage was to a man she'd wed when Montilla was four. According to Montilla, Clarence McClaine, an army commander, forever changed Montilla's life, as well as the lives of her siblings and mother. "He came into our lives like we were his cadets in the army," Montilla said. "It was a nightmare when my mother married him. Physical abuse, mental abuse, just torture."

Montilla moved with her family to Kansas and Texas, Clarence's army assignments, before returning to Louisville, and she described being made to rise daily at 5 a.m. to dress and to eat breakfast; latecomers would go without food. Montilla remembers Clarence's constant refusal to let the children drink from cups; instead, she said, they were forced to capture what they could in their hands. At Christmas, Montilla and the siblings her mother brought to the marriage, as well as the five additional children that Montilla's mother eventually had with her husband, were told by Clarence, "Santa Claus don't come to this house because you all bad." Each year December 25 would pass without a tree, without a family meal, without gifts. However, Montilla stressed that Christmas had been special before her mother married Clarence. As we listened to Montilla, it seemed that all the joy went out of her life after the arrival of Clarence, a lack that would later be exacerbated by her great-aunt's behavior.

Montilla told us she was eight when Clarence started asking her, "If I can't have sex with you, why do you have to live in my house?" But Montilla claims that Clarence never attacked her sexually, even though, she says, he sexually abused her mother.

"Was this when he was drinking?" we asked. "No," said Montilla. "When he was drinking he wouldn't speak to you."

Montilla described how Clarence hit her mother, Shirley, when she was pregnant. "He'd push her toward the TV—choke her and stuff." While in prison Montilla wrote, "[When we lived in Texas] I [once] made a promise that if he hit my mother again, I'd kill him. One day I came home . . . and he was fighting my mother. I got my brother's bat and started hitting him in the head. I hit him so hard that I knocked him out. He just lay there on the floor. My mother gathered us all up and took us to a friend's house to stay. The next morning we went home. He told my mother he was sorry and he would never do that again. He lied."

When one of Montilla's sisters came home late from a date, Montilla remembers that Clarence shot a 357 Magnum through the ceiling. "The bullet came through the upstairs and put a big hole right by the closet," Montilla said.

According to Montilla, her great-grandmother, her mother's grandmother, proved the family's sole salvation. "When [Clarence] would put us out in the middle of the night, my [great-]grandmother would call and tell us to catch a cab and come down there [Cotter Homes, a Louisville public housing project] and stay with her. . . . My mother told my grandmother she felt she should get a divorce."

We asked Montilla what Clarence would do when the family fled to Cotter Homes.

"He would either call, and my [great-]grandmother would say, 'No, you can't speak to her, and don't call my house,'" she said, "or he would come down there with a gift—candy, roses. You know—trying to lure her back in. He would tell her, 'Oh, I'm so sorry. It will never happen again.'"

"Did she believe it?" we asked.

"Yeah."

"Every time?"

"Yeah."

But, Montilla said, in 1978, when her great-grandmother died, Shirley began to drink and take prescription tranquilizers. According to Montilla, a severely depressed Shirley saw alcohol and pills as her only means of escape. "My [great-]grandmother died in '78, and my mother drank all the way up until about 1983," she said.

Shirley had raised her children Catholic; they were parishioners of St. Anthony's Church and attended Catholic schools. Montilla commented that even though Shirley went to Sunday mass, neither the rituals nor the homilies appeared to effect much response. Yet in 1983, Montilla believes, a miracle occurred. "One day . . . it was Derby Day, and my mother had been in bed for . . . months. She wouldn't even come out of [her] room. . . . She just got so little 'til we thought she was just going to die because she wasn't eating. Then . . . my sister said, 'Come on, Momma. I'm going to take you to church with me. There's this minister. He's laying hands on people and you need to go.' [Mama] got dressed. She left. She came back in. . . . She threw away all the beer. . . . She went outside and started throwing it in the garbage can and breaking up all the bottles. She said, 'God's going to help me, but *he* cannot come around us.'"

The "he" to whom Shirley referred was Clarence McClaine, who taunted Shirley's newfound religion as well as her fresh resolve. "Oh my God," Montilla said. "[Clarence] told her she was a fool. Why would she believe in Christ? There was no such thing as God. . . . Why would she believe in something she couldn't see?"

But in the late 1980s, Shirley, now strengthened and focused, filed for divorce. Montilla recalls how Clarence threatened to kill her mother, how he broke into the house perhaps to make good his threat, and how the police intervened. After that, said Montilla, Clarence left Shirley alone. In 1990 the family learned that Clarence had died.

"Had Clarence himself ever been abused?" we asked. Montilla replied that he had, that he'd been raised by a tyrannical father who'd beaten his mother and who'd provided her a weekly allowance of ten dollars to purchase food for his family of thirteen. But when Clarence married Shirley, she added, Clarence took his father's restrictive treatment one step further. Instead of providing too few funds to meet the family's needs, he offered her no money at all, he refused her transportation, and after their first few years of marriage, he forbade her to work. According to Montilla, Clarence not only purchased their groceries but he also appointed himself the family's sole liaison with the outside world.

We asked whether Clarence's abusiveness had extended to his work. "Yes," said Montilla, "he'd started drinking. He'd started getting incident reports where he was running into jeeps, hitting trees, paying $500 for a tree if he destroyed it in the army. [His superiors] would send him to AA [Alcoholics Anonymous]. He wouldn't go. He'd come right out of AA with two six-packs and brag about it." Yet Montilla noted that any reprimand that Clarence suffered fell far short of a military discharge; Clarence McClaine retired from the U.S. Army after serving thirty years.

There's no question that Montilla's stepfather terrified her from the time he entered her life, when she was four, until he died, when she was twenty-eight. But the familial abuse that most haunts her, she insists, was not by Clarence McClaine, but by her beloved great-grandmother's twin sister, a woman to whom she refers as Auntie.

In the life history that Montilla wrote while incarcerated, she revived the image of her great-aunt, who, she declared, "destroyed her life":

"My aunt babysat my brother and I. She was very abusive with me. My brother was spoiled rotten and got his way about everything. If he didn't happen to get his way about something, then he'd run and tell [our] aunt on me.

"I remember one day in particular when my brother ran off and told my aunt [that] I was going to run away. She came out on the porch and grabbed me by the arm. 'Bitch, you aren't going to run nowhere.' When she got me into the house she slapped me so hard . . . I saw black spots. When I started crying she yelled at me to shut up and I told her 'No!' She took me to the hallway closet and put me in it. Then she locked the door on me. I started beating on the door and screaming, I was so scared. Then my brother unlocked the door and let me out. My aunt came running from the living room demanding to know why he let the 'Little Bitch' out. So I spoke up and said that I had to use the bathroom. She told me no, then she locked me back in the closet.

"I didn't cry or scream, I just sat on the floor. Then I went to the bathroom on myself. After a really long time she came and let me out. When she saw that my shorts were wet, I told her I couldn't help it; I had to use the bathroom.

"She took me into the bathroom and ran some water in the tub. She told me not to get in until she got back. When she came back she had a switch in her hand. She started hitting me with it and yelling at me, 'You're a bad little bitch and this will teach you a lesson.' When she finally stopped hitting me she put me in the really hot water in the tub. With all those fresh switch marks, the water burned me real bad. When I started to cry she took me out of the tub. When she took me out of the tub she put some soap into my vagina and wouldn't let me get it out. She told me since I was so bad I had to go back into the closet. So after she mopped the closet out she locked me back in there. I didn't make a sound. I just stayed really quiet and prayed my 'Hail Mary, full of Grace' prayers."

Montilla said that she felt that God didn't love her because of all the bad things that happened to her. "People said that you're not supposed to be angry with God, but I said, 'Why didn't He protect me?' I used to say for a long time, 'God, you didn't love me; why'd you let her hurt me?' When [Auntie] would wash me, she would put soap in my vagina and never wash it out. I would say, 'It's burning me.' She said, 'Well, it's gonna burn you all day long.' She would put my clothes on and put me back in the closet to stay until she knew it was time for my mother to get off from work."

Her mother's late-afternoon arrivals provided Montilla's only respite, other than weekends, from her great-aunt. While Montilla's verbal and written stories often reveal statements that appear contradictory, her reports about her great-aunt remain consistent.

Montilla's great-aunt babysat her and her brother while their mother worked. She wrote, "I started school when I was five. I thought [my battering] would stop then, but it didn't. . . . [Auntie] still had to watch me after school until my mother got home. One day my big sister was sick and stayed home. When I came home from school that day I was so glad she was there. My sister caught my aunt beating on me and told her not to hit me anymore. [Auntie] made my sister go to her room and then she hurt me really bad. She backhanded me so hard that she busted my mouth. When my mother got home, [Auntie] told her that I fell.

"My aunt did something worse to me than beating me. She sexually abused me. When I was real little, around four, she started taking me to the bed and undressing me. She'd lay me down and stick her fingers in and out of my vagina and rectum. She would lick on my vagina and make me do that to her. This didn't stop until I was about eight years old."

Medical documents that Montilla provided, including psychiatric and psychological reports, tell the same story. Montilla believes that her great-aunt's abuse destroyed her life. Indeed, the physical and mental battering that she suffered may well have rendered her incapable of trust. She recalled, "I would want to tell my mother, and then I would think about what [my great-aunt] said: 'If you tell anybody, I'll kill you, and they'll never know that I killed you.' She took all my dolls and told my mama . . . that I threw them away." Deprived of her dolls and of any hope of rescue by a responsible adult, Montilla resigned herself to living in a virtual prison in which her nightmares and her fears would prove more frightening than did any physical confinement.

Montilla was twelve when her great-aunt died. Yet instead of her abuser's death freeing Montilla, the news triggered memories so painful that, to escape her thoughts, she overdosed on drugs. Obtaining the pills, Valium and other prescription tranquilizers, was easy. Montilla said that her mother, who, at the time, still depended on drugs and alcohol as her own means of escape, served as her role model. "My mother used to take pills," Montilla told us. "She would go to the doctor and get [them]. I said, 'Momma, why do you take those pills that make you sleep?' She said, 'Because I don't want to think about some things.' So, I just felt that taking pills was a way out."

"Would you take just one or two?" we asked.

"Oh, no. I was taking six or seven at a time. I walked around one day not knowing that I had been asleep for a week without waking up. My stepfather tried to have me committed, but my mother wouldn't let him."

When asked what her Mother thought when Montilla didn't wake up for a week, Montilla replied, "This is what happened. . . . God must have been with me. I came in on Sunday, and my [great-]grandmother had fixed Sunday din-ner. I told her, 'I'm going to lay down and not wake back up no more.' She said, 'What do you mean?' I said, 'I won't be back up no more, 'cause when I lay down, I'm laying down for good.' So I had went to the bathroom . . . [in] my [great-]auntie's house, because she wasn't at home and my sister was at her house. So, I went in her medicine cabinet and stole all these pills. I said, 'Well, I'm just going to kill myself.' . . . I poured me some [liquor] and mixed it with a little water. I went in the bathroom and I took the pills. It seemed like forever, but when the pills really hit me, I just lay in bed. It was like everything had shut down. They were shaking me, beating me. They would walk me. [My mother] said the last day, on Wednesday, I sat straight up in bed and said, 'Well, God, if you loved me, why didn't you let me die?'"

We asked Montilla why, if her family loved her, they hadn't taken her to a hospital.

"Because my Momma was afraid they would put me away. She was afraid . . . if they did, [of what] I would tell these people. . . . Is there something going on in the family that's making me do this? You know, people say all this is hush hush. You don't go out in public and tell this. You keep this in the family. Our family was like that."

"And after you came out of that?" we asked.

"I never took another pill in my life, until I was put on medication, [because] I figured out then you can't stop the events that are going to happen. Things happen for a reason."

Montilla recalls age sixteen as the next turning point in her life, the year she entered ninth grade. She swore that she had remained a virgin until then, but that a boy a year or two older than she, a friend from the local roller skating rink, encouraged her, on her birthday, to drink too much rum. She said he spiked her drink with a substance that made her woozy, after which he raped her. According to Montilla, that single encounter with him resulted in her first pregnancy, and she dropped out of school when she gave birth to her daughter, Chantilla.

But before Chantilla's birth, when a doctor confirmed Montilla's condition, Montilla's life, as she described it, continued to disintegrate. She recalled that her mother literally discharged her fury by shooting at the boy and by insisting that he marry Montilla. His father intervened, declaring that his son would not be forced to marry *any* woman. But her mother's wrath targeted Montilla, too. Telling Montilla that she'd expected more from her than from her other children, Shirley scolded her daughter by flinging from the stovetop a skillet of steaming pork chops, followed by a scalding spoon. And Clarence, Montilla's stepfather, relegated her to the porch to sleep until Chantilla was born. After the birth, he commanded Montilla to leave his house and to survive wherever and however she could.

Meanwhile, the boy from the skating rink, who was first drawn to Montilla, as she was to him, by their shared experiences of familial abuse, turned increasingly violent toward Montilla until his battering of her became ritual. Montilla remembered how, for nine years, she showed up in Louisville's Norton Hospital emergency room as a bruised and black-eyed regular. She said, "I went to Norton so much and lied to these people that I'm having all these accidents 'til this one doctor . . . said, 'Let me tell you something. I've never seen a woman come in my emergency room every other night with a bump, a bad bruise, or a footprint on her chest and tell me that she's fallen.' He said, 'I'm going to ask you something, and I'm not going to tell anybody, but is that man holding that little girl the one that's abusing you?' I said, 'Yeah, but please don't tell him I told you, because you'll get me killed.' He said, 'That's all I needed to know.'"

Despite his promise to keep Montilla's secret, the physician phoned the police, who came that night to Norton and arrested her abuser. Montilla recalled, "[A policeman] walked up and said, 'You Montilla Seewright?' I said, 'Yes.' He said, 'Is this your boyfriend?' I said, 'Yes.' He said, 'Well, . . . you're under arrest.' [The boyfriend] said, 'For what? What did I do?' [The policeman] said, 'Well, right now, I have a list of things you've done to her.'"

As soon as the boyfriend was released from jail, he broke into her apartment. An attorney had suggested to Montilla that in order to avoid her abuser she give him a twenty-five-minute head start exiting the courthouse. His head start granted him time to beat Montilla to her Village West apartment where, when she arrived, the sound of her television alerted her to his presence. She said, "So I looked in the bedroom and I thought, 'Oh, my God! How did he get in this house? He don't have a key.' So he said, 'Yeah, well, didn't nobody see me come in. Now you've got to pay.' I mean, he beat me almost to death in that apartment. First he started choking me on the bed, so I started trying to fight him back. Then my hair was long; that's the reason I don't like long hair. He grabbed me by the hair and was . . . kicking me, stomping me, and telling me that because of me [he went] to prison. . . . Finally, he calmed down. He said, 'Well, since nobody seen me, I should just kill you and leave you in this apartment to die.' I said, 'Well, then, if you feel like that, then I want you to do that, 'cause I want to die.' So then he leaves and I didn't see him for a week, and then he told me he got a new job. He was the only person I know who would work, and then he would lose his paycheck. How can you lose your paycheck *every* Friday?"

It wasn't long before Montilla learned, she said, that the break-in had been abetted by an apartment security guard related to her boyfriend by marriage, who had unlocked Montilla's apartment with a master key. Montilla soon learned, too, that her boyfriend had been spending his pay on diet pills known on the street as black widows, tiny black capsules the size of small roaches that provide an adrenaline rush.

Yet despite her boyfriend's alleged deceit and violent behavior, two months after he "almost killed her," Montilla invited him to move in with her. "I know this is going to sound strange and off the wall," she said, "but I felt that the only reason a person beat me [was that] they loved me. He *had* to love me. He was beating me for a reason, so he loved me."

But Montilla admits that contrary to her fantasies, their living together failed to change her boyfriend. She said he told her he worked at a downtown hotel, but he actually earned what money he had pushing marijuana. Montilla's brother tipped her off regarding her boyfriend's illegal activities, then drove her downtown to observe his dealing. Later, after Montilla confronted him with what she'd seen, he beat her, she claims, with curtain rods—sharp metal shafts that proved particularly effective in slashing and lacerating her into submission. She wrote, "The first beating was after my cousin's funeral. [He] was dragging me down the street, kicking me all the way. He tore all my clothes off . . . and there I stood on the street. . . . When we got home he beat me with a curtain rod. He stomped me and kicked me. . . . I had no idea I was pregnant again, and when he kicked [me] I started bleeding really bad." That beating, which caused Montilla to begin to miscarry, resulted in an abortion.

Ever since dropping out of the ninth grade, Montilla had wanted to return to school, and, she said, when she started working as a housekeeper for a woman who encouraged Montilla to obtain her GED, she did. Later, in the early 1980s, Montilla enrolled in Louisville's Mid-America College of Funeral Services, thinking that mastering the mortuary trade might secure her independence in a field in which "no one talked back." But her boyfriend refused to help her study for tests, so when she ran into an old male friend who offered to quiz her for an hour, she accepted. Montilla told us that she and her male friend were sitting in her living room practicing test questions when her abuser walked in. After Montilla's friend left, her boyfriend railed that Montilla had "totally disrespected him" by spending time with another man, and she stated he once again beat her with her own curtain rods, leaving scars she still bears.

Montilla's attempts to hide those wounds while dressing according to her mortuary school's strict requirements met with mixed success. A friend from school noticed Montilla's bruises and her efforts to hide them beneath long sleeves and high collars. She pressed Montilla to confess her abuse. Montilla confided in her classmate and found relief, she said, in finally sharing her secret. She also recalled the day when Montilla's confidante confronted her boyfriend. "One day," she said, "[my friend] came over and said [to him], 'So why are you abusive to her?' [He replied,] 'Well, because she wants to go to school and be somebody.' But after my friend left, [my boyfriend] smashed [my head] into the wall because I'd told my business. . . . He told me [my friend] couldn't come back to my house no more."

Montilla's battering continued until 1983 when, despite her boyfriend's threats and objections, she graduated from mortuary school. Her achievement provided Montilla more than a trade; it gave her the courage to command her abuser, once and for all, to move out. She told him that she no longer needed him, and even though he assured Montilla's mother that he'd kill Montilla if he ever saw her again, he "just faded away."

For a year, then, following her 1983 graduation, Montilla hoped her fate had changed. She found a job working for a local funeral home, but just months later she quit, citing dissatisfaction with her employer.

Soon thereafter Montilla returned to her former housekeeping job, a position she maintained until, in her mid-twenties, she became pregnant with her second daughter, Sheetara. According to Montilla, Sheetara's father, Ralph, is the only man in her life who never abused her. Yet she went on to say that Ralph, a friend from her past to whom she was reintroduced by her brother, failed to tell her, when he asked her to be his girlfriend, that for more than twenty years he'd been living with a woman who he introduced to Montilla as his sister. And Montilla, he assured his girlfriend, was "just a friend." Montilla said that her relationship with Ralph lasted for a couple of years and then evaporated, until the late 1980s when Ralph reappeared and proposed.

With two children to support, Montilla survived for a while on welfare before resuming her housekeeping job. She said that her life had begun to assume an even keel when, on the next New Year's Eve, she returned to her childhood Hill Street neighborhood to attend a party. There she encountered a former acquaintance, Roy. Montilla wrote, "We danced and he asked me if I had any children. I told him about my two daughters. He took me home that night and tried to kiss me, but I wouldn't let him. I told him that even though I knew him from the old neighborhood, I didn't know him that well yet. So I gave him my number and told him he could call me sometime.

"The next day he called and then later came over to dinner. When he showed up he had a bottle of red wine with him. I called the girls out to meet him. After we had dinner, he helped me do the dishes. While we were watching cable he tried to kiss me, but I wouldn't let him. I told him I thought he was very aggressive. He left around 11 p.m. and then about 11:30 p.m. he called me and asked me to be his lady. I told him 'yes.'

"I wasn't what you would call sexually active. I waited until July 1989 to have sex with him even though we started dating in 1988. In September 1989 I told him I was pregnant and he flipped out on me. He started hitting me with his fists and I hit him back. My mother always taught me that if a man hits me, I'd better hit him back. It didn't do any good. He beat the hell out of me. When he left I had a black eye and a busted lip. I'd started spotting blood. When I went to the doctor he told me to stay off of my feet and get lots of rest, so I did.

"Two days later Roy came and said he was sorry. He asked if we could talk and I said yes. He kept talking and talking and finally talked his way into moving into my house. I was so scared that he'd hit on me again. I was right.

"I had to call my brother and he came over to talk to Roy. After their talk, Roy left. Then the calls started. He kept telling me over and over again that he was going to kill me and 'that unborn bastard.' I got my number changed. He came over and broke out all of my windows. I replaced the windows and moved to Shively. No one knew where I lived except my family. My cousin lived around the corner from him.

"One day I was at my cousin's house and when I went up the front steps something hit me really hard in my back. I turned around and he hit me in the jaw. . . . My cousin's whittling knife was laying there on the porch, so I picked it up and tried to stab Roy. But he grabbed the sharp end and wound up cutting his hand. He pushed me down and started kicking me with his hard shoes on. My mother heard me screaming, and she came running from the house. She was yelling at him to get off of her daughter. Roy said, 'I'm going to kill this bitch!' Then he ran away. After this incident my mother wanted me to get a warrant on him, so I went and swore one out. I was scared of him, so I never went to court, and so he never got served with a warrant.

"I started a new job and things were looking up when my cousin betrayed me and told him where I lived. He showed up at my apartment one day while I was at work and my sister who was there babysitting for me told him that he wasn't welcome in that house. When I got off of the bus that night at 7:15 he was waiting for me. I tried to ignore him; I didn't say anything to him. He started in on me, 'Yeah, Bitch, you tried to have me locked up, but my friend stopped the warrant!' I always knew he had some police friends, but I never knew who they were. The Shively Police Department was right in front of my apartment house, so I went inside and got a policeman. When we came out he was gone.

"By November I had broken down again and let him move back in. Things were going great, [but] in December my job ran out. When I came in from work the morning of my last day, there was Roy, in bed with my daughter. I started screaming at him to get out of that bed. He slapped me hard and I hit the floor. I just knew that he had molested my oldest daughter. He left and after I calmed down I called my mother and told her what went on. As it has turned out, I was right. I know now that he did, in fact, molest my daughter. She has since confessed this to me.

"Christmas and New Year's past [sic] quietly. In February somebody started calling me, saying 'Bitch, I'm going to kill you.' My cousin had betrayed me again and given Roy my phone number.

"In March I had a baby shower and he came over. I wasn't afraid because my sisters and friends were there, and I wasn't alone. We talked for a couple of minutes and then I told him he could come back over later. He did come over later. I told him that my youngest daughter's father had asked me to marry him. Roy knew that I was still seeing him from time to time.

"In April I had the baby [Roy, Jr.]. I came home on Monday and on Tuesday night he jumped on me and blacked my eye. I called the police and told them and they told me to take a warrant out on him. I knew that it wouldn't do any good. He knew every move I made and seemed to spend all his time and energy stalking me and terrorizing me.

"In August I was standing in a parking lot at a shopping center talking to a friend of mine. All at once her eyes got real big . . . so I asked her what was wrong. She said, 'Roy's behind you and he's running toward you.' There were some black people there and a black boy that was getting carts in. Roy was pulling my hair, beating me in the face, and kicking me. I tried hard to fight him back. Some white man started screaming, 'You get off of her!' The man ran toward me to try to help me. A policeman was coming out of the store and the white man got him and tried to tell him what he saw. Just think—this man tried so hard to help me, and Roy could have very easily killed him. I used to pray and ask God to let me see this white man again so that I could thank him properly, but I never saw him again.

"On August 11, my brother found my stepfather dead in his apartment. Roy came over and I saw a side of him I never knew was there. Roy started crying because I was crying. I was crying because of all the terrible things my stepfather had done to me. I was thinking of some old memories of the man that used to be my stepfather, who was now dead. Like the time he kicked the bathroom door in and tried to yank the towel off of me. My mother was scream-ing at him to leave me alone and he said, 'I'm not fucking her, why should she take a bath at my house?' All kinds of terrible things he'd done to me were going through my mind.

"On August 15 my brother got shot in the head. Having this happen almost killed me inside. He lived, but he has many problems from it. He stays very depressed all the time and has almost no memory. . . . He has seizures all the time.

"Roy was trying hard to destroy me. All the beatings I'd taken from him were taking their toll on me. He was breaking into my apartment. He'd call [at] all hours of the night just to wake me up and tell me he was going to kill me.

"When I couldn't take any more of being terrorized I took a bunch of pills. I wanted to die so I didn't have to go thru this anymore. My kids called my sister and then she and her boyfriend took me to Norton's hospital. When I woke up I had a long tube down my throat. I pulled the tube out and just begged those people to let me go on and die.

"When I went home from the hospital Roy was hiding in the closet. I was laying there on the bed and the closet door opened and he stepped out. He said, 'Bitch, no one seen me come in and I should just kill you.' I started scream-ing and he hit me in the mouth. I started to bleed and he started to choke me.

I just laid there not moving. He finally stopped and said, 'Mousie, I'm sorry. I don't know what's wrong with me.' He left and I thought it was for good. So I thought.

"I always straightened up my house before I went to bed at night. I made sure that the ashtrays were clean and the messes all cleaned up. All of a sudden I started finding cigarette butts in the ashtrays and a glass in the sink. I thought for sure I was losing my mind. This went on until November fifth.

"He called me and asked if we could talk. I said yes. When he got there my mother and brother were in the kitchen, so we went into the bedroom to talk. I told him that I'd set a date to get married [to Ralph]. He turned the TV up loud and started twisting my arm up behind my back, telling me, 'Bitch, before you marry him, you'll die first.' He threw me down on the bed and started choking me. I managed to scream and my mother busted through the door. She yelled at him to get off of me. He said to my mother, 'Mama Shirley, I'm going to come back and kill this bitch!' My brother was crying because he wanted to kill Roy right then. My mother told Roy to leave and not ever show up again.

"The next day I went to the doctor and the nurse asked me what happened to my neck. When I told her, she told me that he was trying to kill me. She told me to leave him alone before he did kill me.

"I was so thrilled about the fact that I was about to marry my second daughter's daddy. On the following Wednesday I took the kids over to my sister's to stay. The phone rang when I got back. 'Bitch, I know you're home alone.' Click. I got a big knife out of the kitchen drawer and turned off all the lights. The phone rang all night long, but I didn't answer it. I sat up all night on the couch holding that knife listening to the phone ring and not answering it.

"The next morning I got into bed after it got light outside. The phone rang and I answered it. It was my daughter's father. I told him what had gone on all night. He told me I wouldn't have to worry much longer. We were going to get married on Thanksgiving.

"But Roy . . . destroyed my life and my future that night. I was already in bad shape. I was under the care of a doctor, being treated for depression. I'd been taking anti-depressant medication for awhile when November eighth rolled around.

"Roy entered my apartment without my knowledge. I was in the shower and when I finished I went into the bedroom to get dressed. Roy stepped out of the closet and we started yelling at one another. He pushed me down on the bed and I fought to get away from him with all my might. I kicked him in his groin and he released me. I ran from him and he caught me in the hallway. He threw me down on the floor and had sex with me in my rectum.

"When he got finished with me he left. I laid on the floor bleeding from my rectum. I laid there for a while. I finally was able to get up and I went to call my mother. She wasn't at home. I went and took some of the prescribed medicine. I just could not believe that I was raped and sodomized by my baby's father. I kept taking pills to dull the pain—physical, mental, and emotional pain. I took pills until I finally lost touch with reality.

"My very next memory is of waking up in a hospital. My mother told me that Roy had been shot and that I did it. Later I learned that Roy was shot while at his workplace and was hit in the chest. During surgery he had a stroke that has caused him to be paralyzed in one arm and disabled. [Since then] I haven't had any contact with him."

Psychiatrists and other healthcare professionals concur that people can repress traumatic memories. In our visit with Montilla and in her request for clemency, she was consistent in saying that she didn't remember shooting Roy. But she did say she must have been responsible for Roy's injuries because she had been recorded by the store's video camera. She could not deny that she had entered the convenience store and had fired the gun.

As grim as Montilla's written account of her life with Roy is, in conversation with us she emphasized that drugs and alcohol, as well as abuse, had dominated their relationship. She told us that Roy, to whom she referred as a cocaine addict and an alcoholic, worked at convenience stores only long enough to obtain enough cash to support his habit. And she said that while living with Roy, she, too, remained high on drugs, on prescription medications like those she'd abused at age twelve as well as on Roy's illegal stash. She indicated that drugs served as psychic bandages because she "never knew when [she] was going to get beat up." Numerous pills, washed down by straight gin, numbed her pain and induced blackouts like the one she experienced on the night she shot Roy. Referring to that night, Montilla told us, "All I remember, . . . after he did this to me, [was] taking medicine and going to bed. I took Ativan, Prozac. I had a number of drugs in my body. . . . The man in the ambulance told my sister that I took thirteen doses over the amount of medication I was supposed to take. He said, 'She doesn't even know she is in the world.'"

Montilla told us that had she not, during her trial, seen the video of herself shooting Roy in the Five Star Food Mart at Thirty-eighth Street and Broadway in Louisville's West End, no one could have convinced her that she had pulled the trigger. Not being able to remember anything about that night after overdosing still causes Montilla to obsess, she stressed, over the same questions that her attorneys, as well as Roy's, wanted answered. "How could I live down in Shively [Louisville's South End], how could I get from Shively all the way down to the West End?" she questioned, as though hoping that one of us would hit on the answer. "I didn't," she pointed out, "have a car." Montilla added that she'd asked a psychologist if he would hypnotize her so she could recall the events of that night. "I want to remember because I want to know for myself," she said. "I don't want to go by what people are telling me. I need to know. [To] this day . . . I still want to know." But Montilla said that her psychologist refused her request on the grounds that being hypnotized would endanger her.

Montilla told us that she's received ongoing mental health care since before she shot Roy, since the occasion a nurse realized that Montilla's swollen neck, purple with handprints, was the mark of a strangulation attempt. Montilla insisted that she's been diagnosed manic-depressive and that she takes several prescription drugs to cope with her condition. Yet Montilla also referred to having heard voices most of her life, to having heard voices in her head instructing her to hurt herself, to punish herself for being inherently bad. When Montilla mentioned her voices, we wondered whether she could be schizophrenic, a condition manifested by, among other indices, internal voices, but a condition that cannot coexist with manic depression. But further reflection caused us to believe that Montilla's voices—their messages the very real admonishments she'd heard all her life—might well have been internalized as surrogate abusers, as an echoing chorus that could chant familiar litanies in the absence of actual batterers. "You are why my marriage to Clarence McClaine failed," Montilla said her mother had told her. "You little bitch, you made me hurt you!" Montilla said her stepfather, great-aunt, and all but one of her boyfriends—the man who spoke a caring language she couldn't comprehend—had told her. Montilla Seewright's cursing, masochistic voices, like Karen Stout [Stelzer's] abuses since her parole, could have been created as subconscious self-protection by a shattered ego in need of a familiar crutch. And the voices that Montilla said encourage her to punish herself may encourage her in an admittedly unhealthy but curiously effective way to alleviate her guilt and to gain power over her immediate destiny. By cutting herself, Montilla substituted physical pain for psychic suffering. A plausible explanation of Montilla's voices may be that what she calls voices are actually personified compulsions, cries that constitute an intensely human response to the inhumanity of abuse. Montilla's diagnosis differs from one court document to the next, so we cannot supply definitive data regarding her mental health. But it makes sense to us that Montilla would internalize the messages that shaped her and that she would find her abusers' commands difficult to silence.

Asked to describe her experiences during her arrest, detention, and trial, Montilla responded that no attorney was ever present while the police questioned her. Asked how the police interrogated her, Montilla replied, "That man told me, 'Sign a piece of paper so I can read you your rights.' And I signed a piece of paper; when I was down to Sixth District, I just signed it." She said her medication had made her unable to focus.

Montilla was taken to the top floor of the Hall of Justice, which then served the city of Louisville as a place to hold people awaiting trial who had not yet posted bond as well as a place to house inmates serving relatively short sentences. Montilla was booked there, she said, and she added that there, too, police officers set her bail and bond. She remembers spending one night in jail and being released the next day when her mother posted bond. She lived in her home until after her trial, which took place more than a year later.

A state physician evaluated Montilla. He diagnosed her with clinical depression, but he noted that because she could distinguish right from wrong, she was competent to stand trial. Montilla said that she thought the doctor had tested her for literacy, not mental competence. She commented, "My trial started December eighth of '92. After the trial ended on Friday, which was December 11, the jury found me guilty of first-degree assault. But there were three things they could have did. First-degree assault, with a finding of extreme emotional distress, a lesser degree of assault, or a not guilty verdict." She added, "I don't understand the court system. I really don't understand that legal stuff. I really don't." When asked if she had testified on her own behalf, she answered, "I tried to, but my lawyer said it wouldn't be a good idea." Montilla's attorney may well have been right; her testifying that she could not remember anything might have been considered untruthful by jury members, and lawyers must weigh the legal risks of any action against the benefits of not taking that action. But Montilla recalled other reasons that she had been dissatisfied with her attorney. Her lawyer, she told us, spoke to the jury about himself, not about her. She also said that she had given her lawyer a list of witnesses that should be called and that the lawyer told her that he would take care of getting subpoenas so that those witnesses could testify. But, she stressed, he did not. Montilla's mother offered testimony, but Montilla claims that her mother was questioned less than five minutes.

Montilla attempted to dismiss her attorney and to hire another one at about the time of the trial. She said, "I asked [my attorney] could I get a new lawyer. He said I couldn't get a new lawyer because we were starting into the trial and the judge wouldn't change over the lawyers going into trial." Although judges can replace lawyers at their discretion, they may be reluctant to do so when a trial is about to begin or is already under way.

At some point during the trial, Montilla's attorney offered her a plea bargain. But Montilla rejected the deal, believing that she wasn't guilty. The jury for her case found her guilty, and because her act of assault occurred after Kentucky's new domestic violence laws took effect, her sentence was fifteen years.

After her conviction, Montilla stayed in the County Correctional Center for three months before she was taken to the Kentucky Correctional Institution for Women in Pee Wee Valley. When requested to describe her experiences after her arrival at prison, she provided a detailed account:

"You go to the back [of the prison] and they'll bring you in. The gates will close behind you and lock. They'll get you out of the car. They help you out . . . because you're shackled. They got you so shackled up there's no way you can get out. . . . They open the gate, you go up these steps, about eight or nine flights [of] little metal steps. You go straight in [a room], and there's [people] taking pictures, fingerprinting you and stuff, and I'm like, 'Oh, my God!' I'm down here with a bunch of women that are different personalities—I mean just different everything. I didn't want to be there. I wanted just to die. But then the night after we were fingerprinted, they decontaminated you with this crab shampoo, . . . and that night you go and you register. You go walk around and get your stuff taken care of at the canteen. Make sure your money's on the books over there, get all your paperwork done, 'cause you got to get ready to go to class and take tests all day. You're going through the fishtank, is what they call it, but you're in a blue uniform [with] pants [and a] smock, and you stay in there for up to ten days. Being so crowded, we stayed thirty days in blues, and, at that time, the voices [telling me to hurt myself] had started coming back."

Asked what life on parole had been like, Montilla responded by talking about what it means to be a convicted felon and attempt to rent an apartment. She was able to get Section 8 public housing, she said, because she told her landlady the truth about the nature of her conviction and incarceration.

Montilla spent almost four years in prison, an experience that she claims frightened her at first, then helped her once she joined the B.O.S.H. Group and began sharing with other battered women memories of her abuse.

When Montilla left prison on February 12, 1996, she intended to start over. Her plans to marry Ralph had fizzled, but thoughts of a clean slate, a new beginning, gave her hope. Yet within weeks of her release, Montilla claimed that she met up with a man she'd known before her imprisonment. She said that she became sexually involved with him before finding out about incest in his family, information that she could not reconcile with her religious or moral beliefs. Montilla broke up with this man, but not before becoming pregnant with her fourth child, Yasmine.

At eighteen months, Yasmine continued to coo, then wail, while our tape recorder rolled, and Montilla's patience with her active, vocal child appeared endless. But beyond the rainbow-splashed walls of Montilla's kitchen lay darker realities. Not long after Montilla's parole, her second daughter, she said, had attempted to stab her. Since then, that child had been in and out of mental health facilities, and at the time of our interview, she was living with Montilla's mother, who had recently informed Montilla that she'd made the twelve-year-old a doctor's appointment. She suspected that the girl had become sexually active.

At eighteen, Montilla's oldest daughter had three children and was planning to marry for the first time in August. And according to Montilla, both of her oldest daughters had been hospitalized because they, like their mother, "heard voices."

Montilla's son, Roy, Jr., was eight when we interviewed his mother. "He says he loves me," said Montilla. "He says 'Momma, when am I going to see my daddy?' It hurts me to answer that."

Montilla told us about her oldest sister's breakdown, about her younger sister's current battles with domestic violence, and about her own desire to become self-supporting. Yet, as we listened to Montilla, we heard a woman talking about having coped the only way that she believed she could. Her great-grandmother's positive influence had proved insufficient to counteract the abuse perpetrated by Auntie, her beloved great-grandmother's evil twin, or to neutralize the effects of her stepfather's daily abuse. Montilla was taught to consider herself nothing without a man, and almost every man she's encountered trampled her, then tossed her aside. At the end of our interview, Montilla recounted a conversation in which she'd offered a reason for her family's abusive behavior. In response to the question, "Did you ever do anything to your family?" Montilla said she'd replied, "Yes, I did—be born. Be born was the worstest thing that could ever happen."

Deadline

January 15, 1991

The night before war begins, and you are still here.
You can stand in a breathless cold
ocean of candles, a thousand issues of your same face
rubbed white from below by clear waxed light.
A vigil. You are wondering what it is
you can hold a candle to.

You have a daughter. Her cheeks curve
like aspects of the Mohammed's perfect pear.
She is three. Too young for candles but
you are here, this is war.
Flames covet the gold-sparked ends of her hair,
her nylon parka laughing in color,
inflammable. It has taken your whole self
to bring her undamaged to this moment,
and waiting in the desert at this moment
is a bomb that flings gasoline in a liquid sheet,
a laundress' snap overhead, wide as the ancient Tigris,
and ignites as it descends.

The polls have sung their opera of assent: the land
wants war. But here is another America,
candle-throated, sure as tide.
Whoever you are, you are also this granite anger.
In history you will be the vigilant dead
who stood in front of every war with old hearts
in your pockets, stood on the carcass of hope
listening for the thunder of its feathers.

The desert is diamond ice and only stars above us here
and elsewhere, a thousand issues of a clear waxed star,

a holocaust of heaven
and somewhere, a way out.

Barbara Kingsolver

Excerpted from The American Voice Anthology *(Univ. Press of Kentucky, 1998) and reprinted with the permission of the* American Voice *and Barbara Kingsolver.*

Epilogue

Since their appearance on the *Donahue Show*, the Sisters in Pain have had few opportunities to hear about, much less to meet with, one another. On April 4, 1997, Tracie English, Sue Melton, Sherry Pollard, Paula Richey, and Karen Stout (Stelzer), with permission from their parole officers, reunited for dinner at Masterson's, a Louisville restaurant, before attending at the University of Louisville the concert premiere of an original musical composition written, sung, and played in their honor. In an attempt to heighten public awareness and understanding of the dynamics of domestic violence, several Louisville-area social service agencies, in conjunction with arts and education organizations, served as local sponsors for a national Meet the Composer grant. The grant funded music by Louisvillian Steve Rouse with lyrics contributed by Oneida, Kentucky, writer Anne Shelby. The experimental endeavor culminated in a performance that communicated via orchestra and solo soprano the anguish of abuse and the miracle of survival.

Before that concert the paroled women gathered for a group photo taken in front of their quilt. Since its display at the 1995 Kentucky State Fair, the quilt had been in the custody of Shelly Zegart, cofounder of the Kentucky Quilt Project and the Alliance of American Quilts. Elaine Hedges, an author and women's studies scholar who, before her death in 1997, wrote about the political aspects of quilts, said of the B.O.S.H. Group's creation, "This quilt is probably the greatest icon quilt of its type because it had a measurable result in the public forum." Tracie and Karen, the Sisters whose stories have received the most media attention, resumed their public stand in that very forum, where they were again interviewed by members of the local media, WAVE-3 TV's Connie Leonard included, while their cohorts sat in silence before the patchwork depiction of their decades of abuse.

Members of the B.O.S.H. Group reunited at the University of Louisville in May 1997 for a concert held to increase public awareness concerning domestic violence. *Above, left to right,* Tracie English, Karen Stout (Stelzer), Sue Melton, and Sherry Pollard. *Below, left to right,* Chandra McElroy, Marguerite Thomas, Sherry Pollard, Sue Melton, Karen Stout (Stelzer), Tracie English, Linda Smith, and Paula Richey. Photos by Thomas R. Oates.

Another domestic violence support group established at the Kentucky Correctional Institution for Women since the B.O.S.H. Group disbanded has produced, under the auspices of Louisville art therapist and Kentucky Foundation for Women visual art grant recipient Collis Marshall, a second quilt. Its makers, like the designers of the B.O.S.H. Group quilt, indicated that their textile project, intended to provide public education, also offered catharsis and comfort to the quilt's creators. And the Sisters in Pain depicted in this book continue, of course, to experience changes in their lives.

Since her release from prison, Karen Stout (Stelzer) has relocated within her county, and, in addition to working for the attorney who first defended her, she supervises a telemarketing business at night. Sue Melton has moved, too, but not because of her health. Against medical odds, her condition continues to improve.

Teresa Gulley Hilterbrand's and Montilla Seewright's lives appear to have altered the least, but *Lexington Herald-Leader* reporter Cheryl Powell wrote in her January 1997 series that revisited the Sisters in Pain one year after their parole, "[Teresa Gulley Hilterbrand] says she doesn't trust anyone—not even her husband.

"She clings to her solitude, spending most of her days working on her tobacco and hay farm.

"After she was released from prison in February, it took her two months before she would leave her home in Fleming County to go to the grocery store.

"Most days, she wouldn't even answer the phone.

"'I don't want to be bothered,' she said. 'I don't trust people. I don't believe anyone can be trusted with anything.'"

Montilla still lives in the Louisville apartment that she felt so lucky to obtain. She's still raising Yasmine, but other of her children exhibit increasing emotional and behavioral difficulties. She's still hoping to find a job that she can tolerate and to which she can commute without owning a car of her own.

Sherry Pollard, like Sue Melton, also seems to have beaten the odds. In 1997 she married a long-distance truck driver she'd met while working at the only employment she could find—serving as a clerk on the Staunton, Illinois, truck stop's graveyard shift. Because of the conditions of her parole, Sherry was forbidden, at first, to live with her husband, who resided in Missouri. After applying for her parole supervision to be transferred out of state, she learned that she could have relocated but, after talking with her would-be Missouri parole officer, a man who, she said, threatened to watch her every move, Sherry chose to remain in Illinois. Her husband left Missouri, found employment in Illinois, and, with Sherry, bought a house. The house that she and her husband purchased includes two guest bedrooms. Sherry decorated one of those rooms for her son and the other for her daughter. She hasn't heard from them, but she's still hopeful that if and when she's released from parole, her children will contact her and will one day stay in the rooms she's remade.

In 1998 Tracie English married a Cuban refugee and gave birth to twin girls. But a few months after the babies arrived, Tracie filed for divorce. Her husband had begun to batter her, she said, so she initiated legal steps to leave him.

Margie Marcum remains close to her mountain home, locked in, like Teresa, by such fear and distrust that she refused to have her photograph taken for this book. Neither her advocate nor her counselor could convince Margie that our publishing her picture would not return Margie to prison.

The other women to whom, at Governor Jones's behest, the parole board granted clemency—Charlotte Haycraft, Mary Ann Long, Johnetta McNair, Paula Richey, and Martina Stillwell—continue, like their above-named Sisters, to live lives that are far from ideal but that have remained free of further convictions. Their lack of education, trust in themselves and in others, self-esteem, and money keep them mired in habits and habitats that are difficult to transcend. But occasional reports that one or more of the Sisters have found better jobs or have negotiated counseling that they can afford offers hope to counter hushed rumors that one or more among them have also entered new abusive relationships, dependencies that shame them into lives bound by secrecy, isolation, and depression.

Significant, though, is the fact that the paroled Sisters' legal records have remained clear of additional charges. Chandra McElroy, their prison counselor, who later became a classification and treatment supervisor at the Kentucky State Reformatory, a men's facility, and who currently cares for her two young children at home, commented that, while working in a women's prison, she preferred counseling women who had murdered their abusers to counseling women who had committed crimes that she viewed as more calculated—crimes such as forging checks or dealing drugs. "Someone who has been convicted of murder or manslaughter—that's usually a once-in-a-lifetime thing. And I don't call [killing an abuser] a crime of passion," she said. "I just call it a heat-of-the-moment situation—you know, fearing for their lives. There's no doubt that these women will never do something like this again. But as far as writing [bad] checks or using drugs—in my profession, I see such women come in and go out [of prison], come in and go out. These women just begged for one chance, and they're doing great."

Sherry Currens, executive director of the Kentucky Domestic Violence Association, has on numerous occasions voiced the message that she believes to be most crucial concerning the Sisters in Pains' parole: "I think it's vital that [the public] understand what actually happened. [These women] weren't simply pardoned. There was a parole process. I think, clearly, the big issue that everybody has is why didn't [these women] leave [their abusive relationships]? If I could impart anything in the world to anyone—or everyone—it would be to make them understand that. When I started this job, I had no concept of that. Now, after having been here for ten years, I don't see how anyone *ever* leaves, especially when [the abusers] are as violent and volatile as the ones we're talking about in these situations."

Our question, too, after having heard the Sisters in Pains' graphic and poignant testimonies and after having learned from the professionals who worked so closely with their cases is, like Currens's question, how could these women have survived? Clearly, any crimes that they committed cannot and should not be excused. The women themselves stress that fact. But neither should explanations be confused with excuses. Excuses can be ignored; explanations require research. Violent confrontations that offer women or men the choice of saving their own or their sons' and daughters' lives by assaulting or killing potential murderers can no longer be condoned as the single option for survival open to too many individuals in a civilized society. And a judicial system that discourages attorneys and their clients from entering as evidence testimony about their abuse requires reform.

Once we, as increasingly interdependent citizens of an ever-smaller world, acknowledge that we do not each, after all, share equal opportunities or facilities to resolve our dilemmas, we may begin to shift the burden of moral blame away from abuse victims who have not yet escaped their fates. Instead, we may focus fault on individuals and institutions that have failed to help those survivors seek relief and that have neglected to insist that batterers change their behavior. It is up to us to understand that domestic abuse, a term that veils raw and violent coercion with a euphemistic "family values" veneer, deserves no protection or respect. If we as a culture ignore abuse we deem "merely" personal, our inheritance will consist of detritus from the shattered lives that have already begun to crowd our courts, prisons, hospitals, mental health clinics, and schools—and that crowd them at our expense. It is in our economic and social interests, as well as in our essential human interests, to accept accountability for each other's fates, for it is only by so doing that we can hope to command our own.

Appendix A

Issues Related to Research, Reform, and the Law

Two significant issues vital to any discussion of abuse and of society's treatment of batterers are current research regarding social programs that focus on abuse prevention and reform, and legal considerations regarding batterers and their victims.

Mental health and other experts view abusive behavior either as a manifestation of mental illness or as a learned pattern of thinking and acting, or as a combination of these. In the 1970s, prevention programs for male abusers became popular throughout the United States. Today, more than 200 such initiatives exist as convicted batterers' primary alternatives to incarceration. Unfortunately, despite some successes, most such programs have thus far proved limited in permanently altering the behavior of abusers (Landes, Squyres, and Quiram 1997).

According to Daniel G. Saunders in his essay "Husbands Who Assault: Multiple Profiles Requiring Multiple Responses," published in Zoe Hilton's *Legal Responses to Wife Assault* (1993), reasons for program failure determined by drop-out rates exceeding 50 percent and of recidivism rates estimated to be between 35 and 60 percent may relate to a variety of factors. These factors include the inability of researchers to agree upon or target the reason or reasons that men abuse. In addition, some programs reject participants who are "drug and/or alcohol abusers, [have] psychological problems, [lack] motivation, or [have] a history of violence outside the family," the very abusers whose needs and offenses tend to be the greatest. Many programs conducted few, if any, follow-up studies of their participants. And the courts that sentence batterers to attend such programs often fail to sanction participants due to their "personality disorders that conflict with authority" typical of abusers or for other reasons. Experts agree, however, that because of the nature of the continuing relationships between most batterers and their victims in domestically violent relationships, treatment of abusers cannot be correlated with treatment of other types of criminals. Abused women, often more concerned that the violence committed against them cease than that their abusers get punished, often remain as reluctant to report their abuse as abusers—who lack internal motivation—remain resistant to change (Landes, Squyres, and Quiram 1997). University of Indiana researchers of abuse treatment programs Maureen Pirog-Good and Jan Stets-Kealey revealed in "Male Batterers and Battering Prevention Programs: A National Survey" (1985), quoted in *Violent Relationships, Battering, and Abuse Among Adults*, that men who enter such programs of their own volition, as well as batterers referred to such programs by their spouses, social workers, and judges, are the men most likely to complete such programs. But Landes, Squyres, and Quiram noted that same study as claiming that court-ordered mandates for men to participate in abuse prevention programs "[add] legitimacy to the program and [emphasize] to the man, the volunteers in the group, and the rest of society that wife battering is a crime." In addition, wrote the editors, Pirog-Good and Stets-Kealey found that it is "far better to have the courts require attendance [in such programs] rather than the wife or girlfriend," because men whose significant others return to them based on the men's entering a treatment program often drop out of treatment. However, in some instances, batterers who choose to go into treatment succeed in modifying or changing their behavior more than do court-ordered participants, who resent authority and who therefore resist attempts to change.

But whether or not batterers volunteer to participate in programs designed to alter their attitudes and behavior, experts and organizations such as the National Woman Abuse Prevention Project stress that "in some areas, criminal courts give the batterer the option to have charges dropped by completing a counseling program, thereby avoiding the entire trial process. This dangerous practice can reinforce the idea that domestic violence is not a crime and gives the abuser a method of avoiding consequences for his violence. Batterers must not be diverted from prosecution. Court-ordered counseling needs to be part of sentencing or probation after adjudication" (Landes, Squyres, and Quiram 1997).

Clearly, though, all counseling and prevention programs must, to earn their legitimacy with the public as well as with their program participants, maintain accurate records and conduct long-term studies of the abusers they counsel. And clearly, all courts must, to earn the respect of the public and of abusers, establish, enact, and enforce appropriate counseling referrals. Finally, the quality and quantity of domestic violence research itself—the shortcomings of which still include "small sample size, lack of control groups, inconsistency of variables across studies, and infrequent use of psychological tests to determine changes in the subjects" (Landes, Squyres, and Quiram 1997)—must improve before mental health, legal, and other experts achieve consensus as to the causes and possible cures of domestic violence. As Esta Soler of the Family Violence Prevention Fund pointed out, "People say that batterers' programs don't work. How can they when the media, the churches, and the workplace give different messages? We need public outrage and an orchestra of messages that surround individuals" (Landes, Squyres, and Quiram 1997).

Until quite recently, as discussed earlier in this book, our society tended to view domestic violence as a private matter, as almost a dirty secret. Shame, fear, and confusion as to who is responsible for abusive acts, batterers or the people they batter, caused abused women to deny their painful experiences and encouraged many law enforcers as well as much of the public to regard those reported cases of domestic violence as nothing more than nuisance calls. Fewer than thirty years ago, according to the editors of

Violent Relationships, Battering, and Abuse Among Adults (Landes, Squyres, and Quiram 1997), official policy for Detroit Police Department dispatchers was to dismiss reports of domestic violence without any investigation unless dispatchers suspected "excessive" violence. A 1975 law officers' manual, *The Function of the Police in Crisis Intervention and Conflict Management,* instructed police to handle any such abuse cases that they did encounter without arresting the abusers and by convincing the victims that pressing charges could only cause those victims more grief. And all of this was—as remains the case in too many communities—true, despite the fact that domestic violence complaints constitute the single largest category of calls received by police.

Too many women, discouraged by law officers' cavalier attitudes, assume that dismissive responses to their initial calls to police represent the sentiments of the entire judicial system. Instead of pursuing help, they learn to further hide their experiences. Yet a 1986 study of domestic violence, *Preventing Domestic Violence Against Wives,* conducted by Patrick A. Langan and Christopher A. Innes, revealed that the percentage of women who report abuse by spouses or significant others to law officers endure fewer instances of subsequent abuse than do women who fail to report such battering.

But again, how police regard domestic violence reports indicates the efficacy of their responses, which, in turn, can, in part, predict the potential for change in batterers' behavior.

There's no doubt that police, inundated with repeat calls from or about couples in constant turmoil, grow weary—and wary—of people and circumstances that they come to regard as hopeless. Landes, Squyres, and Quiram (1997) stated that a 1993 study of the attitudes of Phoenix, Arizona, law enforcers regarding arrest revealed that "among the most influential factors in police attitudes were the officers' background beliefs about race and class. Women from low-income, minority communities were more likely to be seen as 'enmeshed in a culture of violence.' A specific violent event was likely to be viewed as part of a larger pattern of culture and therefore beyond the scope of police intervention."

Such frustration is valid because it is real. Police challenged to contend with victims whose fear of their batterers and whose limited alternatives can cause victims to remain in self-destructive relationships; police challenged to contend with batterers savvy enough to minimize or to lie about their violence and its causes (and who may also prove dangerous); and police challenged to contend with a judicial system and a society more eager to evade than to confront the complexities of abuse cannot be expected to alter their attitudes without societal support. Law enforcers often blame battered women for their own plights, just as they blame judges for issuing protective orders that cannot, for various reasons, be enforced. And judges reply that the restraining orders that they issue would work if only police would enforce them. The anger and resentment that result from such perceptions breed distrust, curtail communication, and reinforce the status quo. Bardstown, Kentucky, police officer Kyle M. Willett commented, "For a police officer, the 'domestic' is his most frequent and frustrating type of call. Many times there is no simple solution to the domestic problems the officer encounters, and those difficulties require much more attention than an officer can provide. Although I've been trained to mediate disputes, I am neither the social worker nor the marriage counselor I often feel batterers and their victims expect me to be."

Yet some cities bent on eradicating such systemic gridlock by initiating radical change are experiencing success. For the past fifteen years police, prosecutors, probation officers, and judges in Duluth, Minnesota, together have enforced a zero-tolerance policy for domestic violence. In that city, most first-time offenders are jailed for thirty days and are then compelled to complete a twenty-six-week counseling program. Truants who miss just days of counseling find themselves back in jail. Additional communities, whose police and judicial liaisons and policies may not be as stringent, are nevertheless insisting that domestic violence constitutes a crime, just as they are also insisting that law enforcers' responses to that crime be the consistent arrest of abusers and the protection of victims (Landes, Squyres, and Quiram 1997).

Until recently, because what the law calls simple assault and battery constituted a misdemeanor rather than a felony in most states, the law required that any charges pressed against abusers be filed by their victims; police could make probable cause arrests without warrants only in cases deemed felonies. At this writing, West Virginia remains the only state that now prohibits police from arresting abusers—their crimes still termed misdemeanors—for probable cause. But more than half of the states that have revised their laws also require victims to suffer visible injuries and/or to report their battering within a specified number of hours for a police arrest to be legal (Landes, Squyres, and Quiram 1997).

Mandatory arrests of abusers, now in effect in fifteen states and in the District of Columbia, depend only on police being called to a scene involving domestic violence. If police encounter situations in which both parties appear to have been physically harmed, both parties can be arrested, a situation, some critics contend, that can cause further problems if any children involved end up in foster care (Landes, Squyres, and Quiram 1997).

Preferred or presumptive arrest policies, directives growing increasingly popular with police across the nation, call for law officers to arrest abusers unless they see "clear and compelling" evidence of why they shouldn't do so. Because neither the abused party's consent to arrest her abuser nor her abuser's desire to cooperate weigh in an officer's decision, such policies appear to be effective in providing victims immediate relief from violence as well as some specific relief from their batterers' blame regarding the arrests.

But domestic violence cases that involve any type of arrests are often decided by considerations more pragmatic than just. Judges and juries, plagued by the same prejudices and frustrations common to police, often view keeping a family, especially one that includes children, intact as more important than punishing perpetrators of violence. Husbands and fathers who are batterers and who are also families' sole breadwinners may escape jail sentences if judges, juries, and, to complicate the issue, their victims believe that their households depend on the batterers' incomes. Also, because abusers tend to batter their victims in private, survivors of abuse often experience difficulty providing evidence sufficient to convince courts that abuse occurred, especially if one spouse claims sexual abuse against another. The notions that a woman can be raped by her husband or that a man can beat a woman without her having provoked him remain doubtful, if not foreign, to numerous judges and jurors raised to believe that men have the right to rule their homes and families as they see fit (Landes, Squyres, and Quiram 1997). Also, according to *Violent Relationships, Battering, and Abuse Among Adults* (Landes, Squyres, and Quiram 1997), the "decisions to charge offenders in cases of domestic violence are notable for having less to do with legal criteria than with an evaluation of the victims' and offenders' personal attributes." The publication's editors point out that "negative characteristics in the offender (alcohol or drug use, failure to comply with the police or courts) make it more likely that charges will be pressed, while these same attributes in the abused call into question her status as an innocent 'victim.' . . . More than a third of misdemeanor domestic violence cases would have been felony offenses of rape, robbery, or aggravated assault if they had been committed by a stranger."

Landes, Squyres, and Quiram (1997) also stated that "to pressure women to testify, some prosecutors have charged them with filing false police reports and perjury (lying), and in rare instances even jailing them. Some prosecutors see this as the worst kind of paternalism and a further abuse of an already demoralized woman, while others claim that allowing the woman to drop charges is sending her the message that the courts do not take her problem seriously."

Communities such as Quincy, Massachusetts, that have instituted county offices to help battered women file charges and that have organized support groups for those same abuse survivors have witnessed astonishing success in getting battered women to testify against their abusers in court. More than 98 percent of abused women who file charges in Quincy now defend the charges they filed, as compared to fewer than 30 percent of such women in Brockton, Massachusetts. These numbers indicate that education and support can be critical factors in the behavior of abuse victims and argue that fear of an impersonal and immense-seeming judicial system and feelings of isolation may, without such programs as those now in place in Quincy, influence the willingness of victims to testify against their abusers more than do other considerations (Landes, Squyres, and Quiram 1997).

In our society, abuse victims of all ages and of either sex turn more to protection orders (POs)—sometimes called emergency protection orders (EPOs)—as their first line of defense than to any other type of legal protection. These court orders, that remain in effect from six months to a year in most states, but that can be valid for as many as three years in California and Hawaii, prohibit abusers from further abusing, and usually from further contacting, their victims. Although many well-intentioned courts now issue protection orders before an abuser's pretrial release from incarceration, the strength of such orders depends on the maintenance of accurate records by police and on their arresting and even jailing abusers who violate them (Landes, Squyres, and Quiram 1997).

Many battered women also seek protection from the antistalking laws enacted in the past decade in all states and in the District of Columbia. Defined as "the act of following, viewing, communicating with, or moving threateningly or menacingly toward another person," stalking, stated Landes, Squyres, and Quiram, who quote a 1993 Institute of Justice report, includes, as its greatest category of victims, "former lovers, former spouses, or spouses" whose "relationships have almost always been abusive in the past." They added that "the Violence Against Women Act of the Violent Crime Control and Law Enforcement Act of 1994 made it a federal offense to cross state lines to pursue a fleeing spouse or partner." In addition, they added, "[It] became a crime for anyone under a restraining order for domestic abuse to possess a firearm. This provision of the law has proved very unpopular with policemen who are placed under restraining orders since they can then only take a desk job that does not require being armed" (Landes, Squyres, and Quiram 1997).

Several women, including Sandra Baker in 1966 (*Baker v. City of New York*) and Tracey Thurman in 1984 (*Thurman v. City of Torrington*), sued the Cities of New York, New York, and Torrington, Connecticut, respectively, for the failure of police to protect them from their batterers, despite the women's repeated pleas and despite their having obtained legal protection orders. Baker and Thurman, like other domestic violence victims since, won their landmark cases on the grounds that cities' duties extend to protecting all of their citizens. As a consequence of society's increasing awareness of the dynamics of abuse and its decreasing tolerance of domestic violence, more and more law officers regard protective orders as serious charges that are vital to enforce (Landes, Squyres, and Quiram 1997).

Yet even as some court rulings have set precedents that favor protecting victims of abuse, other decisions have reversed those gains. The editors of *Violent Relationships, Battering, and Abuse Among Adults (1997)* wrote: "The due process clause of the Fourteenth Amendment provides that 'no state shall deprive any person of life, liberty, or property, without due process of law,' protecting against state actions that are extremely unfair or arbitrary. It does not, however, obligate the state to protect the public from harm or provide services that would protect them. A state may, however, create special conditions in which that state has constitutional obligations to particular citizens because of a 'special relationship between the state and the individual' (*Escamillo v. Santa Anna*, 796 F. 2d 266, 269 [1986]). Abused women have used this argument to claim that being under a protection order put them in a 'special relationship.'"

The editors continued by noting that "the 'special relationships' and the gains for women achieved in *Thurman* lost their power with the Supreme Court case of *DeShaney v. Winnebago County Department of Social* Services (489 U.S. 189 1989)." They cite the circumstances of that case as originating with a child who "was repeatedly abused by his father. Despite repeated hospitalizations," they stated, "the Department of Social Services (DSS) insisted that there was insufficient evidence to remove the child. Finally, the father beat the boy into a coma, causing permanent brain damage. The mother (who had not had custody) sued the DSS for not intervening. The Supreme Court ruled that the due process clause does not grant citizens any general rights to government aid and that a 'special relationship' is a custodial (i.e., incarceration) relationship." Landes, Squyres, and Quiram wrote that since this decision, abused women "have been unable to win a case on the basis of due process or equal protection" (1997).

The most significant setback to date, however, occurred on March 5, 1999, when a federal appeals court declared unconstitutional the 1994 Violence against Women Act and deemed it a "sweeping intrusion" into states' rights. This ruling reverses several landmark domestic violence decisions and will stand unless reversed by the Supreme Court.

The number of women who kill in this country remains small compared with the number of men who murder. And a predominant cause of women committing murder is to escape an intimate abuser. According to Landes, Squyres, and Quiram (1997) a 1995 Bureau of Justice Statistics study, *Spouse Murder Defendants in Large Urban Counties*, revealed that in cases involving one spouse charged with killing another, more husbands are convicted than wives. And although convicted females in such cases are almost as likely as their convicted male counterparts to be sentenced to prison, women convicted of murder tend to receive shorter sentences. The fact that more women than men claim self-defense—with 44 percent of women stating that their spouses had been battering them at the time of the killing and with 58 percent of women saying that their husbands had assaulted them before the killing, as compared with only 10 percent of men charged with murdering their wives claiming self-defense or spousal assault—may serve as partial explanation for women's lower conviction rates.

The most significant research to date that compares abused women who kill their abusers with abused women who do not suggests a correlation between an abuser's level of physical violence and/or sexual torture of his victim and the nature of a victim's response. In *When Battered Women Kill* (1987), Angela Browne of the Family Research Laboratory at the University of New Hampshire reported that her study of forty-two women who killed their abusers and of 205 battered women whose abusers were still alive resulted in her finding that the most violent batterers tend, ironically, to exhibit the most romantic (and, therefore, attractive) characteristics at the beginning of an abusive relationship. A man's instant desire to accompany his significant other and to monitor every aspect of her life can flatter a woman who doesn't suspect that such seemingly solicitous behavior disguises a dictator bent on control. A pattern that Browne found in documenting case after case of battered women who kill is that their batterers, after winning such women, would isolate them first from neighbors and friends, then from family, and always from the truth of their own perceptions. What such women had believed to be romantic, even ideal, partnerships had become prisons. Such abusers, like most of the men who battered the Sisters in Pain, accused their victims of having sex with other men, wore uniforms to designate their power while they tortured their victims sexually, drank until drunk every day, had arrest records, wielded guns to taunt their victims, tortured and killed their family pets, and repeatedly threatened to kill their victims or, if their victims would attempt to escape, threatened to kill themselves. In most instances, women killed their abusers, intentionally or not, in battering relationships wherein the physical and psychological violence had escalated to a level so constant and intense as to transcend rational response or human endurance. But it is especially interesting to note that among the battered women who Browne studied, 48 percent of those who killed their batterers had, before their batterers' deaths, threatened or attempted suicide as the only means that they could conceive of exiting their abusive relationships. Browne's research depicted battered women who murder their abusers—most of whom, she noted, like Sue Melton, knew nothing about their abusers' pasts before marrying their abusers—not as calculating criminals but as creatures so tortured that their thinking grows distorted. They learn to adapt to abnormal situations in which either they and their children *or* their abusers can survive.

Legal issues specific to battered women charged with first- or second-degree murder, which are defined as, according to Landes, Squyres, and Quiram (1997), "murder with malicious intent either with or without premeditation," include "self-defense, equal force, and imminent versus immediate danger." These issues present problems peculiar to abuse victims because certain legal definitions, such as the meaning of self-defense, fail to take into account such broader considerations as past instances of abuse to explain defendants' motivations. Since U.S. law defines self-defense as a response to a stranger's attack, abuse victims who strike out in response to a history of abuse or who act out of fear cannot successfully plead self-defense. Only battered women who kill in the midst of being assaulted by their abusers can hope to win their cases. But courts insist that battered women be certain that their batterers' force was deadly and, in some cases and in some states, insist that battered women produce evidence that before their deadly confrontations they had attempted to flee.

However, growing numbers of courts educated by specialists educated in the dynamics of domestic violence are allowing expert witnesses to testify about mitigating circumstances and issues common to battered woman syndrome and/or experiences specific to particular abused women. And, based on such testimony, these courts are adopting new, subjective standards that redefine self-defense in light of specific victims' experiences. Thus, fewer battered women now have to prove that they were in "imminent danger" to convince judges and juries that, although not always immediate, the danger to which they responded was lethal and real. Other courts, in an attempt to strike a balance between traditional, objective legal standards and newer, subjective standards now strive to consider cases in accordance with victims' experiences and perceptions and in accordance with efforts to determine whether most individuals who share those victims' perspectives would have acted in similar ways (Landes, Squyres, and Quiram 1997).

But another aspect of self-defense that can prove complicated for women is the law's contention that, to protect one's self from immediate physical harm or death, a person may respond to force with equal force. Women who are often smaller in physical stature, weaker in physical strength, and less than experienced in combat than are their batterers may believe weapons to be their only equalizers in violent physical confrontations, an opinion with which some courts concur (Landes, Squyres, and Quiram 1997).

Without a doubt, the U.S. judicial system is becoming increasingly knowledgeable about domestic violence as critical research recognizes truths concerning abusers and abuse. Yet in her 1994 article "Jurors' Decisions in Trials of Battered Women Who Kill: The Role of Prior Beliefs and Expert Testimony," published in the *Journal of Applied Psychology*, Regina Schuller and her cohorts (1994) posited that judges' and juries' personal philosophies—their world views—still determine their attitude toward abuse victims more than does evidence based on research. As Landes, Squyres, and Quiram (1997) reported, the "researchers examined whether a person's belief in a 'just world' influenced how [he or she] received expert testimony. A strong belief in a just world says that a person deserves his or her fate. In other words, bad things happen to bad people. Therefore, if a woman is abused, she must be responsible for the beating in some way, or she must deserve the outcome and the husband is not the only guilty party. The study found that women who did not accept the concept of a just world were especially open to and influenced by expert testimony. Men, however, were more resistant to the influence of expert witnesses."

It is human nature to judge that which we know as well as that which we only think we understand. Schuller and her colleagues' research revealed that despite the significant findings concerning the dynamics of abuse discovered in the last twenty years, public perceptions about domestic violence still remain more righteous than objective, more judgmental than just.

Appendix B

Warning Signs for Women: Predictors of Violence in Men

- Did he grow up in a violent family? Those who come from violent homes may claim they will never behave that way but often resort to violence when they are faced with problems of marriage and parenting.

- Does he tend to use force or violence to "solve" his problems? Does he overreact to little problems and frustrations, such as not finding a parking place . . . ? Does he punch walls or throw things?. . . Do not minimize a tendency he may have to be cruel to animals. Cruelty to animals is a common behavior of men who are cruel to women and children.

- Does he abuse alcohol or other drugs? Do not think you can change him.

- Does he think poorly of himself? Does he guard against his masculinity by trying to act tough? He may think he's acting like a man, but in fact, he may be acting like a future batterer.

- Does he have strong traditional ideas about what a man should be and what a woman should be?

- Is he jealous of you—not just of other men that you may know—but also of your girlfriends and your family?

- Does he play with guns, knives, or other lethal instruments? Does he talk of using them against people or threaten to use them to "get even"?

- Does he expect you to follow his orders or advice? Does he become angry if you do not fulfill his wishes, if you cannot anticipate what he wants?

- Does he go through extreme highs and lows, as though he is almost two different people? Is he extremely kind at one time and extremely cruel at another time?

- When he gets angry, do you fear him? Do you find that not making him angry has become a major part of your life?

- Does he treat you roughly? Abuse during dating is a guarantee of later abuse, and more violent abuse. . . . If he does abuse you, you are already a battered woman.

- Do you feel threatened by him? Have you changed your life so you won't make him angry?

Excerpted from "Predictors of Domestic Violence," published by the National Coalition Against Domestic Violence.

* * *

Why She Stays, When She Leaves

Abused women have reported these reasons for remaining in or for fleeing a violent relationship:

- Hope for change: Many abusive men become contrite after beating their spouse. The wife, who is in a committed relationship, often with children, hopes that this time her husband means it. "When the batterer acknowledges the error of his ways, when he breaks down and cries out his despair and concedes the need for dramatic change, hope is often born anew for battered women."

- Isolation: Men who batter are often highly possessive and extremely jealous. They believe they own their partners and are entitled to their exclusive attention and absolute obedience. Batterers isolate their spouses from potential support from family, friends, or institutions because they fear this support will threaten their control.

- Societal denial: Abused women discover that many institutions trivialize their complaints (doctors prescribe tranquilizers, priests recommend prayer, and the police do not always remove the abusive husband from the home, etc.). In addition, many violent husbands hide their behavior behind closed doors and appear pleasant in public, leading the woman to fear no one will believe her if she leaves.

- Preventing leaving: Batterers may put up barricades to a woman leaving the home. He may threaten (or carry out his threats) to commit suicide, to keep the children from her, to withhold support, or to escalate the violence. In fact, many battered women who are killed by a partner are killed after they have left the relationship.

- Belief in batterer treatment: Many battered women are reluctant to leave a partner while he is in a treatment program. They assume the programs will help their spouses make the profound changes necessary to stop the use of violence. It is crucial that battered women receive full information about the success of treatment programs.

Violent Relationships, Battering, and Abuse Among Adults editors Alison B. Landes, Suzanne Squyres, and Jacquelyn Quiram write, "According to Hart, the most likely predictor of whether a separated woman will stay away is whether she has the economic resources to survive without him. It is important, therefore, that a woman learn about child support awards, job training, and other economic opportunities. In many cases, a woman leaves several times before finally separating from her abuser. She is usually testing the response of the outside community and gathering information before the final break."

Barbara Hart. From the manual "Stopping the Violence," produced by the Pennsylvania Coalition Against Domestic Violence and excerpted from Violent Relationships, Battering, and Abuse Among Adults *(Wylie, Texas: Information Plus, 1997).*

Appendix C

Private Artifact to Public Act

The following is the proposal that author and Women's Studies scholar Elaine Hedges wrote and that was accepted by the American Studies Association for a paper to be delivered at the fall 1997 meeting. It is probably her last polished piece of writing on quilts.

The Quilt as Accusatory Text

As I have argued in previously published work, American women in the course of the nineteenth century redefined and transformed the quilt, from a domestic artifact, symbol of their confinement to the private sphere of the home, into an instrument of their public, political emancipation. Women in the anti-slavery, temperance, and suffrage movements used quilts for political statement and as fundraisers—as a means of entering into political discourse and thus claiming for themselves greater public space. The contemporary quilt revival, begun in the 1960s in the United States and now a worldwide phenomenon, has seen a dramatic expansion of the political uses of the quilt. Quilts currently address issues ranging from environmental degradation to nuclear proliferation to racism, poverty, homelessness, and AIDS. Where nineteenth-century women felt it necessary to justify the political use of their needlework as a logical extension of their sphere role as custodians of morality, and because sewing was condoned as an appropriate female activity, contemporary women are more likely to choose the quilt as a form of public discourse in order ironically to deploy the quilt's traditional associations with warmth, comfort, security, and protection to disrupt and disturb viewer's expectations. They create accusatory texts that intentionally subvert the idealized, domestic-sentimental script of the traditional quilt. Nowhere is this more apparent than in contemporary quilts that address the—until recently—private and even taboo subject of sexual violence against women—both domestic violence and violence in war. Such quilts, being produced in increasing numbers since the late 1980s, and intentionally problematizing conventional categories of private and public, will be the specific focus of my paper.

The quilts I shall discuss include both individual and group-made United States and Canadian quilts that address domestic violence: Faith Ringgold's story quilts, including one based on Alice Walker's *The Color Purple* (a novel in which sexual abuse of

black women is a major theme); the 1996 Kentucky Prison Quilt, made by prison inmates who had murdered their abusers and which, after being publicly displayed, led to
their parole; and the Star Quilt project, an exhibition of several hundred quilts by women
from the United States, Europe, the Middle East, and Asia dealing with domestic violence and rape in war, displayed at the NGO Forum of The Fourth United Nations
World Conference on Women in Beijing in 1995 and intended to influence government officials and policymakers as they drafted the official Platform for Action of the
Conference.

Women thus continue to use what was originally a set of private cultural practices in order to enter in ever larger numbers into public discourse and to affect public
policy. In the process, they are continuing to redefine and enlarge the content and
nature of previously male-gendered public, political space.

Reprinted by permission of the Feminist Press at the City University of New York, from Elaine Hedges:
A Tribute. *Copyright © Elaine R. Hedges.*

* * *

The Nineteenth-Century Diarist and Her Quilts

"The long sacrifice of women's days passes without a thought, without a word." So
began a scrapbook kept by a Missouri woman named Rebecca Foard in 1860. Making
scrapbooks—a salvage art not unlike making quilts—was typical of many nineteenth-
century women. But Mrs. Foard's scrapbook, which now rests in the Missouri State
Historical Society Library, is, so far as one knows, the only remaining evidence of her
life, and it serves as an especially poignant and revealing document. The quotation with
which she began the scrapbook sets the tone for many of her future entries: a poem
entitled, "Tired Women," a newspaper clipping, "Women's Drudgery," another poem,
"Endurances," and yet another that urged daughters not to let their mothers slave and
toil. Too reticent, perhaps, to record life in her own words, Mrs. Foard spoke at a
remove, through the words of others. Yet the clippings managed to convey a very personal view of her life.[1]

Recent research has focused on these "ordinary women" whose household work
comprised, defined, and often circumscribed their lives: the work of cooking, cleaning
and sewing that women traditionally and perpetually performed and that has gone un-
heralded until now. In the faded ink of letters, in ledgers and marbled schoolbooks
converted into diaries, in the single remaining copy of an autobiography that a woman
might have privately published for family and friends—in these, have been sought the
words that Rebecca Foard lacked, but knew she needed. These records open wide a
door that has been hitherto only slightly ajar, a door behind which are women, in all
periods and in all phases of history, faithfully recording and commenting on domestic
work that was otherwise ignored.

Rebecca Foard's newspaper clipping, "Women's Drudgery," captured a good deal
of what many nineteenth-century women felt about much of what they did. There are

many diaries like that of Mary Ann Morse who described her life in New York State in 1862:

January 6   All sorts of housework took most of the day
January 7   Sewed all the time I could get
January 10   Sewed all the time I could get²

Litanies of such entries, month after month, year after year, a monotony of repetition and routine, culminated as a Georgia girl's diary of the 1860s did: "Fannie and I sewed ourselves sick/stitched day after day from morning until night."³

In the period before the 1846 invention of the sewing machine, and until much later in areas where machines were not available or were too costly, hand-sewing remained a major domestic task. "The good wife makes breakfast, makes the beds, then sits down to sew or knit," wrote a Virginia mother to her daughter in 1873.⁴ Women sewed their own and their husbands' and children's clothes, and all towels, bed linens, and table cloths. In addition, they quilted. Quilting was necessary work since warm bedcovers were essential in cold New England winters and in drafty log cabins when chinks could not keep out the snows of Iowa, Minnesota, and Nebraska. But for innumerable nineteenth-century women, quilting became, unlike mere clothing construction, not only necessary work but also a creative outlet, a form of personal artistic expression. Such creative activity enabled women to transcend the limiting daily routine.

Awesome quantities of quilts were produced by nineteenth-century women. An 1883 issue of *Arthur's Home Magazine* estimated that as many as three-quarters of the bed coverings in the United States were quilts.⁵ Furthermore, we know from the records women left and from extant quilts, many in mint condition, that women created more of them than necessity demanded. Quilts became a vehicle through which women could express themselves; utilitarian objects elevated through enterprise, imagination and love to the status of an original art form.

Women's autobiographies frequently begin with a childhood memory of learning patchwork from a mother or grandmother. "Each granddaughter helped grandma piece and quilt her own quilt," wrote a Texas woman in the 1900s. "Grandma taught the girls how to piece and quilt the simpler patterns."⁶ Children might begin with a ninepatch and, as in the case of the daughter of Harriette Kidder of New Jersey in 1847, be encouraged to complete a first quilt by a certain birthday. Harriette's daughter finished piecing her quilt in time for her fifth birthday, and the event was celebrated appropriately by a quilting party.⁷ Throughout youth and adolescence young girls continued to piece quilts. They held "calico parties" at which they exchanged scraps, and they attended quilting bees (which could also be an occasion for meeting young men).

Training thus received—"every stitch honestly taken"—was preparation for a lifetime of industrious work.⁸ That they were proud of their accomplishments is apparent from the accounts left behind. A girl, not quite fifteen, married, and ready to leave for Texas in 1895, listed in her autobiography the featherbed, two pillows, and quilts which her mother had made and packed for her, but also, "Of course . . . the quilts of my own, . . . for I had always prided myself on the way I could piece and quilt them."⁹

This pride in creation sustained women through life's hardships. Even in records which relentlessly confined themselves to a listing of daily chores, one finds relaxation when quilts are mentioned. Women noted carefully the dates when quilts were begun, put into frames, and taken out. They also recorded names of the patchwork patterns. Nancy Holman, a Missouri homesteader in the 1860s and 1870s, wrote that her quilts included an "Irish chain," a "Bird comfort," a "lincy quilt," a "Temperance tree," and a "Basket."[10]

Completing a quilt was especially gratifying when it involved the participation of other women. Especially in areas where homes or homesteads were separated widely, the quilting party, or bee, was a special occasion. It was anticipated eagerly and invariably enjoyed as a time for socializing, for conversation, and for contact.

> Wednesday. Aunt Abigail came over from Pembroke to pass a week or two with us, this forenoon we put in the quilt, and this afternoon Mrs. Thomson, Mrs. Storer and Miss Gott came to assist us. We had a fine time, and were all cheerful.[11]

Accounts of quilting parties like the foregoing from Portland, Maine, 1810, abound in women's diaries. So important were these occasions that one woman even confided to her diary concerning a quilting party to which she was *not* invited. In lives which led women to write, "I am so nearly played out now that I sometimes don't know where I am going," or, "I wish I could live without so much hard work," the quilting party was a special event, a time for work and pleasure; a time for renewal of energies.[12]

Given the repetitive nature of women's everyday work, the pride exhibited in quilts is understandable. The twentieth-century poet Marge Piercy calls a quilt "the only perfect artifact a woman would ever see."[13] Dishes washed became dirty; food cooked is consumed; a quilt endures. Eliza Bell, who at the age of 77 in 1890 made a quilt for President Benjamin Harrison, may have been more meticulous than most women in the detail with which she recorded her achievement; but other women who recorded their quilts would have understood her pride in saying, "Every stitch [was] done by my own hand, and the needle was threaded 777 times, entirely by myself." They would have responded with interest and appreciation, also, to her further description of the quilt as containing "one hundred and thirty nine yards of straight work. Twelve yards of Chain-work. One square yard of Small shells in the center. Thirty three Feathers. Ten Stars."[14]

Women made quilts for all occasions: to commemorate the births of children and their coming of age, to celebrate marriages, to mark the departures of children from the home, and to pay obligations to the dead. Quilts, and the fabric that composed them, were a lifeline connecting families otherwise far-flung geographically. The Nebraska State Historical Society Library contains a set of letters written by the Shaw family. The parents, Stephen and Hannah, were both born in 1801 and had, by 1856, migrated from New York to Connecticut, thence to Wisconsin and Nebraska. Of their nine children, only Margaret had remained, with her husband and children in Poughkeepsie, New York. The correspondence among Hannah, several of the daughters, and Margaret is a moving record of the way in which fabric and quilts bound together members of a dispersed family.

"I have been looking for something to send you, but I could not send anything that I could send in a letter bitt (sic) a piece of my new dress," Hannah writes to Margaret from Wisconsin in 1850. As the correspondence proceeded throughout the 1850s and 1860s, the sending of dress scraps from mother to daughter, and from sister to sister, continued: "Here is a piece of my gingham Lydia made me"; "a piece of my dress of delanes"; a piece of my bonnet, trimmed with green plaid ribbon"; and finally, "I will send you some pieces of my new dresses for patch work." In 1865, a sister, Amelia, wrote to Margaret, "Hear (sic) are some peaces (sic) for Mary's quilt." The family also exchanged quilt blocks, and sent each other samples of calico to be matched for use in a quilt. For the Shaw women, fabric scraps and the quilts made from them were what photographs would be to a family today: they verified existence and became the loving ties that bound. They were tactile communication and reassurance. Even in the third generation, Margaret's sister's children sent her scraps from aprons, dresses, and pants. Reassuring connections were established in yet a fourth generation when in 1851 the grandmother of the family died. Hannah then wrote to Margaret that daughter Rebecca, who had been "peacing (sic) calico for me . . . has finished my stars I had worked at so long . . . [and] will now peace (sic) up your grandmother's dresses in quilts / I think [that] will [do] more good so than any other way / She [grandmother] had a new quilt peaced (sic) / I have that and am going to join it with one of her dresses and when you come [Margaret was expected for a visit] I know you will help me quilt them all."[15]

In 1845, a Lowell, Massachusetts woman described quilts as "the hieroglyphs of women's lives."[16] And so they were. Hannah Shaw knew the importance of a quilt and its value as a permanent memorial. She was anxious to see her daughter: "don't wait to (sic) long for I am growing old and my teeth are falling out . . . father is afraid I will look old and snaggy so don't wait till you don't know your own mother." When they met, they would likely celebrate the reunion by quilting together. Unfortunately, the records of the Shaw family end without telling us whether Margaret ever arrived to complete her grandmother's quilt.

Today, in seeking to understand more fully the everyday lives of nineteenth-century women, we must piece together scraps as they once did. From entries in diaries, autobiographies and letters, and from pieced quilts themselves, we are uncovering a strong tradition of industry, creativity, and human expression that has been hidden too long. Quilts, and informal written accounts of their construction and original meaning, have proven rich resources of the American woman's heritage. Stitched together by twentieth-century interpreters they become, again, a completed fabric.

Notes

"The Nineteenth-Century Diarist and Her Quilts" is an abridged version of the text for the catalog *American Quilts: A Handmade Legacy*, which accompanied the exhibit of the same name at the Oakland Museum in Oakland, California, January-April 1981, curated by Pat Ferrero, Linda Reuther, and Julie Silber. This version was first published in *Feminist Studies* 8, no. 2 (summer 1982).

1. Rebecca Foard, *Scrapbook*, Univ. of Missouri Library, State Historical Society, Columbia.

2. Mary Ann Morse, *Diary, 1862*, MS, Collection of Electa Kidder, Nebraska State Historical Society, Lincoln.

3. Anna Green Cook, Journal of a Milledgeville Girl, 1861-1867. Ed. James C. Bonner (Athens: Univ. of Georgia, 1964), p. 12.

4. Mrs. Virginia C. Ayre, "Letter, 1873," Willa Cather Family Papers, Nebraska State Historical Society, Lincoln.

5. *Arthur's Home Magazine*, 1883, quoted in Ruth Andrews, ed. *How to Know American Folk Art* (New York: E.P. Dutton, 1977), p. 132.

6. Dorothy Howard, *Dorothy's World: Childhood in Sabine Bottom, 1902-1910* (Englewood Cliffs, N.J.: Prentice-Hall, 1977), p. 133.

7. Harriette Smith Kidder, *Diary*, MS, Rutgers Univ. Library, Rutgers, N.J.

8. *Reminiscences of Martha White Long, 1904*, MS, Univ. of Missouri Library, State Historical Society of Missouri, Columbia.

9. Sue Sanders, *Our Common Herd* (Garden City, N.Y.: Barton Syndicate Country Life Press, 1939), p. 72.

10. Nancy Holman, *Diary*, MS, Univ. of Missouri Library, State Historical Society of Missouri, Columbia.

11. M.H. Jewell, ed., *Diary of Sarah Connell Ayer, Portland, Maine* (Portland, Maine: Lefavour-Tower, 1910), p. 167.

12. Elizabeth Welty, Letters, MS, Univ. of Missouri Library, State Historical Society of Missouri, Columbia.

13. Marge Piercy, "Looking at Quilts," in *Living in the Open* (New York: Alfred A. Knopf, 1974).

14. Eliza Bell, "Account Book, 1888-1891," Joseph Downs Manuscript Collection, Henry Francis du Pont Wintherthur Museum, Wintherthur, Del.

15. "Shaw Family Papers," Nebraska State Historical Society, Lincoln.

16. Harriet Farley or Rebecca C. Thompson, "The Patchwork Quilt," in *The Lowell Offering*, vol. 5, 1845, pp. 210-203 [*sic*], as reprinted in Benita Eisler, ed., *The Lowell Offering* (New York: Harper and Row, 1980), p. 154.

Appendix D

National Domestic Violence Organizations and Kentucky Spouse Abuse Centers

The following list of national domestic violence organizations and Kentucky spouse abuse centers was prepared by the National Resource Center on Domestic Violence and the Kentucky Domestic Violence Association.

Domestic Violence Organizations

HOTLINE

National Domestic Violence Hotline (800) 799-7233
3616 Far West Boulevard, Suite 101-297
Austin, TX 78731-3074
Office: (512) 453-8117
FAX: (512) 453-8541

Resource Only Information (not for crisis calls)

National Resource Center on Domestic Violence
Pennsylvania Coalition against Domestic Violence
6400 Flank Drive, Suite 1300
Harrisburg, PA 17112-2778
Office: (800) 537-2238
FAX: (717) 545-9456

Battered Women's Justice Program—Civil Justice Issues
c/o PCADV—Legal Office
6400 Flank Drive, Suite 1300
Harrisburg, PA 17112
Office: (800) 903-0111 or (717) 671-4767
FAX: (717) 671-5542

Battered Women's Justice Project—Criminal Justice Issues c/o Minnesota Program Development, Inc.
4032 Chicago Avenue South
Minneapolis, MN 55407
Office: (800) 903-0111
FAX: (612) 824-8965

Battered Women's Justice Project
c/o National Clearinghouse for the Defense of Battered Women
125 South 9th Street, Suite 302
Philadelphia, PA 19107
Office: (800) 903-0111 or (215) 351-0010
FAX: (215) 351-0779

Health Resource Center on Domestic Violence
c/o Family Violence Prevention Fund
383 Rhode Island Street, Suite 304
San Francisco, CA 94103-5133
Office: (888) 792-2873
FAX: (415) 252-8991

Resource Center on Domestic Violence: Child Protection and Custody
NCJFCJ
P.O. Box 8970
Reno, NV 89507
Office: (800) 527-3223
FAX: (702) 784-6628

American Bar Association Commission on Domestic Violence
740 15th Street, NW
9th Floor
Washington, DC 20005-1009
Office: (202) 662-1737
FAX: (202) 662-1032

Center for the Prevention of Sexual and Domestic Violence
936 North 34th Street, Suite 200
Seattle, WA 98103
Office: (206) 634-1903
FAX: (206) 634-0115

Center for Women Policy Studies
1211 Connecticut Avenue, NW, #312
Washington, DC 20036
Office: (202) 872-1770
FAX: (202) 296-8962

Domestic Abuse Intervention Project
206 W. 4th Street
Duluth, MN 55806
Office: (218) 722-2781
FAX: (218) 722-1545

Family Research Project
University of New Hampshire
126 Horton Social Science Center
Durham, NH 03824
Office: (603) 862-1888
FAX: (603) 862-1122

Family Violence Prevention Fund
383 Rhode Island Street, Suite 304
San Francisco, CA 94103-5133
Office: (415) 252-8900
FAX: (415) 252-8991

Family Violence and Sexual Assault Institute
1121 East Southeast Loop 323, Suite 130
Tyler, TX 75701
Office: (903) 534-5100
FAX: (903) 534-5454

Mending the Sacred Hoop, National Training Project
206 West Fourth Street
Duluth, MN 55806
Office: (218) 722-2781
FAX: (218) 722-0779

National Clearing House for the Defense of Battered Women
125 South 9th Street, Suite 302
Philadelphia, PA 19107
Office: (215) 351-0010
FAX: (215) 351-0779

National Coalition Against Domestic Violence—Administrative Office
P.O. Box 18749
Denver, CO 80218
Office: (303) 839-1852
FAX: (303) 831-9251

National Coalition Against Domestic Violence—Public Policy Office
119 Constitution Avenue, NE
Washington, DC 20002
Office: (202) 544-7358
FAX: (202) 544-7893

National Institute of Justice
633 Indiana Avenue, NW
Washington, DC 20531
Office: (202) 307-2942
FAX: (202) 307-6394

National Network to End Domestic Violence
701 Pennsylvania Avenue, NW, Suite 900
Washington, DC 20004
Office: (202) 347-9520
FAX: (202) 434-7400

National Resource Center on Child Abuse and Neglect
American Humane Association
63 Inverness Drive, East
Englewood, CO 80112
Office: (800) 227-5242
FAX: (303) 792-5333

Older Women's League
666 11th Street, NW, Suite 700
Washington, DC 2001
Office: (202) 783-6686 or (800) 825-3695

Self-Help Clearinghouse
St. Clare's-Riverside Medical Center
25 Pocono Road
Danville, NJ 07834
Office: (201) 625-9565

Sexual Assault Recovery Anonymous Society (SARA)
P.O. Box 16
Surrey, British Columbia
V3T 4W4 Canada
Office: (604) 584-2626
FAX: (604) 584-2888

Kentucky Domestic Violence Service Organizations

Contract Management Branch DSS/CFC
275 East Main Street
Frankfort, KY 40621
Phone: (502) 564-6746

Adult Services Branch DSS/CFC
275 East Main Street
Frankfort, KY 40621
Phone: (502) 564-7043

Sexual and Domestic Violence Program
MHMRS
275 East Main Street
Frankfort, KY 40621
Phone: (502) 564-4448
FAX: (502) 564-9010

Governor's Office of Child Abuse and Domestic Violence Services
Room 146, State Capital Building
Frankfort, KY 40601
Phone: (502) 564-2611
FAX: (502) 564-6657

Attorney General's Office
Victims Advocacy Division
P.O. Box 2000
Frankfort, KY 40602-2000
Phone: (502) 573-5900 or (800) 372-2551
FAX: (502) 573-8315

Chris Kubale & Lucky Collins
P.O. Box 5
Danville, KY 40423
Phone: (606) 236-0853
FAX: (606) 236-0854

Kentucky Domestic Violence Association
P.O. Box 356
Frankfort, KY 40601
Phone: (502) 695-2444
FAX: (502) 695-2488 (24 hours)

Kentucky Spouse Abuse Centers

Barren River Area Development District (Counties served: Allen, Barren, Butler, Edmonson, Hart, Logan, Metcalfe, Monroe, Simpson, Warren)

BRASS
P.O. Box 1941
Bowling Green, KY 42102-1941
Office: (502) 781-9334 or 781-9332
Crisis: (502) 843-1183 or (800) 928-1183
FAX: (502) 782-3278

Big Sandy Area Development District (Counties served: Floyd, Johnson, Magoffin, Martin, Pike)

Big Sandy Family Abuse Center
P.O. Box 1279
Prestonsburg, KY 41653
Office: (606) 285-9079
Crisis: (606) 886-6025 or (800) 649-6605
FAX: (606) 285-3581

Bluegrass Area Development District (Counties served: Anderson, Bourbon, Boyle, Clark, Estill, Fayette, Franklin, Garrard, Harrison, Jessamine, Lincoln, Madison, Mercer, Nicholas, Powell, Scott, Woodford)

YWCA Spouse Abuse Center
P.O. Box 8028
Lexington, KY 40533-8028
Office: (606) 233-9927
Crisis: (606) 255-9808 or (800) 544-2022
FAX: (606) 226-9424

Buffalo Trace Area Development District (Counties served: Bracken, Fleming, Lewis, Mason, Robertson)

Women's Crisis Center
111 East Third Street
Maysville, KY 41056
Shelter: (606) 564-6708
Crisis: (606) 491-3335 or (800) 928-6708

Cumberland Valley Area Development District (Counties served: Bell, Clay, Harlan, Jackson, Knox, Laurel, Rockcastle, Whitley)

Family Life Abuse Center
Christian Appalachian Project
P.O. Box 674
Mount Vernon, KY 40456
Family Life Services: Route 3, Box 37
Office: (606) 256-5623
Crisis: (606) 256-2724 or (800) 755-5348
FAX: (606) 256-5622

FIVCO Area Development District (Counties served: Boyd,Carter, Elliott, Greenup, Lawrence)

Safe Harbor/FIVCO
Box 2163
Ashland, KY 41105-2163
Office: (606) 325-5138
Crisis: (606) 329-9304 or (800) 926-2150

Gateway Area Development District (Counties served: Bath, Menifee, Montgomery, Morgan, Rowan)

D.O.V.E.S.
P.O. Box 1012
Morehead, KY 40351
Office: (606) 784-6880
Crisis: (606) 784-7985 or (800) 221-4361
FAX: (606) 784-6880—Call first

Green River Area Development District (Counties served: Daviess, Hancock, Henderson, McLean, Ohio, Union, Webster)

Owensboro Area Shelter and Information Services
P.O. Box 315
Owensboro, KY 42302-0315
Office: (502) 685-0260
Crisis: (502) 685-0260 or (800) 882-2873
FAX: (502) 685-1764

KIPDA Area Development District (Counties served: Bullitt, Henry, Jefferson, Oldham, Shelby, Spencer, Trimble)

The Center for Women and Families Domestic Violence Program
P.O. Box 2048
Louisville, KY 40201-2048
Office: (502) 581-7200
Crisis: (502) 581-7222
FAX: (502) 581-7204

Kentucky River Area Development District (Counties served: Breathitt, Knott, Lee, Leslie, Letcher, Owsley, Perry, Wolfe)

LKLP Safe House
P.O. Box 1867
Hazard, KY 41702
Safe House: (606) 439-3961 Shelter: (606) 439-1552
Crisis: (606) 439-5129 or (800) 928-3131
FAX: (606) 439-3790

Resurrection House
68 Resurrection Road
Beattyville, KY 41311
Office: (606) 464-8481 or in Owsley Co. (800) 928-4638
FAX: (606) 464-8492

Lake Cumberland Area Development District (Counties served: Adair, Casey, Clinton, Cumberland, Green, McCreary, Pulaski, Russell, Taylor, Wayne)

Bethany House Abuse Shelter, Inc.
P.O. Box 864
Somerset, KY 42502
Office: (606) 679-1553
Crisis: (606) 679-8852 or (800) 755-2017
FAX: (606) 679-3994

Lincoln Trail Area Development District (Counties served: Breckinridge, Grayson, Hardin, Larue, Marion, Meade, Nelson, Washington)

Caring Place, Inc. (Washington, Marion, and Nelson Counties)
P.O. Box 945
Lebanon, KY 40033
Office: (502) 692-9300
Crisis: (502) 692-9300 or (800) 692-9394

Lincoln Trail Domestic Violence Program
P.O. Box 2047
Elizabethtown, KY 42702
Office: (502) 765-4057
Crisis: (502) 769-1234 or (800) 767-5838
FAX: (502) 766-1081—Call first

Northern Kentucky Area Development District (Counties served: Boone, Bracken, Campbell, Carroll, Gallatin, Grant, Kenton, Owen, Pendleton)

Women's Crisis Center
835 Madison Avenue
Covington, KY 41011
Office: (606) 491-3335
Crisis: (800) 928-6708
FAX: (606) 655-2656
Shelter: (606) 781-6606
FAX Shelter: (606) 781-6630

Pennyrile Area Development District (Counties served: Caldwell, Christian, Crittenden, Hopkins, Livingston, Lyon, Muhlenberg, Todd, Trigg)

Sanctuary, Inc.
P.O. Box 1265
Hopkinsville, KY 42240
Office: (502) 885-4572
Shelter: (502) 885-5421
Crisis: (502) 886-8174 or (800) 766-0000
FAX: (502) 886-4260

Project PRISM: (502) 885-2565

Purchase Area Development District (Counties served: Ballard, Calloway, Carlisle, Fulton, Graves, Hickman, Marshall, McCracken)

Purchase Area Spouse Abuse Center
P.O. Box 98
Paducah, KY 42002
Office: (502) 443-6282
Crisis: (502) 443-6001 or (800) 585-2686
FAX: (502) 443-9146

Bibliography

Bachman, Ronet, and Linda Saltzman. *Violence Against Women: Estimates from the Redesigned Survey.* U.S. Department of Justice, Bureau of Justice Statistics, Washington, D.C., 1995.

Boodman, Sandra G. "Poor Women Experience High Level of Abuse." Louisville *Courier-Journal*, 26 May 1997, G-1.

Bowker, Lee. "A Battered Woman's Problems Are Social, Not Psychological." In *Current Controversies on Family Violence*, ed. Richard Gelles and Donileen Loseke. Newbury Park, Calif.: Sage Publications, 1994.

Browne, Angela. *When Battered Women Kill.* New York: Free Press, 1987.

Clay, Richard H.C. Louisville *Courier-Journal*, 11 April 1999, D-1.

Dusky, Loraine. *USA Weekend*, 17-19 Jan. 1997.

Dutton, Donald. *The Batterer: A Psychological Profile.* New York: Basic Books, 1995.

Gelles, Richard, and Donileen Loseke. *Current Controversies on Family Violence.* Newbury Park, Calif.: Sage Publications, 1994.

Gelles, Richard, and Murray Straus. *Physical Violence in American Families: Risk Factors and Adaptions to Violence in 8,145 Families.* New Brunswick, N.J.: Transaction Publications, 1990.

Hall, Evelyn J. "The Counselor's Perspective." In *I Am Not Your Victim: Anatomy of Domestic Violence*, ed. Beth Sipe and Evelyn J. Hall. Thousand Oaks, Calif.: Sage Publications, 1996.

Hilton, Zoe, ed. *Legal Responses to Wife Assault.* Newbury Park, Calif.: Sage Publications, 1993.

Hotaling, Gerald, and David Sugarman. "A Risk Marker Analysis of Assaulted Wives." *Journal of Family Violence* 4 (March 1990): 1-13.

Kentucky Commission on Women. "A Report on the Status of Women's Health in Kentucky." Frankfort, Ky., 1997.

Landes, Alison B., Suzanne Squyres, and Jacquelyn Quiram. *Violent Relationships, Battering, and Abuse Among Adults.* Wylie, Texas: Information Plus, 1997.

Langan, Patrick A., and Christopher Innes. *Preventing Domestic Violence Against Wives.* U.S. Department of Justice, Bureau of Justice Statistics, 1986.

McCrea, Laura, and Honi Marleen Goldman. "Violence Against Women Is a Man's Problem." Louisville *Courier-Journal*, 8 Sept. 1998, A-9.

Miller, Susan L. "The Fatal Flaw: Inadequacies in Social Support and Criminal Justice Responses." In *I Am Not Your Victim: Anatomy of Domestic Violence*, ed. Beth Sipe and Evelyn J. Hall. Thousand Oaks, Calif.: Sage Publications, 1996.

Powell, Cheryl. "Parole Board Seeks More Power in Cases of Victims of Abuse." *Lexington Herald-Leader*, 23 Aug. 1995.

Rubiner, Betsy. "Free Program Gives Hope to Abuse Victims." Louisville *Courier-Journal*, 8 Aug. 1996, H-3.

Saunders, Daniel G. "Husbands Who Assault: Multiple Profiles Requiring Multiple Responses." In *Legal Responses to Wife Assault*, ed. Zoe Hilton. Newbury Park, Calif.: Sage Publications, 1993.

Schuller, Regina, et al. "Jurors' Decisions in Trials of Battered Women Who Kill: The Role of Prior Beliefs and Expert Testimony." *Journal of Applied Psychology* 24, no. 4 (1994).

Sipe, Beth, and Evelyn J. Hall, eds. *I Am Not Your Victim: Anatomy of Domestic Violence*. Thousand Oaks, Calif.: Sage Publications, 1996.

Stark, Evan, and Anne Flitcraft. *Women at Risk*. Newbury Park, Calif.: Sage Publications, 1996.

Straus, Murray, and Richard Gelles. *Intimate Violence: The Definitive Study of the Causes and Consequences of Abuse in the American Family*. New York: Simon and Schuster, 1988.

Straus, Murray, and Glenda Kaufman Kantor. *Changes in Spouse Assault Rates from 1975 to 1992: A Comparison of Three National Surveys in the United States*. Durham: Family Research Laboratory, Univ. of New Hampshire, 1994.

Walker, Lenore. *Why Battered Women Kill and How Society Responds*. New York: Harper and Row, 1989.

Websdale, Neil. *Rural Battering and the Justice System: An Ethnography*. Thousand Oaks, Calif.: Sage Publications, 1998.